Women's Paid and Unpaid Labor

In the series
WOMEN IN THE
POLITICAL ECONOMY
edited by
Ronnie J. Steinberg

Women's Paid and Unpaid Labor

The Work Transfer in Health Care and Retailing

NONA Y. GLAZER

Temple University Press

Philadelphia

Temple University Press, Philadelphia 19122
Copyright © 1993 by Temple University
All rights reserved. Published 1993
Printed in the United States of America

⊗ The paper used in this publication meets
the minimum requirements of American National
Standard for Information Sciences—
Permanence of Paper for Printed Library
Materials, ANSI Z39.48-1984

LIBRARY OF CONGRESS CATALOGING-IN-
PUBLICATION DATA
Glazer, Nona Y. (Nona Yetta), 1932–
    Women's paid and unpaid labor : the
work transfer in health care and retailing
/ Nona Y. Glazer.
        p.   cm. — (Women in the political
        economy)
    Includes bibliographical references and
    index.
    ISBN 0-87722-979-1
    1. Women—Employment—United
States.   2. Women—United States—
Economic conditions.   3. Capitalism—
United States.   4. Self-service
(Economics)—United States.   5. Service
industries—United States.   6. Retail
trade—United States.   7. Medical care—
United States.   8. Home care services—
United States.   I. Title.   II. Series.
HD6095.G53   1993
331.4'81'0973—dc20   92-19837

Contents

v

List of Tables

Acknowledgments

Many friends, colleagues, and organizations gave me generous support while I wrote this book. The Center for the Education, Study and Advancement of Women, the University of California, Berkeley, supported my initial research on the retail industry with a grant from the Ford Foundation. The Berkeley Women and Work Group to which I belonged critiqued early versions of my work. The Andrew W. Mellon Fund supported a one-year fellowship at the Henry A. Murray Center of Radcliffe College, Harvard University, where I found invaluable materials in the archives and permanent collections of the Arthur and Elizabeth Schlesinger Library of the History of American Women, Baker Library, Littauer Library, and Widener. The National Science Foundation funded my field research with health service workers in 1984–1985. Professors Virginia Olesen and Carroll Estes hosted the award at the University of California, San Francisco, and Troy Duster gave me a niche at the Institute for the Study of Social Change, the University of California, Berkeley.

Portland State University provided continuous support. I thank Grant Farr for encouragement, Bob Liebman for a thoughtful and thorough critique of the entire manuscript, and my students for comments. The Faculty Development Committee award and Provost Frank Martino gave me a reduced teaching load and funded an assistant.

Jeanette Harvey toiled at the word processor in the heat of an Oregon summer with good humor and wise counsel. Ellen Morrison, Janna Allquist, Brooks Nelson, Sharon Smith, and Jean Campopiano helped with research. Stephanie Limoncelli was my mainstay in the final stages of editing. She provided a high level of editorial skill, an astute sociological sense, and moral support. I am also grateful to Sarah Laughlin, artist-cartoonist, for using on this book the skills she honed at a small press before resuming her studies in sociology at Portland State University.

I worked on this book in 1989–1990 at the Mary Ingraham Bunting Institute, a unique community of women scholars, artists, poets, and political activists. I thank Ann Bookman for encouraging me to come to the institute. My sister Bunting Fellows were a well of good humor, intellectual stimulation, and constructive criticism. I especially appreciate the support of Susan Kellogg, Zella Luria, Janet Seiz, Florence Ladd, and Mitzi Goheen. Bill Simon and Steve Mintz, semiattached to the institute as spouses, gave me helpful critiques. The Thursday night regulars in the Social Science Interest Group mixed light-heartedness with shrewd criticism.

Roz Feldberg, as usual, was a sharp and constructive critic, and gets my gratitude and appreciation. Joan Acker, Sally Hacker, Bart Hacker, Rachel Kahn-Hut, Marj Lasky, and Judith Lorber read bits and pieces of the manuscript and gave me friendly and supportive advice. I thank students in my Spring 1991 seminar on Feminist Issues for vetting the book as women's studies and sociology undergraduates and as sociology graduate students. Last, but not least, I am grateful to my editors at Temple University, Ronnie Steinberg and Michael Ames.

Friends have complained to me that I have "ruined" their fun in shopping and have given them new worries about home care. What once they saw as normal, they now find irritating and threatening! So be it. I hope that women service workers and their officers in associations and unions can use this work in organizing and improving the conditions of their employment. I thank them for their most generous gifts of time, patience, and wisdom.

Some sections of this book, especially in the chapters on health care, draw on earlier articles I have written on the subject. Although nothing has been quoted verbatim, I would like to note these articles and the journals in which they appeared:

"Servants to Capital: Unpaid Domestic Labor and Paid Work," *Review of Radical Political Economics* 16(1984):61–87.

"Overlooked and Overworked: Women's Unpaid and Paid Labor in the American Health Services 'Cost Crisis,'" *International Journal of Health Services* 18(1988):317–339.

"The Home as Workshop: Women as Amateur Caregivers in the U.S. Health Services Industry," *Gender & Society* 4(1990):479–499.

"'Between a Rock and a Hard Place': Women's Professional Organizations in Nursing, and Class, Racial and Ethnic Inequalities," *Gender & Society* 5(1991):351–372.

Introduction

This book explores the transformation of work from paid to unpaid. It looks at how the major reorganization of women's paid work results in job losses or vastly different paid jobs and increases in women's unpaid domestic labor. I call the shift of tasks from a paid worker to an unpaid family member or friend the *work transfer,* and I consider it to be one among many mechanisms that managers use to change the labor process in service jobs. My interest in the transfer of work from paid to unpaid comes from puzzling over the persistence of women's unpaid domestic labor in the United States, despite the industrialization or commercialization of much household production. The work transfer seems one obvious source of the increase in unpaid domestic labor. Although it is not the only mechanism that managers use to change the labor process, the work transfer is important to feminist scholarship and activism because it mostly affects the labor of women, in harmful as well as beneficial ways. The work transfer also demonstrates the inaccuracy of considering the social world as divided between the public sphere of labor and the private sphere of love. These are my major intellectual concerns.

But the personal is political too. In the mid-1970s, when I began to think about women's domestic labor, my income dropped sharply after divorce. This economic consequence astonished me as much as the affluence of marriage, for though somewhat younger than the generation in Elder's *Children of the Depression,* I remembered "relief" and charity-supplied goods and services and had my Social Security card and first job at age twelve. The cycle of contrasts in what services I could afford during and after marriage helped me to see how much labor I did that had nothing directly to do with serving members of my household. With less income, I began to transport, shop, keep books, and pay bills, as I could no longer afford delivery and lost services from my former partner's workplace.

I chose retailing and health services for my case studies of the work transfer because of their dramatic restructuring. I had also experienced retailing from the inside. As a small child, I lived behind our "Mom and Pop" grocery store for which my family supplied the labor for intensive customer service. As a college student, I worked in Chicago's State Street department stores as a tagger, wrapper–cashier, and salesclerk, and I heard tales from my stepmother, who sold "better hats" at a State Street store. My familiarity with the health services industry is less experiential. As a doctor's wife, I saw the early stages of the corporatization of medicine, the fights of progressive physicians for prepaid care and socialized medicine, and I observed the infantilization and lack of respect of physicians and managers for registered nurses and other health workers.

In discussing changes in paid and unpaid work, I have several agendas. One is to understand what is happening to paid women workers from diverse racial and ethnic backgrounds as owners and managers try to cope with crises in capitalism. I want to show the impact on women's unpaid domestic labor, which is drawn into the labor process of firms far removed from the household. By connecting paid and unpaid labor, I hope to show that it is false to argue that capitalism inevitably only commodifies labor and that the marketplace inevitably expands to supply more and more services to households.

A second and perhaps impossible agenda is to find grounds for more solidarity among women across racial, ethnic, and class lines and hence, for a more broadly based struggle against capitalist and state practices. There are impediments. Most women are affected by the work transfer, but the effects differ by race, ethnicity, and class. Whether in the household, the labor market, or the marketplace, women share few common experiences except being disadvantaged compared to most men similar to themselves. Nor do women share a common experience of state subsidies: the poor experience the degradation of welfare and Medicaid, while more affluent women lose tax credits and deductions and must pay greater shares of health costs (Brown 1988). But women are twice-affected compared to men, as workers in service jobs and as unpaid domestic workers.

My last agenda is to explain my ideas so that readers without formal training in sociology can understand, judge, and maybe use them. My model is C. Wright Mills, the only sociologist I read, as a student during the 1950s, who wrote political analyses for the public. Also, I do so with respect for the grass-roots origins of women's studies. Community activists, without whom women's studies would not exist, insisted on socially useful research and understandable reporting. Nonetheless, I also consider debates in feminist theory and sociology and use jargon, which I explain briefly. Professional scholars should understand that definitional asides are not for them.

I work as a feminist and a Marxist. In the United States, feminist scholarship is moderately acceptable in academia, as is liberal feminist action in politics. Most feminists and many others accept the premise that gender differences, such as the household division of labor, or femininity and masculinity, are not natural but socially constructed. Even among feminists who claim that women are essentially different (and better) than men, some view many of the differences as socially constructed. Thus, gender has been "denaturalized" significantly, as have "racial" and "ethnic" differences and sexual preference.

In contrast, capitalism has continued to be seen as "natural" by most people in the United States. It is seen as socially progressive as well as a perfect reflection of a human nature presumed to be individualistic, competitive, and acquisitive. The belief that capitalism is natural, normal, and desirable permeates and is disseminated through social institutions—schools, religion, mass media, political propaganda, academic knowledge, architecture, art, and popular culture. Even the terms commonly used in public debates about community and social needs (e.g., health care, schooling) are from the vocabulary of the marketplace: "cost–benefit," "value for money," "demand," and "efficiency" (Hall 1988: 40). Marxism is jarring in this intellectual and political climate because it denaturalizes capitalism, considering it one among a series of societies or social formations built by humans in their everyday lives.

In addition, Marxist scholarship is often unfamiliar to many in this country, except as caricature or the debunked "scientific socialism" of the former Soviet Union. Contemporary Marxism is rarely studied seriously in high schools or colleges. Most intellectuals in the United States also know little of the debates within what is called "Western" Marxism (to separate it from Soviet Marxism). Few realize that most other advanced capitalist countries have long-standing and sometimes powerful political parties influenced by Marxism. In the United States, there have been repeated and successful attempts to repress political organizing, Marxist or not, that is critical of capitalism with its lack of economic rights and participatory democracy. The result: there has been no de-naturalizing of capitalism that parallels the denaturalizing of gender. There is only a weak critique of widespread and increasingly polarized class forms of social inequality in the United States and a continued sense that the poor, including women, have what they deserve.

The result of the marginality of Marxist scholarship is that some readers may find my language "ideological." Others may be offended by a critique of capitalism that may seem to violate the ideal of a "value-free" social science. My analysis assumes that capitalism is a socially constructed political–economic system, and as a humanly contructed system, it is a subject for criticism, reflection, and replacement as much as gender relations, race relations in the United States, and other systems of the late twentieth century.

The Data and Their Limits

In retailing, my data describe mainly white urban women from northern and western states. Only limited data are available about women of color in retailing. In the health services industry, government documents and the census provide considerable data, in part because the federal government, the states, or both have been funding and legislating in the area for at least fifty years.

For retailing, I draw only on census data, archival materials, and magazines; I do not use interviews because the changes I describe began in 1912 and were substantially completed by 1960. In my analysis of health services, I use interviews with health service workers in 1984–1985, as major changes were under way in their labor.

Though some similar changes in retailing have occurred in Canada and Western Europe, I consider only the United States. The same is true for health care. Nor do I examine the work transfer in Eastern Europe, where retailing has not undergone similar changes, and health delivery was never similar to that in the United States.

I want to caution that I am not proposing a "theory of consumption," nor do I expect the observations to apply ahistorically, say, to peasant and socialist command economies and to other advanced capitalist societies. Nor am I predicting that all service work will be decommodified in advanced capitalist societies. Work—paid and unpaid—is historically specific, and the work transfer is one among many strategies used by capital and the state, intentionally and inadvertently, to resolve crises. These crises are specific to time and place: faltering accumulation, state "overspending," declining rates of profits, struggles between capitalists and unions, and other organized protest movements over the costs of social reproduction and social entitlements, capitalist problems with labor militancy, labor shortages, and overproduction because of reduced customer buying.

Plan of the Book

Chapter 1 explains the key concept of this book, the work transfer, which changes the labor of women as paid and unpaid workers. Chapter 2 considers how the work transfer operates within the service economy. Chapter 3 considers conceptualizations of the private–public worlds in historical perspective and their limitations; it proposes an alternative view of the relationship between the private world of the family and the public world of paid labor and critiques the wide variations in interpretations of *work*. It suggests, in general terms, how paid and unpaid labor are connected in retailing and health services, gives definitions and theories of the service economy and self-service, and examines the use of self-service to increase the productivity of service labor. The next three chapters focus on the retail trade industry: Chapter 4 discusses structural changes in the industry, Chapter 5 considers how paid workers were affected, and Chapter 6 relates how customers were transformed into unpaid workers. Chapters 7 through 10 focus on the health services industry: Chapter 7 discusses structural changes in the industry, Chapter 8 considers how paid workers in hospitals were affected, Chapter 9 describes the impact on home health care workers, and Chapter 10 relates how family caregivers have been transformed into workers who complete technical processes begun by paid health workers. Chapter 11 concludes the book with reflections on sociological theory and practice and implications for women.

Part One
Changes in Women's Lives

1

From Paid to Unpaid Work

Women do unpaid domestic labor that completes steps begun by paid workers in organizations outside the family. Women's everyday lives as shoppers and caregivers for their families change with structural changes in retailing and health care delivery systems and the changes in the labor process within these systems.

Consider typical shopping in the 1990s:

> Forty-five-year-old Mary O'Hanlan is on her way home from her Silicon Valley factory job. She stops at the local supermarket, races up and down the aisles with a cart,[1] unloads her groceries at the check-out counter, and may bag them.
>
> In Memphis in the 1920s, Mary's grandparents counted on a neighborhood family-run grocery store for credit until Father got his wages each Friday and during hard times. Mother telephoned the order to the grocer. A "boy" (often a middle-aged African American man on a bike) delivered the order to their home. Memphis already had a chain of self-service Piggly Wiggly grocery stores, but these gave no credit, would not take telephone orders, and did not deliver.

What is Mary O'Hanlan missing? If she had been shopping at the Farmers' Market in Portland, Oregon, in 1970, she would have done less work. Consider the following scenario:

> At 8:30 A.M., Nancy Field, white, married, and a college teacher, telephones her shopping list to Jack, who owns a fruit and vegetable stand in the Farmers' Market. Jack takes her order for his produce, but also for meat and poultry, bread and cheeses, candy and flowers, gathered from other stands. En route home that evening, Nancy toots her horn, and Jack places her groceries in the back seat of her car. She pays Jack once a month, and he repays the other stands. Convenience, not credit, is her need. She

pays prices slightly higher than those at the supermarket, but she gets top-quality produce and spends less time than if she shopped in her neighborhood stores.

More has changed over the past fifty years than shopping. Family members have also been brought into the institutionalized delivery of health care to acutely sick family members, as Mark Walker is well aware.

> Mark Walker, a low-income African American long retired from his job in an auto parts factory, is home five days after his lower leg was amputated because of diabetes. Most of his postsurgery care takes place in his home. Between visits by a home health care RN, his wife, Jessie Lee, cares for his stump wound and encourages him to walk between visits from the physical therapist.
>
> Because Mrs. Walker is also ailing, a home health aide will come every day for three weeks to give personal care to Mr. Walker and help him walk. If Mrs. Walker was not living with him, the aide would also do light cooking.
>
> Mr. Walker is happy to be home rather than in the hospital, and Mrs. Walker is glad to care for him and eager to learn to nurse him. Sometimes things seem to be "too much," and the Walkers regret not having more help with everyday routines.

In 1975, Mrs. Walker had a very different experience after cataract surgery.

> When Mrs. Walker had cataract surgery, she stayed in the hospital for thirteen days. All presurgery tests were done on her during the first two days. For six days after surgery, she was immobilized. Then, for five more days, she was monitored in the hospital as she regained her physical strength and all body functions. On her last two days of hospitalization, she helped with sicker patients by changing the water in flower vases and getting books from the gift shop.
>
> For a month, a white RN from the visiting nurse association came to her home several times weekly, checking on her eyes and general recovery. An African American home attendant helped with housekeeping, shopping, banking, and bill payments. The aide also drove her to the doctor's office.

Since then, treatment for cataracts has been simplified by the use of lasers instead of surgical knives, and Mrs. Walker would now be expected to recover at home and rely less on paid helpers there.

Basic care is increasingly given in outpatient clinics and by home health service agencies that provide an RN, a chore worker, and a twenty-four-hour emergency line. Not all patients receive the same support, as the cases that follow illustrate.

Laurel Di Stefano and Missy Porter Kenworth are each recovering from a lumpectomy and are receiving chemotherapy and radiation treatments.

Laurel is thirty-four years old, white, and unmarried; she lives alone in a small cottage on a friend's property. She has no health insurance, "spent down" her assets, and is on Medicaid, the federal program for the indigent. Four days after surgery to control metastatic breast cancer and to replace a hip joint destroyed by the disease, she was discharged to her home. A white home health RN comes every three days to check her responses to drug therapies and supervise her physical therapy. Marie, a home health aide trained as an RN in the Phillipines but unable to pass the state's licensing examination, comes every other day to cook, bathe Laurel, and do other personal care. But Laurel must depend on friends for grocery shopping, library books, her mail, hot evening meals, and other necessities of life.

Missy is white, married to a corporate executive, and the mother of three girls. Before her illness, she taught fifth grade, and she still has health insurance through the school, which covers what her husband's insurance does not. A white home health RN visits her four times each week; a Malaysian-born physical therapist came every day for three weeks and now comes twice a week. Missy gets help from an African American chore worker for two hours, five days a week. However, she also hired a housekeeper to work twenty more hours, and Missy relies on her to do light housekeeping, cook dinner, and do some childcare. A catering service makes weekend meals, and a cleaning service does the house weekly.

The vignettes[2] illustrate self-service in retailing and health care. They show how women's domestic work, done directly for the benefit of the family or one of its members, also complements and completes the work of employees in stores, hospitals, and clinics. And the vignettes illustrate the class and racial–ethnic differences in paid service work and women's self-service labor.

Why Has Work Been Reorganized?

Capitalism reduces or reorganizes paid work, in part, by using women's unwaged domestic work in the labor process. The capitalist *labor process* refers to management-designed use of tools, knowledge, raw materials, and relations among workers, organized to produce goods and services for the market and for capitalist profit (Braverman 1974). As a mode of production, capitalism is distinguished from earlier modes by the *commodification* of labor power. Labor power is bought by capitalists who own and control the means of production and is sold by workers who do neither. Workers must sell their labor power for wages and salaries and spend their earnings on goods and services. Their purchases in the marketplace include things they produced as well as those provided by independent artisans, professionals, state employees, and other workers.

In combining the unwaged domestic labor of women with the waged labor of service workers, also mostly women, employers invented a new social relationship. The *work transfer* is the redistribution of labor from paid women service workers to unpaid women family members, but one that maintains a connection between the work. Most important, the work transfer is completely at odds with the belief that social life is divided between the public and private spheres because it actually draws on both paid and unpaid labor.

Labor is decommodified, in part, when employers cease buying the labor power of service workers or buy less of it and from fewer workers. But the need for the service labor does not disappear, and so the work remains. Employers force a new division of labor through the work transfer, redistributing tasks between paid service workers and customers—clients (and their caregivers). The new labor process is at odds with the view that the trend in capitalism is always to commodify labor power, including services, and never to decommodify.

In the work transfer, the labor process is reorganized to depend on what has been called "self-service" or "self-care." The work that still needs doing is reassigned, deliberately or unwittingly, and most often to women as family members (Abel and Nelson 1990; Szalai 1972). Men do unwaged work too, but less often than women because of women's subordination in the sex—gender system and their responsibility for domestic activities. The reorganized everyday activities in shops and health care delivery coerce women into doing work in the new division of labor. Advertising, political ideologies, or both are used by employers and state agencies to persuade women that the new work guarantees freedom of choice, keeps the family together, is convenient and cheap, respects individual rights, and so on. The work transfer exemplifies the capacity of capitalism to shape even the most intimate details of social life, in this instance even the tending work that women do as family members.

The Choice of Industries for Research

Self-service occurs in many organizations in the United States: self-service gasoline stations displaced young male workers and until women increased their ownership of cars made more work for men than women customers. Automatic teller machines (ATMs) displaced mostly women clerical workers, but both women and men use the machines. Do-it-yourself law involves largely poor women clients and legal aides who substitute for lawyers by preparing restraining orders against batterers and in landlord–tenant disputes. Do-it-yourself law benefits lawyers by relieving them of poorly paid jobs. The work transfer of clerical work passes the responsibility for insurance paperwork to clients or asks charge customers to do paperwork that minimizes that of office workers. Computerized libraries require scholars to become experts in computerized searches, reduce the assistance of research librarians, and encourage libraries to hire aides and library assistants in place of professionals.

In both the retailing and health care industries, women predominate as paid workers. There are similarities and differences in the history of each industry, in relevant changes in the structure of capitalism and state power, in dependence on gender systems, and in reliance on ideologies of individualism. Women as wage earners and women as unpaid domestic workers find their work altered in both. The former face job loss, deskilling, speed-ups, and job consolidation; the latter, a lot more everyday work and technical tasks once done by the former. More women of color work in the health services industries than in retailing. As members of households, low-income women must do more work than affluent women and men to gain goods and services.

Self-service has an extensive history in each sector. In retailing, it was used first in restaurants in the 1890s and tried with varying success in food stores from 1912 on. Self-service was introduced to department, variety, and specialty stores during World War II. Self-service (self-diagnoses and self-prescription, self-care and family care) was basic to health care until the late nineteenth century. From the 1930s onward, the hospital supplanted the home. But in the decades after World War II, hospitals tried a variety of self-care and patient–family care units in hospital facilities, as well as a modest level of paid home health services.

The outcomes of each industry differ in importance. In retailing, the labor demanded of the customer occurs regularly, with some inconvenience but without life-threatening consequences. In health services, caregiving occurs irregularly, only for those with sick children, parents, and spouses. But the consequences can be very serious: stress, overwork, relapse, and even death.

These two industries contrast in the specific causes of the initial shift to self-service. Retailers tried the work transfer to solve problems of labor shortages, high labor costs, and a decline in customer–client spending. They considered self-service (and freely discussed it in their trade journals), but never said that customers clamored for self-service.

In contrast, in health services, the expansion of home health services resulted from large institutional buyers of insurance pressuring the government to control expenditures in the United States on health care. The federal government capped hospital payments, encouraging the substitution of home health care (and patient financial and domestic responsibilities) for hospitalization. Also, sick people and their families had sought insurance payments for home health care for decades, especially for children and young adults.

In both industries, the direction of change from paid workers to self-service has not been unilinear, nor has it occurred without conflict. In retailing, merchants fought among themselves. In health services, institutional buyers and institutional sellers of services, as well as insurers and the sick, have been in conflict.

There is an important difference in the services provided in each industry. In retailing, the service enables the purchasing of goods, and the service itself can be minimal, provided by persons who may be completely ignorant of the purpose, quality, and appropriateness of the goods. Sometimes the salesclerk is, of course, highly skilled, and the skills as well as the goods benefit the buyer. In health care, most services depend heavily on the schooling, experience, and skills of the persons providing them. It is the service itself that is purchased, even if it sometimes enables the use of goods (e.g., of medications). Hence the "services" in the two industries are, typically, quite distinct.

The Heterogeneity of Capital

Capital includes distinct though overlapping business sectors in retailing, health services, and other industries. Sometimes businesses in each sector compete, and sometimes they cooperate. They try to shape economic policies that they see as maximizing accumulation, ensuring a more cooperative and compliant workforce, or both. They try, but they do not necessarily succeed. Nor do businesses engage in identical practices or agree on what impedes accumulation or on solutions.

Divisions and dual interests in capitalism are common. From 1905 through the 1950s, retailers in the United States sought conflicting state policies, fought over markets, and organized boycotts against one another. Supermarkets, regional and local chains, prominent local merchandisers, and "Mom and Pop" stores competed with one another. But they also warred within each subgroup over product standardization, brand names, price setting, and labor organizing. Large retailers diversified, buying land and factories to be able to manufacture goods for stocking their own stores, and they adopted self-service. Smaller retailers and local merchants tried, through local ordinances or boycotts, to prevent chains and supermarkets from using self-service to lower their prices. From the 1940s through the 1960s, retailers pared their workforce and deskilled the salesclerk. But in the late 1970s and through the 1980s, "boutique" groceries, food shops, clothing stores, and finally some department stores began to reemphasize clerk service. Nordstrom of Seattle (with stores in California, Oregon, and New York) was the exemplar, with its use of commissions to encourage salesclerks to increase their sales and its use of emotional labor (Hochschild 1983).

In health services, a division exists between major American corporations in the *Fortune* 500, which buy health insurance for their workers, and corporations that sell health insurance, medical goods (such as pharmaceuticals, computers, supplies), and services (such as nursing, medical emergency care, and laboratory analyses). The former want to pay as little as possible for insurance for their workers and tax dollars for federal programs, while the latter relish high prices for health goods and services to ensure high rates of profits. Some corporations may try to circumvent the high cost of medical care for their workers by selling insurance to themselves and running health maintenance organizations (HMOs) for their employees. Others may sell goods and services to providers of health care and simultaneously buy insurance from them, creating lines of both cooperation and conflict (Waitzkin 1983).

Since the 1970s, the health services industry has been undergoing a transformation from a public "human service" industry to a private investor-owned industry. Ironically, the corporatization of health services resulted from public funding: Medicare, Medicaid, and direct federal and state grants for training, services, and equipment and buildings. Today, health services are neither "private" nor "public"; they are a mix. Users—patients and their families, public interest groups, unions, and so on—have also sought more control, wider choices, and improved quality in health services. Their struggles have sometimes been coopted or subverted, transformed by corporate capital through the state into a narrow focus on *financial* self-responsibility. Users asked for medical and nursing care at home for its social, physiological, and emotional advantages. Congress and corporate buyers, however, embraced home care as a cost-saving strategy and ignored the cost and labor that was shifted to the individual and family.

Capitalist managers and state policymakers have set the context for the new work relations described in this book. Their efforts at cost containment enlarge women's unpaid labor in the household and shift the costs of social reproduction from capital and the state back to the individual and the family. Using ideologies of "professionalization," "self-responsibility," and "free choice," congressional and corporate cost-containment programs have produced the work transfer in health care.

Linking the Private and the Public

Zaretsky (1973) lamented that the concept of a private sphere of "personal life" obscured the connection between capitalist production and daily life. Both scholars and citizens have come to recognize women's double day in advanced capitalist countries (Finch 1983; Hochschild and Machung 1989; Lapidus 1982; Pleck 1985; Szalai 1972). But the concept of a split between the private and public obscures a third burden: women's work in linking or knitting together for-profit enterprises and state programs with daily family life. Unpaid domestic labor is double-edged in retailing and home health, serving the family but serving organizations too. Much of the activity of shopping today is work that in 1900 was done by salesclerks, stock clerks, wrappers, "box boys," and others employed in the retail food industry. In 1900, the typical clerk filled the order, cutting meat to the customer's wishes, weighing out an exact quantity of dried beans, fresh fruits, and grains, measuring to the customer's needs. Today, the shopper (still most often a woman) must locate the goods she wants to buy and collect them in a basket she wheels up and down aisles. She unloads her selections at the check-out counter and may even bag them as well as carry them home. Stores have been able to do with fewer paid workers by rearranging their physical layouts and then convincing buyers that it is desirable or inevitable that customers work in order to buy.

Health service work has changed too. Today, the patient and the family do both trivial and highly technical work because of shorter hospital stays and increased treatment in outpatient clinics. Until the early 1970s, hospitals and clinics depended on low-paid service workers for routine recordkeeping, transporting of laboratory specimens, and supervision of patients undergoing diagnoses. Recent trends in acute-care hospital employment eliminate or reduce the numbers of lower-grade service workers, and patients do much of the work that remains, carrying lab specimens and records and doing paperwork for insurance claims. Organizational strategies to reduce costs and reorganize work vary: earlier discharge of patients from the hospital; increasing use of outpatient or ambulatory services; layoffs of wardclerks and runners.[3] Most important, patients spend little time in hospitals and increasingly are treated only as outpatients. The new nurses are family members.[4]

Self-Service

THE THIRD BURDEN

The double day for women with family responsibilities is extended with a third burden. The burden solves problems for capitalists and the state, but not necessarily for wives and mothers. Women's unpaid work in retailing and health care delivery makes capital more efficient and is expected to reduce corporate expenditures on health insurance and tax expenditures on the health care of the elderly and poor. Married white women and those with children under five years of age increased their paid labor outside the household beginning in the 1950s, but without decreasing their unpaid domestic labor to a like degree or drawing on their husbands' labor (Berk 1985; Berk and Berk 1979; Meissner et al. 1975; Oakley 1974).[5] In the mid-1960s and early 1970s, employed married women spent more time on obligatory work, paid and unpaid, than married unemployed women, and their husbands gained free time instead of spending more time on housework and childcare (Robinson et al. 1977). Industrial societies seem similar in this respect. In the 1980s in Australia, women did more total work than their husbands (Antill and Cotton 1988). In Canada, wives and husbands spent the same amount of time doing paid and unpaid work, but men did only one activity at a time, while women did many (Harvey 1989). In the United States, only one study (of the 1970s) concluded that women had reduced their paid and unpaid work so that the total "work" time of spouses converged (Pleck 1982), but the data showing changes in men's behavior are "cloudy at best" (Coverman and Sheley 1986).

Gender differences in work persist in the two tasks with which I am concerned, retail shopping and health care. As recently as the early 1980s, spouses shopped together mainly for expensive items. Otherwise, the wife bought groceries and household supplies more often than the husband and was twice as likely to shop with him for his clothes than he was for hers (Atkinson and Huston 1984). Few studies have researched health care in the household division of labor. In Finland, the care of the elderly, the sick, and persons with handicaps appears to be women's unpaid domestic labor (Kilpio 1981; Santii et al. 1981). In the Netherlands in 1980, women assisted other households, helped relatives, and gave medical care outside the home (Aldershoff et al. 1983). Staying home with a sick child, and missing a paid job to do so, remains the mother's responsibility in the United States (Nyquist et al. 1985). We know that women give the overwhelming majority of care—about three-quarters of it—to the chronically ill and help a good deal when men are the primary caregivers (see Chapter 7).

SELF-SERVICE AND POLICY

The conceptual split into private and public is reflected also in solutions proposed by policymakers, opinion leaders, and even women themselves to the burdens of combining employment and family responsibilities: flexible hours, childcare centers in the workplace, personal-leave time for eldercare and emergencies, part-time work, split shifts, and the like. None of these remedies relieves women of work. Some, such as legislating work leaves to care for sick parents and spouses, legitimate new work. The solutions promote a view of woman as a "sponge," capable of absorbing new responsibilities without dropping old ones. Few women are wealthy enough to hire "substitutes for themselves" (as if the tasks were inherently gendered) or want to give up a personal life so as to have a career (Glazer 1980).

Solutions to women's family burdens do not challenge wage labor as a fundamental way of organizing production, or the legitimacy of connecting health, housing, vacations, and other rights to employment rather than citizenship. For example, childcare is described as *for* "working mothers." These solutions do not challenge the domination of family life by capitalism. Instead, changes occur when employers decide solutions to women's problems will maintain a stable workforce. Women workers are not seen as having the right to a decent family life that is independent of the needs of capital.

What is missing in public debates is the question why "families" are responsible *for* their members, while workers are responsible *to* their employers. The family continues to appear as a unit outside society, outside the influence of the *private* ownership of capital and capital's domination of the *public* sphere.

SELF-SERVICE MEANINGS

Self-service has two meanings. In the marketplace, it refers to customer coercion by retail organization and/or persuasion by extensive advertising to take part in the labor process of enterprises. Thus grocers rearranged floor plans and reduced the numbers of salesclerks or eliminated them altogether. The system forced customers to do tasks once done by clerks. Today, health care in the United States is undergoing a similar reorganization of the delivery of medical and nursing services. By reducing payments to hospitals, the federal government has encouraged hospitals to force acutely ill patients to do a substantial amount of self-care at home, rely on family members for services once provided in hospitals by trained health care workers, or both. This is the self-service I examine.

But social critics of the welfare state imbue self-service with desirable family and community social values. They see self-service as liberating people from destructive dependency on the state, best exemplified by George Bush's "thousand points of light."

Self-service is portrayed as having other benefits. It reduces costs for citizens–clients who are angry at spending tax dollars on state services for the elderly and the poor and is an alternative to impersonal services from technocratic experts. Serving oneself or being served by an unpaid family member reduces the ambivalence people experience when being "served," increases customer control over choices, and reduces the reliance of the sick on experts. It enables customers to reject obviously defective, inappropriate, or unwanted goods. (Living in England in the early 1970s, I encountered a greengrocer who insisted on selling blemished produce to me, philosophizing to my complaints that "you have to take the bad with the good, dearie.") It may also make people feel righteous to provide for the needs of loved ones at some sacrifice and inconvenience.

Does self-service lower costs for the ordinary customer or client? In retailing, there seems little evidence of marked savings in money, time, convenience, or otherwise for people who do for free the work that once was done by waged workers. This is largely because once self-service markets were able to drive stores with the same volume of sales from the market, they could raise prices without fear of competition. Nonetheless, buyers may prefer to shop without salesclerks, whom they may view as a hindrance or uninformative. Shoppers may rarely fantasize about a retail system in which their needs could be met quickly and reliably, a reality only for the rich. In health care, the financial saving of shifting work to patients and their families is not reflected in reduced out-of-pocket costs but in reduced costs to businesses and the federal government. There are many psychological and social gains for the sick, who prefer their own homes and more control over their daily lives to impersonal, noisy, and even dangerous hospitals. Yet home care without appropriate discharge from the hospital and adequate support at home (good equipment, comfortable rooms, adequate food, and sufficient support from RNs and home health aides) creates other problems: hospital readmissions, increased mortality, emotional distress, and interpersonal crises for family caretakers as well as patients.

In this chapter, I have argued that retailing and health service work, firmly rooted in the marketplace, are susceptible to being reorganized so that they are done jointly by paid and unpaid workers, largely women. In subsequent chapters, I examine the pressure to reorganize the labor process in two industries. In retailing, services perform a distributive function, that is, clerks transfer goods to the buyer. In health care, the services themselves are largely what is distributed to customers, that is, nursing personnel provide care as well as goods.

2

The Work Transfer
in the Service Economy

Women's new unpaid "self-service" labor expands because work has been taken from women's paid service jobs. Hence the work transfer occurs in the service rather than the manufacturing sector. I call women who do paid and unpaid service work "servants to capital" to mark how capitalists orchestrate the contraction of paid service work and to suggest that the results transform many women into what John Kenneth Galbraith (1973) labels "crypto-servants." Women do work that makes it possible for their families to consume pleasantly and painlessly at high levels. They do what servants do for the rich and some of what paid domestic workers may do for more affluent women in professional–managerial strata (cf. Glenn 1986; Rollins 1985).

As household members, women have responsibilities assigned to them by custom, law, and circumstances and justified by ideologies. The assignment is then expanded by decisions made by men (and some women) in the capitalist class, in federal and state legislatures, and on the boards of social agencies. Sometimes even consumer advocacy groups promote arrangements that call for unwaged or self-service work by women.

Liberal and radical theories conceptualize free domestic labor as private, limiting women's opportunities by draining their time and energy from paid work but having only *indirect* consequences for capital. I offer an alternative view. Capitalists and managers are innovative, forever inventing new ways to reorganize the labor process so as to lower labor costs. In the work transfer, women's unpaid labor flows over the purported boundary between the private sphere of the family and the public sphere outside it. By connecting the "public" world of formal organizations and the "private" world of the household, women's unpaid domestic labor as customers, clients, and as relatives of patients aids capital accumulation directly.

I use the terms *customer, client, user*, rather than *consumer*, to reflect difficulties with this last term: its lack of recognition of the importance of production and the uncertain consensus between producers and buyers about social needs. Also, I use these terms to get away from the oxymoronic concept of "the consumer society." The consumer society avoids considering how capitalists control what gets produced, and use advertising in the public media as well as the schools and politics to generate a social need for their products (goods and services). Advertising legitimates purchasing goods and services as the fundamental human path to satisfaction and the good life and unending buying as social progress. The pair *producer–consumer* implies that the spending of wages and salaries establishes a social relationship of equality with corporations, reflecting the assumption of mainstream economic theorists that equal power between producer and consumer is played out in supply and demand.

Consumer implies that distribution is the central issue and that the marketplace offers the services (and goods) that people need and want. This ignores the social relations of production, including the centralization of production, its multinational character, and the virtual disappearance of corporate national loyalty. And it ignores the wage by which women and men buy services and return profit to capital. Finally, *consumer* suggests the atomized individual, with only her or his individualized needs and choices—a house and backyard, a car, a doctor—but without social needs, such as for affordable housing, safe public parks, public transportation, public health, and access to health care (Williams 1980: 188). Customers, clients, and users are also terms that are atomistic and individualistic, but at least they are less tied theoretically to the producer–consumer model.

A New Labor Process

Given my concerns in this book, I use *work* to include activities that are socially assigned to women as customers–clients *and* used by capitalists and the state.[1] Therefore, I use work to mean activities that produce goods and services that directly or indirectly benefit capital, though others use or benefit from them too. This is not to downplay the extensive labor that women do in the household and community, but to specify my concern with showing how capitalist firms and the state tie together women's paid and unpaid labor.

Work includes both paid work and unpaid work (inside and outside the home) organized by firms and state agencies to contribute to capital accumulation and profit. This includes work in (1) the commercial sector, in which labor produces no material objects or services that have exchange value but help to distribute goods and services; (2) unpaid domestic labor in and outside the home that is inserted into the labor process in for-profit and nonprofit enterprises and state-supported programs.

THE WORK TRANSFER AS PROCESS

Women's domestic labor is used for much business and human service work through the mechanism I call the *work transfer*. Managers change the labor process, that is, how work is organized, in efforts to maximize worker productivity. Their widely recognized mechanisms include a detailed division of labor and automation, job consolidation (in which the tasks of two or more jobs are combined), upgrading skills without increasing pay, and speed-ups (e.g., increasing the pace of work and the length of the working day and reducing the piece rate).

In manufacturing, employers increase worker productivity fairly well by using these techniques. But each depends on the objects of labor (the parts of goods) being standardized and interchangeable and on the work being done at a pace that can readily be controlled by management, not by buyers or clients. In service industries, the objects of labor are customers, users, and clients who want services, but unlike in manufacturing, their wants are not readily standardized or interchangeable, and they cannot be easily forced to a measured pace of demand by sellers or providers. People want food *when* they are hungry and to shop *when* they have needs, time, and money or credit; people need most of their medical–nursing care *when* they are acutely ill or are struggling with chronic health problems. Service workers must be on-call continually or for long periods, even though buyers and users may make demands on them only intermittently, that is, when the customers see themselves as needy.

Modern "queueing theory" gives managers predictions of customer–client demands for services, but still does not allow them to force customers and clients to distribute their demands evenly over the working day, which would improve worker productivity. But managers can use queueing theory to reduce the size of their labor force and can increase part-time work and use the labor of customers and clients (or their surrogates) to fill any gaps in paid services. Organizing a store to require self-service or sending a patient home to a family caregiver are two such uses of unwaged labor.

Equally important, self-service in retailing promotes the sale of goods more than the sale of service labor can, given the difficulties of increasing the productivity of service workers (Mandel 1975). Relying on the work of customers, clients, and their families has historical precedent in the United States, as noted in Chapter 1. From the "cafeterias" of the 1890s through food stores in the 1920s to all variety of nonluxury shops from the 1940s on, retailers have adopted self-service to circumvent their inability to control the pace of shopper demands for services and reduce the "wasteful cost" of having salesclerks wait around for customers. Retailers have grasped that the customer's labor can "contribut[e] to company and industry productivity" (Heskett 1986: 106) and that the costs of service workers can be reduced by substituting the free work of customers for that of waged workers.

VARIATIONS IN THE WORK TRANSFER

Grocers have installed expensive machinery—automatic scanners, moving belts, cash registers, and large shopping carts—in order to facilitate the cash transaction, rather than add clerks to their workforce to help customers. That services are costly compared to goods shows also in health care. In anticipation of a growing market, corporations supplying home-care goods tried to form partnerships with nonprofit visiting nurse associations, who would have provided all services used in home care. Associations that refused did so because their managers were well aware that federal reimbursements for supplies and equipment, not services, supported care for Medicare and Medicaid patients (Interviews 1985).

Managers in public agencies and nonprofit organizations, such as health care facilities, have also substituted client labor (and that of their families) for wage work (Lovelock and Young 1979: 66). Throughout most of the nineteenth century in the United States, family members relied on each other, especially on women, for health care. With the development of science-based medicine and the modern hospital, an elaborate hierarchy of workers developed. These workers sold health care services sometimes in the home, sometimes in hospitals, in place of family nursing and birthing. After World War II, hospital administrators tried to increase the productivity of health service workers by reassigning some of their work to patients and family caregivers. This freed professionals and ancillary health workers to do other work, but without reducing direct costs to patients (Blitzer 1981). Hospitals experimented with "hospitals without walls" (Koren 1986), "ambulant wings" (Tunstall 1960), "cooperative care" units (*American Nurse* 1979; Gibson and Pulliam 1987), and "care-by-parent" units (Evans and Robinson 1983). Family members nursed, and patient and family caregivers did housekeeping, arranged treatments, prepared meals (Tunstall 1960). At Loeb Memorial Cooperative Care Unit, the two shared a hospital room, listened to lectures on posthospital care, took meals together, and attended nonalcoholic cocktail hours (*American Nurse* 1979; Interview 1983).[2]

Self-service is used extensively in other industries. In the 1970s, banks adopted automatic teller machines, telephone companies adopted direct dialing and telephone self-installation, and the U.S. Postal Service began to use sender-coded mail (i.e., zip codes), relying on customer work that allowed a smaller paid workforce (Heskett 1986). By the late 1980s, most states allowed "self-service" gasoline pumping for private cars. To save money in 1989, the Portland, Oregon, police department switched to "self-service" crime reports for victims of burglaries, vandalism, and other petty property crimes (*Oregonian* 1989).

Business makes extensive use of customers as unpaid clerical workers: in the 1950s, tellers ceased filling out withdrawal and deposit slips; since the 1970s, many physician and dental offices are likely to expect patients to complete insurance forms that the professionals use for reimbursements; mortgage, charge account, utility, and other bills may include a request for account numbers on payment checks and envelopes to help clerks sort incoming mail and ask for "amount paid" to relieve clerks of a recording task. (Several dentists explained to me that they deliberately require patients to fill out insurance claims rather than hire more clerks.)

The service sector is particularly conducive to this varying use of client–customer labor. Many, but not all, tasks transferred from paid workers require few skills and virtually no "training." In some ways, low-level skills and minimal training characterize a sizable majority of jobs in the new and growing service sector.

Service and Self-Service

Economists and sociologists have no single explanation for the growth of the "service" sector. Some even doubt that the growth is sufficient to call the United States a "postindustrial" or "service society" (Walker 1985; Mandel 1975). Social scientists also disagree on what "services" include and who gets them (Testa 1989).

THE SERVICE ECONOMY

The service economy in advanced capitalist economies refers to the dominance of non-goods-producing jobs and a shrinkage of capital investment and employment in manufacturing. The service sector contrasts with extractive and manufacturing sectors, which, however, also include "service workers." For example, manufacturing firms hire employees to do clerical work, maintenance, research and development, legal work, management consulting, accounting, advertising, and data processing. The increasing purchase of these services by manufacturing firms has resulted in the estimated growth of "augmented manufacturing," that is, work that is not direct production, from 10 percent in 1957 to 25 percent in 1987 (Testa 1989).

Which services support what varies: services include *productive* ones, such as finance, design, and legal services; and *distributive* services, such as transport, communication, storage, and sales. The *social services* (health, education, income transfer) and *personal* services (restaurant service, cleaning, entertainment, hotels), envisioned as the core of the new society with its service economy, are only two kinds of services.

In the so-called postindustrial society, most services may not mainly serve individuals and households. *Producer services* may support other industries, such as banking, advertising, and legal services may support manufacturing or other service industries, such as hospital chains. *Final-consumption services* go directly to the client, as in health, education, and welfare. But some welfare services, such as public education through land-grant colleges, may be established to service agriculture and industries. *Intermediate consumer services* is another category: these keep equipment such as automobiles, television sets, and appliances usable for members of households and may also serve industries through subcontracting (Miles and Gershuny 1983).

Workers in the service sector hold a wide variety of jobs ranging from professionals (e.g., accountants, teachers, and social scientists) and clerical workers (e.g., secretaries, computer operators, and bookkeepers) to blue-collar workers (e.g., packers and cleaners). Only some of these occupations are classified as "service work." Also, many may supply business and industry, rather than household members. Other service industries, such as banks (part of the finance industry in the service sector), serve businesses mainly, not individual depositors.

Activities that seem to be new "services" may fit into manufacturing, too. The fast-food industry supposedly provides "services." But fast foods themselves are "manufactured," and customers are sold ready-to-eat food, not unlike what can be bought in grocery stores. Indeed, fast-food restaurants require some self-service. Customers place orders, pick them up, collect condiments and napkins, and afterward dispose of their trash. (Nobody has yet asked eaters to wipe down their table after eating, but the low level of "service" may make customers do so.) Fast-food outlets may "mark the triumph of industrial food preparation," rather than burgeoning services (Walker 1985).

Explanations for the growth in services vary. The most optimistic is that of Colin Clark (1940), who views economic progress as a move from agriculture to manufacturing to services. Daniel Bell (1976) used Clark's scheme to conclude that the United States was becoming a "postindustrial" society. In Bell's view, the shift from the dominance of manufacturing to that of services signaled major positive consequences for worker satisfaction, class structure, and economic and political power. The old class division between owner and worker was fading because ideas were supplanting objects. Intellectual skills, rather than the control of capital, were becoming the major source of power. Boring, tedious manufacturing jobs would be replaced by challenging service jobs in "transportation, communication and utilities, health, education, research and government, with jobs, typically, professional, scientific and technical, [making] work satisfying, and technology allowing rational social policy" (Bell 1976: 15). Health services and education would burgeon in response to citizen demands.

This utopian vision has not been realized. The theorists of "postindustrial" society believed that a service economy would lead to high-

quality health care, childcare, and public education. They did not anticipate the recurrent economic crises in capitalism, which the United
States has been experiencing since the early 1970s, or the decline in
federal funding during the Reagan and Bush presidencies.

Service jobs have also failed to provide workers in the United States
with work that is more satisfying than work in manufacturing, and with
an improved quality of daily life (Bell 1976; Galbraith 1973; Schumacher
1979). Most jobs in retailing and health care offer low wages, short
career ladders, and high rates of job burnout. Most service jobs substitute a new form of drudgery for the old one, but in nonunionized, low-
wage, and increasingly part-time jobs without benefits. The slowdown
in economic growth since the 1970s and the subsequent cutbacks in
health, education, and other human services show the theories of the
service economy as a progressive stage in economic evolution to have
been erroneous (Gershuny 1978).[3]

Complementary and less elaborate theories posit the growth of the
service sector to be a response to the needs of capital for well-developed
technical management. Worldwide corporate expansion produces and
demands more information for rational planning in increasingly complex organizations. But organizational complexity may simply make
more visible the services that were always present (Pollard 1979). Other
theorists see service jobs as "fill-ins," created by the capitalist class to
reduce the high unemployment that results from high productivity in
manufacturing and market satiation. Jobs in social services, education,
health, and social welfare are make-work for persons whose labor is no
longer needed in manufacturing. Some service work also extends the
period of preemployment and thereby reduces unemployment, since it
requires extensive postsecondary schooling. In turn, jobholders in the
social services (social workers, welfare aides) placate the temporarily or
permanently unemployed with income and in-kind grants. College and
university teachers transmit the values of capitalism—or the futility of
resistance to the material stranglehold and cultural hegemony of the
capitalist class—to those who will transmit these values through public
school teaching, mass media, medicine, engineering, and so on.

Two theories of service growth consider worker and customer demands. One suggests that worker preference forces the growth.
Workers prefer service jobs and refuse to take jobs in manufacturing,
forcing employers to automate and offer service jobs to workers (Pollard 1979). The other posits that the satiation of "consumer" demands

reduces the need for manufacturing, for as households become saturated with durable goods, their members cease buying goods and switch to buying services.

These latter theories are not far from common sense, and they exaggerate individual choices. As long ago as 1939, Louis E. Kirstein, vice-president of the legendary Filene's department store of Boston, explained that his stores provided so many services because public demand and technological improvements had reduced the number of workers in manufacturing and that "some new function had to be developed for these workers to render services" (National Retail Dry Goods Association 1939: 34). Workers' preference seems to be for better-paying jobs in manufacturing rather than minimum wage "Burger King" jobs, though displaced workers seem to have little power.

WHY SELF-SERVICE?

The critical issue to me is why self-service emerges. Some social theorists use "self-service" to refer to activities in the irregular, or underground, economy in which people barter goods and services with each other "off the books," that is, without reporting them to tax authorities. Others use "self-service" largely to mean voluntary social services that may be given to the needy by community groups, neighbors, and friends when the state ceases to provide social services (Cf. Glazer 1983; Henry 1987; Miles 1985) I use it to refer to the use of the labor of customers or clients to complete processes of buying goods or services.

Nathan Glazer (1983) attributes the rise of self-service in social services to the power of citizens, to their disappointment with the welfare state, its bureaucratic snarls, impersonality, and excessive costs. Others interpret self-service as filling a vacuum, giving people with excessive leisure and, perhaps, reduced incomes something with which to fill their free time! Self-service becomes a magic cure-all. It makes up for lost income, reduces welfare expenditures, creates "community," and provides people with "an alternative to mass-produced entertainment and education" (Miles 1985: 593). Managers may justify the work by portraying it to customers as "liberating," a "participative option" that allows customers to "choose" between self- and full-service in banks, gasoline stations, hotels, airports, and restaurants (Langeard et al. 1981: 3).

The explanations for the emergence of self-service are not convincing. Ernest Mandel (1975) offers an explanation that I find more compelling. He rejects the view that advanced capitalist societies are "postindustrial" and notes that in these societies, "mechanization, standardization, over-specialization" and a highly detailed division of labor characterize agriculture and recreation as much as industrial production (1975: 387). He attributes the growth of certain services to a problem indigenous to capitalism, that of securing the growth of capital as areas for investment shrink. While many workers perform services (housemaids, cooks, cosmeticians, cleaning and repair services, tailors), most produce no value for capitalists. But the production of the equipment that these service workers use does. Firms that must constantly establish new markets do so by creating new products, and new markets for these. All manner of equipment is necessary for the new services, the more expensive and profitable the better. The services that have been interpreted as signs of a postindustrial society could not exist without a base of "high-tech" and other expensive material supports. "Service" workers (clerks) run word processors and computers, keeping records for stores, hospitals, and even for the manufacturers of typewriters and computers.

Self-service also usually demands expensive equipment. Entertainment "services" depend on many goods—theaters, television sets, films—and self-service at home requires videocassettes, VCRs, and televisions. Educational services require the material support of textbooks, and even self-service learning requires expensive computers, software, and school buildings. Restaurants often use meals manufactured in factories, but self-service and take-out meals require the restaurants themselves, home microwaves and freezers, delivery trucks, and telephones. Health care depends on very expensive materials—buildings, supplies, and equipment—but uses relatively cheap labor. (While the earnings of physicians are very high, those of most health service workers are quite low.) Home health care uses expensive small-scale equipment, extensive supplies that can be used without hospital support (e.g., premeasured manufactured medications, home-style hospital beds, disposable sterile bandages, needles, and syringes).

Even among service jobs that are of little or no value to capitalism, there are few that require mainly information coupled with high-level skills. These may be artists and performers, writers and editors, cleaners and salesclerks, and perhaps teachers, religious leaders, librarians, and lawyers. But these jobs, too, depend on extensive material support. For example, in the so-called revolution in information dissemination and retrieval, microfilms and microfiches supplanted entry books and cards for cataloguing library holdings. Now they are being replaced by computers with "databases" that library users must learn to use. Expensive equipment and self-service eventuates in lower-cost labor—in this case, more library aides and work–study students and fewer professional librarians. It also calls for more free labor, for self-service to replace the more costly labor of trained research librarians. Unpaid work also depends on commodities that have been manufactured for household use—appliances, ovens, electric lawnmowers, autos, household furniture, and houses themselves, and the latest food driers for preservation and plastic bins for recycling—as if every step for preventing further degradation of the environment *requires* expensive energy-consuming paraphernalia, new manufactured goods and services that are sold because they ensure the usability of the goods.

The sale by Kodak of its developing and printing services to a Japanese-owned company in the 1980s illustrates the relative profitability of goods versus services. Kodak sold its processing unit to Quelux, Inc., which had a reputation for good service. Small processors were providing better services (custom printing, fewer lost films and slides, shorter turnaround time) at the same or lower prices than Kodak. Kodak sold its money-losing service division, but held on to all sales of materials, continuing to supply Quelux with all equipment, chemicals, and other supplies for processing.

Mandel (1975) focuses on the realization of surplus value through the manufacture of the equipment used in the service industry. Service labor can be a source of value, but one from which employers have more difficulty realizing gains compared to labor in manufacturing (or industrialized agriculture). Managers can try to solve the problem of the lower productivity of service workers by using the work transfer, or self-service.

EVERYTHING IS NOT SELF-SERVICE

Not all decommodification results in self-service. For example, university teachers (still mostly men) may be expected to do their own word processing, but their use of computers is not a work transfer. The shift of work is from one *wage* worker (clerical) to another (teachers), and is a "speed-up" for the second, but not the transfer of work to nonwage persons.

Modern pharmacy may seem to be an intersection between retailing and health care. Shoppers serve themselves, selecting over-the-counter remedies. No new health care work results for customers, however, since they are not doing work once done by pharmacists. Contemporary pharmacists compound few prescriptions, not because customers do self-service, but because pharmaceutical companies manufacture drugs in ready-to-dispense forms and varying dosages.

Do-it-yourself assembly work may seem to be a work transfer, but it is a task of consumption, similar to preparing vegetables for the family pot. While assembly-line workers may become unemployed if their company makes do-it-yourself kits, customer work is not substituted in the manufacturing process itself, and the producer and the retailer profit regardless of what the buyer does with the kit.

DECOMMODIFICATION AS GENDER DISCRIMINATION

Decommodification forces women in households to reabsorb the costs of social reproduction that had been shifted to capital and the state after considerable conflict and struggle. Capital presumably pays some of the costs of social reproduction of workers through taxes, which are then spent on social programs, and in worker benefit packages that include health insurance. The state supports social reproduction through spending on schools, libraries, hospitals, and the like, and through social welfare entitlements to the unemployed and retired, the unemployable and working poor, single mothers and children, and so on.

Decommodification is both a strategy and an outcome. In the private sector, the paid labor power of women workers has been decommodified in retailing, banking, insurance, law, and communications. In the nonprofit "human service" sector, in hospitals, clinics, home-care agencies, and schools, the work transfer seems less deliberately planned, resting on a taken-for-granted premise that women are caregivers. Health policymakers rarely discuss the effects on women in their publications, while retailers were aware early on of the cost savings in getting women shoppers to do self-service. Decommodification is both a strategy and an outcome in that some employers used it deliberately to reduce their workforce, while others, including health policymakers and legislators, corporate leaders and planners, followed a strategy aimed at reducing spending on social wages and entitlements. Self-service in the last instance is an unintended outcome. When decommodification is recognized by policymakers and corporate leaders, it is seen by them as helpful to organizational efficiency rather than as a new problem for women as workers or as family members and caregivers.

Whether the resulting work transfer is deliberate or inadvertent, it increases the productivity of mainly women service workers by reducing a major barrier to their continuous work: the pace or flow of customer–client demand for services. Instead of service workers having to be on-call continuously to respond to customers, customers themselves do the irregular work, releasing the labor of service workers for other tasks. Some service work may still be required, but less now that customers and clients serve themselves or rely on women as family members for the lost paid services.

Infrastructures Supporting Self-Service

Self-service requires supporting material infrastructures and ideologies. These supports include product standardization, centralization of control, state and federal regulations of the marketplace, and customers' beliefs that homogeneous products and self-service meet their needs.

State and corporate decisions forced product standardization of goods and services. In 1905, Congress began to standardize measurement units in both manufacturing and distribution by requiring, for example, one measure for a "single bed" sheet and by specifying the size of a pint, quart, and so on. Similarly, federal reimbursement for the health care of the elderly and indigent and regional and state nonprofit health insurers together forced standardization in diagnostic categories. Medical textbooks also standardize diagnoses, but the practicing physician has a good deal of discretion, ranging from rigid adherence to diagnostic symptoms to flexibility and guesses. The standardized categories of insurance reimbursers force health care providers to report their varied work in identical terms so that the reimbursers can decide whether the services are covered by insurance.

Product standardization reassures customers that they can get the goods or services they prefer or need without relying on service workers for information or discretion. For example, a size 14 dress is supposedly about the same in all brands, though there is variation by price, and a twin-size sheet is the same size from California to New York. In health care, a pap smear, gallbladder surgery, and a physical examination are supposed to follow a standardized protocol.

Many self-tests have been passed to the clients or their caretakers. For example, persons with diabetes monitor their insulin levels, once with urine tests and now with a hi-tech glucose scanner. Hospitals give discharged patients elaborate directions on evaluating their health status, including when to call the hospital for advice, readmission, medication adjustment, and the like. Patients may self-evaluate tuberculosis tests using an intaglio card showing variations in skin reaction ranging from normal to possible active disease.

The centralization of control allows the labor of customers—clients to be used on a large scale, making self-service economically useful, lessening labor problems, and making it easier to disseminate an ideology that makes self-service palatable. Chain stores used self-service to their advantage because they employed many workers and saved a good deal by eliminating salesclerks. Small family businesses gained little in labor-cost savings because most relied heavily on "free" family labor. In health care, central control of reimbursement (or disbursement of care in health maintenance organizations, or HMOs) means that hundreds of thousands of patients are affected. Millions of dollars in costs, mostly labor, are saved when administrators change the health care site from the hospital to the clinic and home.

National media help to make self-service acceptable. For example, national magazines, radio networks, and, eventually, television carried advertisements about nationally distributed products, building customer recognition and thereby dispensing with the reliance of stores on salesclerks to sell products. Products that are advertised nationally are the inevitable core of self-service retailing. The media also informs the public about health facilities and pitfalls of treatments, promotes home services, and so on. National regulation also organizes health services with federal, state, and corporate-driven regulations forming the core of expanding self-care and new work for women in the home and drastically altering the paid work of women in service jobs.

To sum up: the work transfer is a process that originates in the effort of employers to rationalize the use of labor. In manufacturing, machines can substitute for workers. In service jobs, the peculiar and uncontrollable pattern of demand is closer to how people act at home than to how manufacturing proceeds: predictable but also erratic, unexpected and yet having to be met when demand occurs. Only human labor, in the absence of some utopian robot, is able to meet such needs, and self-service is one way by which wage labor can be eliminated and the labor of buyers and clients used instead. In the next chapter, I consider in detail how this process interweaves the family and women's unpaid work for its members to capitalism and the state.

3

Women's Work:
Linking Separate Spheres

Public and *private* have complex, multiple, historically specific and gendered meanings that differ across class, race, and ethnic groups. "Public" life supposedly includes social, economic, political, and intellectual life outside family relations, and is man's world. Women's sphere is predominantly the private one of "personal life" (emotional, sexual, socioemotional, supportive, nurturing) in the family, but also in friendships, among extended kin, and in voluntary associations and neighborhoods—and even in the paid workplace.

Less commonly, but relevant to the retail and health care industries, "public" and "private" refer also to sectors of the economy. In capitalism, private refers to the production of goods and services for private profit, while public refers to "nonprofit" organizations and state agencies. The private sector of the economy is in the *public* social world, as is the public sector (government and private charities and nonprofit organizations). Yet this sharp division is inaccurate even in the economy. The federal government regulates private-sector firms and subsidizes them directly with grants and tax relief. In the nonprofit and for-profit health services industry, the federal government underwrites a sizable percentage of the costs of direct care for the elderly and the indigent and provides grants to hospitals, research institutes, training schools, and so on, for training, research, technology, and buildings. This makes health services "neither conventionally 'private' nor 'public' but an admixture" (Stanback et al. 1981: 135).

Separate spheres gives us a social interpretation of gendered worlds that reaches back into the eighteenth century, capturing the new division between the family and the declining feudal state. The public sphere in capitalist countries emerges as a space between the new capitalist class and the absolutist state, creating a domain of political life for newly enfranchised men (Habermas 1974). During struggles in the new bourgeois state between capitalists, the aristocracy, and the church, this concept of the privatized family was progressive, and middle-class women themselves participated in its elaboration (Fox-Genovese and Genovese 1983). The doctrine of separate spheres ensured freedom for some men from the absolutist state, but transformed the family into a domain where women were expected, according to ideologies in liberal capitalist societies, to compensate for the harshness of the public world of the economy and government.

The dichotomy of public and private justified not only an arena of intellectual and moral privacy free from state intervention but from the older, state-established religions that the emerging bourgeois were rejecting for newer, individualistic ones. The ideology also legitimated the dissolution of the remnants of the feudal community and supported individualistic over communitarian systems of property holding. In the end, the family and its household were established as a realm comparatively free from public, meaning state, scrutiny. But the new capitalist class was freed from moral or material responsibility for the results of the new economy: the wretched working conditions and meager wages in the mines, mills, and factories and the consequences for the living conditions and personal lives of workers and their families.

The Problem of Conceptual Opposites

Dualistic and oppositional thinking about the social world blinds us to overlaps and permeable boundaries. This approach is deeply rooted in Western social thinking, in the dialectic (Offe 1984), and in a binary approach (e.g., either–or, male–female, dead–alive) to the social world. Analyses of the decline of household production and the development of the marketplace use a set of categories reflecting this either–or view, including concepts such as exchange versus use value,[1] productive versus nonproductive labor, market versus nonmarket work, and work in the public realm outside the household versus work at home for the family.

The dichotomies in Marxist theory, unlike those in liberal social theory, describe an asymmetrical, hierarchical social relation (Offe 1984). Nonetheless, theorists may use these terms evaluatively, much as liberal social theorists use pairs of concepts to signal social progress (Mies 1986). For example, for pairs such as modern versus traditional society, rational versus charismatic authority, white-collar versus blue-collar jobs, and service versus the industrial society, most theories imply that the first is more desirable or progressive than the second. Hence some socialists may understand "nonproductive" as of lesser value than "productive," as devaluing women's unpaid domestic labor, and argue that the labor would be better called "productive" in the broad sense of satisfying human needs (Mies 1986: 147–148). Actually, "productive" has a narrow technical meaning (the extraction of value in the capitalist labor process). Similarly, the liberal anthropologist Wadel argues that we should call activities "work" (rather than leisure or nonwork) in order to bolster people's sense of satisfaction because work is more valuable than "nonwork" (Wadel 1979). Such pairs of terms reinforce the view that a sharp boundary separates the market economy with its workplaces from the household economy of the family.

These dualistic concepts may have captured some of the dramatic changes in family production that took place between the late seventeenth century and early twentieth century. Today, these ignore the diversity of women's experiences by class, race, and ethnicity, recognizing only white, American middle-class practices. The terms public and private prevent recognition of the interweaving of these spheres in the labor process, in which customers–clients do self-service to complete work begun by paid workers.

The work transfer is an example of connections across supposed boundaries. From one angle, women's unpaid work is done for the family. But from another angle, it is done for corporate capitalism, because of state policies, or both. Paid work is already recognized as having two effects, across public and private. It is done for capitalism, producing goods and services sold for profit; wages return to capital through spending on those same goods and services. Yet, from another angle, women's participation in paid work forces changes in the family and personal lives (Hochschild and Machung 1989). Labor-force participation provides women with some freedoms, such as an alternative to marriage, but it also results in more responsibilities for many women. Similarly, the work transfer shifts wages, responsibilities, and work, with varying benefits and disadvantages for women as paid and unpaid workers.

Rethinking the Family and the Public Realm

Feminist theorists have held a range of beliefs about the public–private split, from accepting it as universal through seeing it as specific to capitalism to rejecting it as class-bound ideology useful for capitalists seeking to obscure how production organizes "personal" life (Rapp, Ross, and Bridenthal 1979; Zaretsky 1973). Social theory mimicked the nineteenth-century ideologies that bourgeois housewives could absorb from domestic advice manuals, ideologies that "mapped the household as if it were a self-contained world" (Fox-Genovese and Genovese 1983: 304). In sociology, major theorists accepted a fixed and impermeable boundary between public and private and viewed the family as, in some peculiar way, "outside" social life (Parsons and Bales 1955).[2]

I assume that the family is "inside" society, not "marginal," and that social relationships of production and to the state change customer–user–client responsibilities by taking unpaid labor from women. Because of crises and changes in capital and the state, women as "consumers" are coerced, persuaded or both, into social relationships instituted by administrators, managers, and perhaps even workers. In a wage relationship, women would sell their labor power to employers. Through the wage, employers take the results of labor as profit. Women's unpaid labor enters the labor process, and their labor is used by organizations, but outside the wage relationship.

The unpaid labor of customers–clients is required and organized, not as an aspect of the wage relationship, but by how corporations structure consumption in the commercial and service sectors. Customers–clients must act in specific ways to buy goods and services. Labor is *taken from* the retail customer–client, and thereby employers spend less on wages than if they had to keep their workers, raise their wages, or hire new workers at the same or higher wages. Customers–clients are not simply doing work called "consumption" for themselves; they are also performing acts that employers would instead pay workers to do. Thus unpaid domestic labor by customers–clients includes some work that is part of social reproduction and other work that is essential to the circulation of goods in retailing and to the circulation of services in the health industries.

Work

Work itself is a problematic concept, whether paid or unpaid (Beechey 1988; Daniels 1987; Duane-Richard 1988). It is also what can be called a "privileged" activity, considered by major Western social theorists, social policymakers, philosophers, and probably most adults in the United States to be a major social good. Making people capable of working is the central goal of schooling, a criterion of successful medical and psychiatric treatment, and an ostensible goal of most welfare policies and unemployment compensation programs. It also imbues our legal codes; for example, families are compensated for lost wages of breadwinners. The ability to work forms the pillars of social personhood in modern Western philosophy, psychology, and ethics.

Feminist scholars along with many others see women's unpaid domestic labor as private, done by women as wives and mothers, adult daughters, and daughters-in-law. Women's unpaid labor is seen as connected to the world outside the family, that is, to capitalism or to society, through the labor that women do for their families. Under the press of feminist criticism, Marxist theorists began to stress social reproduction, or how women's unpaid domestic work supports capitalism *indirectly*, contributing to surplus value through the social reproduction of the working class. Women bear children and care for them and other family members through a vast array of activities, mainly in the home. Women's domestic labor is seen as reproducing the working class, materially and ideologically, and on a daily and generational basis as tending to the needs of adults in the workforce (including the self) and rearing children as the next generation of workers. Social-reproduction work means cooking, shopping, cleaning, doing laundry, and so on. It includes other social and emotional activities such as negotiating relationships with kin and friends and, among those in the household, giving emotional nurturance and perhaps trying to create a "haven in a heartless world." Recently, some theorists have connected women's family culture to providing its members with support for organized resistance against state and corporate exploitation (Janiewski 1985; Sacks 1988).

Mainstream social theory sees women's labor in the home only somewhat differently, with the emphasis on indirect labor for "society," rather than for capitalism. Women maintain society and culture by socializing the next generation, readying them for school, preparing them for adult status (Lopata 1971; Oakley 1976; Parsons and Bales 1955). Both radical and mainstream theorists also recognize that more and more married women and mothers of young children work for wages. But most important, domestic labor is seen as private and only *indirectly* organized by social relations outside the family.

Though both mainstream and radical theorists see consumption as an important part of unpaid domestic labor, they see it as done largely in the household and for the family. Theorists overstate the extent to which household goods and services for the household lessen women's domestic labor. Few appreciate the fact that capitalism has failed to industrialize or commercialize domestic work—housework and child-care—to the same degree as in agriculture or manufacturing. New goods may even make more work for women in the home (Bennholdt-Thomsen 1984; Cowan 1983; Hartmann 1974; Mies 1986). Some who see the new work explain it away as a "choice" (Gershuny 1987).

Radical theorists see consumption as essential to capital accumulation. Through the purchase of goods and services, the wages and salaries of workers return to capital, part of the cycle of worker reliance on the marketplace for goods and services and hence on the wage. Barter and off-the-books income in the underground economy give some flexibility to customers–clients, but these require a good deal of knowledge, social skills, and networking. Consumption is not seen as direct "labor for capital," however, but as a final step in the accumulation process, that is, how money circulates between being a wage paid by employers to being profit flowing back to capital as workers spend their wages.

Some mainstream theorists recognize women's consumption work as central to capital (Galbraith 1973). Feminist scholars, too, sometimes emphasize that *social reproduction* underpins particular aspects of *production*, including the gendering of women's opportunities, responsibilities, prestige, power, and rewards (Beechey 1988). Still, these ignore the possibility that "two" worlds fail to describe accurately women's connecting activities that are of neither one nor the other but both.

Few social theorists recognize that capital can substitute unpaid labor for paid labor in concrete ways, as when "self-service shops and automatic dispensing machines take the place of salesmen and shopgirls [*sic*]" (Seligman 1968). The pioneering work of Batya Weinbaum and Amy Bridges (1976) on the labor process is the sole theoretical recognition that challenges conventional analyses of domestic labor.

Weinbaum and Bridges argue that women's domestic labor in capitalist society includes consumption and that "capital organized consumption work for women" by pulling them into the *labor process* in supermarkets, doctors' offices, and laundromats (Weinbaum and Bridges 1976: 88, 94–95). Unfortunately, these insights have not been taken up by social scientists, except for a broad recognition that women's domestic work in capitalist society includes "consumption."

My analysis is complementary to Seligman, and to Weinbaum and Bridges, emphasizing deliberate as well as inadvertent attempts by capital and the state to insert the customer–client into the labor process. In my view, capital and the state eliminate services in a struggle for markets and profits and over social entitlements (health insurance, pensions and unemployment funds, public education, and the like). Because some services fall into monopoly-like sectors, such as health care through workplace insurance, nearly everyone except the rich is likely to do some self-service or service-to-others. The work transfer affects paid workers too, changing their work or even eliminating their jobs. For paid workers, the results include reduced self-esteem, deskilling, increased productivity demands and reduced income, as well as reskilling and increased job autonomy.

FROM WAGE TO NONWAGE WORK

Commercial capital, such as the retail grocery industry, hires wage labor that itself does not add to value but is work through which capitalists appropriate "a fraction of the sum total of surplus value accruing to the entire capitalist class" (Mandel 1981: 59). To the customer–client, the work transfer means that commercial capitalists hire fewer workers to serve them than earlier. Customers–clients work in their place because the organization of buying and selling is altered to eliminate some once paid-for steps in the labor process. For example, customers–clients locate and collect merchandise, which is usually packaged so that measuring and bagging are not needed. Women as customers–clients do the necessary work. Women's unpaid domestic labor may still have only an indirect relationship to changes in profits, but women's unpaid labor is deliberately used by commercial capitalists to lower their own labor costs.

In the health services industry, employers hire labor that both produces services and distributes goods. Health care includes many different kinds of consumption, not only of "services" but also of equipment, supplies, and pharmaceuticals. Workers in health service institutions (hospitals, clinics, nursing homes, and medical offices) may be eliminated and their service work and the distribution of goods shifted to family members and patients.

The wage does not have to be the sole criterion for distinguishing work from other activities, for labor may be used to run a business without workers actually receiving a wage. During the Great Depression, for example, waitresses in some New York restaurants were not paid a wage for their work and even had to share their tips with their employers.

The use of women's unpaid work in the consumption of goods and services is essential to the form that distribution has taken over the past forty or so years: self-service. What may make it difficult to see and respect the activity as work is that, for example, in retailing, each individual woman does a trivial amount compared to paid workers. She works or shops on an irregular basis, for perhaps twenty-five minutes at a time. The work of many women, added together, substitutes for the work of many paid workers. The same occurs in health services. One woman assuming responsibilities for one sick child or spouse or elderly parent may seem relatively minor for the health services industry and even the family. Over many families and parents, the workload is considerable, saving the state and insurers millions in wages and material goods and changing enormously the daily lives and financial costs to women in the affected families (see Chapter 7).

This substitution of unpaid for paid labor originally made the use of customer–client work attractive to distributors in retailing, though other unexpected benefits (e.g., increased sales) continue to make it attractive. For the private customer–client, there is no necessary quid pro quo, no absolute price reduction or reduction in anticipated price rises that reflect the savings on labor of the retailers and health service providers. But others may benefit, such as corporations, which buy health insurance for their workers, or those who believe that their taxes ought not support social entitlements.

CALLING EVERYTHING WORK

Social scientists seem increasingly willing to revalue activities by labeling them work, without changing the material conditions of life. Until the reemergence of feminist scholarship in the 1960s, women's *unpaid work* was virtually invisible in social science theory (Daniels 1988;

Glazer-Malbin 1976). Sociologists treated women's domestic labor as a natural duty, and economists considered it to be "leisure" because it was outside market relationships. From the 1920s onward, surveys were done of household labor in the United States, Canada, and Europe, but until the studies of Helena Lopata (1971) and Ann Oakley (1976), few scholars saw the importance of housework and childcare for feminist theory and women's emancipation. Most were concerned with the impact of technology or egalitarian ideologies on the gender division of labor. A typical listing of "housework," designed to sample both women's and men's tasks, includes cooking, shopping, housecleaning, laundry, bill paying, taking out the garbage, mowing the lawn, and the repair of household appliances. "Childcare," a separate task, includes child minding, bathing, feeding, dressing, and so on, and a bit of medical care (Berk and Berk 1979; Szalai 1972). Other activities, such as the care of elderly parents, sick spouses, and children, are surveyed infrequently.

Some social scientists treat all socially valued activities as work in an effort to gain respect for volunteers and patients. Daniels (1987) describes the "careers" of upper-class and upper-middle-class women in community associations and philanthropies, using the occupational term to signal women's seriousness and the activities' merit. Lopata (1971) took the same approach to housewives. Fuchs (1968) considers patients' recall of their medical history for their physicians to be work. Strauss et al. (1981) call patients' watchfulness over their treatments by nurses and other providers in the hospital "patients' work." The anthropologist Wadel (1979) sweeps just about all activities (except housework!) under the label work so as to improve people's sense of their worth, as if work is always better than "nonwork." Hochschild (1983) draws attention to "emotional work," meaning the fabricated feelings that, for a wage, flight attendants and other service workers are supposed to feel in order to sell services (transportation) or goods.

Except for Hochschild, the broad and general uses of the concept of work rob it of its connections to political economy. For example, Strauss et al. (1981) help us understand that health care is a negotiated event between an active patient and physician, not just an action by an authoritative physician. But the patient's activities are not related to the labor-force composition of the hospital, community or personal financial crises, staffing levels, and other factors that may shape the patient–physician relationship.[3] Theorists could recognize the social usefulness of activities without equating usefulness, helpfulness, social value, or impact with work, and without ignoring social theories about the political economy. Nor should recognition of usefulness downplay how people's everyday lives are structured by the paid work they must do to subsist or are freed from by wealth, and how capitalism organizes free domestic labor.[4]

Historically, capitalism has extended the marketplace into all domains of human life, commodifying goods and services and, most important, labor. It has reorganized the social relations between people so that these are organized by marketplace relationships. Among economists, the awareness of the commodification process has resulted in peculiar arguments about nonmarket time (e.g., unpaid domestic labor). Some economists have argued that "nonmarket time" is a "major source of untaxed income," though they admit that nonmarket time generates no monies that could be taxed (Leuthold 1981: 267). Another economist argues for taxing home production (if economists could decide how to compute its value) to discourage people from producing in their homes instead of buying in the market. This is perhaps the ultimate in the state's trying to force all activities into the market for the benefit of capitalism (J. F. Due, cited in Leuthold 1981: 278).

Restricting the definition of work to activities linked to capital separates what remains relatively unpenetrated by capital and what people in their everyday life may do to protect themselves from capitalist rationality. People can resist turning all social relations into a market function, but our awareness of this resistance will be blurred by a failure to recognize distinctions among human activities.

CLASS, RACE, ETHNICITY, GENDER, AND WORK

Class, race, ethnicity, and gender figure in both the paid and unpaid work that women do, affecting social practices in retailing and health services. These shape the labor process, access to jobs, assignment of domestic responsibilities, use of the marketplace, and so on—the key concerns of this book. Each has been structured by beliefs about gender, race, ethnicity, and class, and by the vast differences among these groupings in access to material resources and hence to authority and social power. Feminists do not agree whether these interact or are additive or in some other relationship in the United States and other advanced capitalist economies. I recognize these categories in my analysis of paid and unpaid work and use them in the following ways.

Class, race, ethnicity, and gender are difficult to interweave in analysis because they address dimensions that refer to different kinds of social units. While each results from social practices, the similarity seems to end there. The term *class* is located in particular theoretical frameworks and refers to distinct social relations of domination that occur only in particular social formations or societies, those with a social surplus. (This leaves aside the common use of *class* to mean relative ranking of occupational prestige, income, years of schooling, and the like.)

Gender implies discriminatory practices and relations of domination. It recognizes a socially constructed difference based on perceptions of biology, but suggests no particular social formation, society, or historical context. Nor is the term tied to one particular social theory, but only recognizes universal or near-universal social differentiation. *Race* recognizes discriminatory differentiation and relations of domination, and some historical and social location, with its common modern usage in Euro-American societies. *Ethnicity* carries with it both a discriminatory implication and a neutral one; in racist societies, it implies discriminatory practices, but otherwise it may carry no such meaning. It is tied to no particular social theory.

Though these terms differ in such ways, scholars may use them as if they had what I call "theoretical equivalence." By that I mean that the differences I just noted between class, race, ethnicity, and gender are ignored. In the United States, for example, most scholars see all four terms as referring to "social differentiation," that is, to social distinctions, such as capitalist, intelligentsia, and worker; women and men; Anglo-Saxon, Jew, African American, and Irish Catholic. *Stratification* means that these differences are socially ranked, men over women, the capitalist class over working class, Anglo-Saxons over other ethnics. These factors, singly and together, affect the daily life of individuals. But this ignores important differences in the concepts.

Class is defined by Marxist theories primarily, in which the Weberian use shares, despite differences. Within Marxist theorizing, *class* by definition refers to social relations of domination and subordination. In capitalist societies, the fundamental class relation is between the capitalist class and the working class, structured by the ownership and control of the means of production and the need of working-class women and men to sell their labor power to capitalists so as to earn a living. The state may be a terrain of class struggle, but it is also the apparatus by which the capitalist class seeks to establish a social order favorable to accumulation. The social relations of class are elaborated, justified, and disputed within other kinds of social relations: the state, schooling, public media, religion, and so on.

The relationship of domination and subordination is permanent, persistent, and inevitable. Whatever gains the working class may make in wages or political and civil rights, and however much increased productivity may result in increased consumption, longevity, leisure, and the like, the working class is politically as well as economically subordinate to the capitalist class. Despite waxings and wanings in working-class influences in organized resistance in the workplace, the community, and the state, the capitalist class maintains domination.

Classes themselves are heterogenous and internally differentiated with "capitalist" and "working class" capturing only the broad outlines of class relations (Marx 1969). The working class is differentiated by gender, race, and ethnicity and class fractions. By class fractions, I refer to varying social relations to capital within the working class and among capitalists. Within the working class, there are broad occupational groups including those increasingly employed in bureaucratic workplaces: salaried professionals and lower-level corporate managers, employees of the state and educational institutions. Also, those in well-paid blue-collar jobs in unionized industries may differ from those in other kinds of blue-collar jobs, in low-wage service jobs and in female-typed white-collar ones, and so on. Women working in the pink-collar ghetto, and women and men who do so-called unskilled work, are in yet another relation to the capitalist class. Between the capitalist class and workers, there are petty capitalists (small-scale farmers, small business owners), and independent and salaried professionals.

The capitalist class itself is divided, sharing an interest in accumulation and profit, but differing on myriad issues—on what strategies are most useful to accomplish this, what concessions can be made to working-class demands for economic rights, which foreign policies support expansion, and so on. While class differentiation, access to resources, and hence the details of inequalities vary historically, what remains fundamental is that in advanced capitalist formations, the capitalist class dominates all other classes.

Race as a social category refers to differentiation and, usually, to stratification, presuming differences within the human species. Also, it sometimes refers to a national group (the English race), sometimes to a mix of religion and culture (the Jewish race), and sometimes to a broad or narrow geographical area (African Americans as descendants of people from the African continent, Americans as people from a multistate culture) (Williams 1983). It usually but not always implies social superiority and inferiority and, most likely, discriminatory practices within a particular society.

Race has been understood differently in different phases of capitalism. In the nineteenth century, it was considered to be biological. "Inherent" differences were used to account for the inability of people of color and groups of white people, too, to resist Western military and economic imperialism, and to justify colonization. Today, race is recognized as a social construct, but now "historical" experiences of different "races" and ethnic groups may be used to justify continuing exploitation and subordination.

Racism has been fundamental in the development of capitalism in the United States. It has been used to support, institute, and justify conquest, genocide, enslavement, economic and sexual exploitation, political disenfranchisement, appropriation of property, and the destruction of cultures.

Racism, along with gender and class, has been built into the structure of U.S. property relations, state organization, and cross-gender relations, as well as into the composition of occupations. Race in the sense of ethnic variations among descendants of European Christians has had a different history than among other groups, including people of color and European Jews. Most people of European ancestry were assimilated relatively easily into the political and economic system, though informal and family networks often remained relatively distinct. But the assimilation of African Americans into the dominant community has been, at best, slight, compared to Latinos and Asians.

"Racism" thus has greater fluidity than class and gender. "Races" may experience a change in their social relations under capitalism more often than gender groups or class, with rising status, increased political power, and the incorporation of some into the capitalist class. These are, de facto, an impossibility in class relations as the capitalist class maintains its dominance.

Gender is a most general term. Usually, it implies relations of domination. The term recognizes a social position based on biological dimorphism, but the material roots of gender stratification may or may not be connected to procreative differences. The terms *women* and *men* are not analytical categories. Neither reveals other social characteristics (e.g., age, race), historical phenomena (e.g., the breakdown of feudalism, large-scale immigration), social processes (e.g., conflict, cooperation), or structures (nuclear families, bureaucracies). To assume that "women" and "men" automatically include relations of domination depends on an essentialist view. Essentialism may underpin some views that gender permeates every and all structures, but if it is an ahistorical factor, then it cannot very well explain the observed variations in sex–gender relations.

Patriarchy, with all its problems (Acker 1989), comes closer to an analytical match with class than does *gender*, since the term implies a specific social relation, though not necessarily within particular types of societies. (In this it is akin to "class" in Marxist analysis.) Patriarchy implies that sex–gender systems can be understood as historically specific, for example, as more prominent in state societies than in others. (*State societies* refers to those with a large economic surplus, military institutions, and a specialized administrative apparatus.)

Feminists have tried to reconcile these categories in theory. One of the most widely debated is the "class first" perspective. In this view, capitalism is primary, and capitalists use and construct gender, race, and ethnicity to suit their needs, or the relationships emerge as a reflection of struggles among capitalists and between capitalists and other classes.

A second major approach, "dual systems," treats capitalism and patriarchy as two autonomous or semiautonomous and interacting systems, so that patriarchy can be analyzed apart from capitalism as well as in relation to it.

A third solution is to conceptualize class, race, ethnicity, and gender "as not autonomous, nor even interconnected, but as the same system" (Armstrong and Armstrong 1986: 226). Acker (1989: 259) concludes "gender and class relations may be produced within the same ongoing practices. Looking at them from one angle, we see class, from another we see gender, neither complete without the other."

CAPITALISM AND WORK

My approach is to emphasize capitalist relations of production and to see how women, as a gender group and within race and ethnic groups, are affected differently. My analysis tries to bring capitalism back into an analysis of women's lives, to highlight the effects of the changing nature of political economy on the working and domestic lives of women. (See Milkman 1987; Sacks 1988; Smith 1987 for such an approach.) My research emphasizes the impact on women's unpaid and paid work lives of strategies used by capitalists to rationalize the labor process. This complements and is distinct, for example, from a more usual focus on women's family burdens, lack of educational opportunities, and gender stereotypes as critical in shaping the labor process in female-typed jobs and accounting for variations by class, race, and ethnicity. Yet, I am not arguing for a "capitalism first" approach that would be mechanistic, nor do I see capitalism as mapping out social life automatically. But for the issues I am investigating, the relation between paid and unpaid work and the imaginary boundary between them, I see capitalism as the central feature. For other issues, for example, sexuality, biological reproduction, mothering, the hegemony of the capitalist class would certainly be influential, but other dynamics may reveal as much or more than starting with the assumed centrality of capitalism.

Self-Service and Caring and Tending

Self-service rests on practices of racial and ethnic discrimination, the subordination of women, and the legal definition and customary expectations of the family. It assumes that despite the ideology of individualism, the family is responsible for its members (Barrett and McIntosh 1984). The practice and ideology of "racism" (meaning both race and ethnicity) shape self-service. For example, self-service flourished in the 1920s in Tennessee, where owners hired African Americans only for backroom or menial front jobs. The shift to self-service in health care has also had a racial dimension, with a decrease in middle-grade and an expansion in lower-grade jobs held disproportionately by women of color. It has also meant disproportionate unpaid work for women of color, for single mothers, and for others with low incomes.

As paid workers, women of all races are more likely than men to be affected by the new labor process. Women predominate in service jobs in retailing and health care, usually as low-wage salesclerks and nursing personnel. Their jobs are the most susceptible to elimination or reduction by self-service. This reverberates also on the continuing gender division of labor in the household, where men, on the average, do not accept the ideology of joint responsibility for social reproduction, their own or their children's. If they do, practice does not reflect ideology. Men do not share equally with women in the self-care and family care of the acutely ill (see Chapter 7).

Most of the work transfer falls on women because of the social ideologies and practices of family care, and because of women's continuing responsibility for unpaid domestic labor (see Chapter 10 on women as amateur caregivers). Women "care for" family members, drawing on feelings of love and affection as well as responsibility whether they are shopping or doing health care. Women do the "care of" family members, which Parker (1981) suggests is better called "tending" because women need skills to do the work, even if it is also a labor of love. "Caring for" and "tending" are interwoven, with love legitimizing coerced and voluntary labor.

Because of their dependency and relative powerlessness compared to men in the home, workplace, and political life, women are more easily coerced into doing the work of social reproduction. Women also acquire the skills and the commitment to tend and care for others, reproducing the labor force on a daily and generational basis. They do the majority of housework, nurturing, childcare, and so on that prepare employed family members for daily work and prepare children to be the next generation of workers. Shopping and health care (nontechnical and technical) for husbands, partners, and children is one among many tasks of social reproduction for which women are responsible.

Women's domestic labor entails another contribution that few theorists of work or family life have recognized: the care of family members who are socially *dependent*. This includes the retired, the acutely ill, and the chronically sick, all of whom may need physical, emotional, and financial assistance (Leonard and Speakman 1986; Strong-Boag 1986). The state may finance many welfare services, but expects families to support their dependent adult members unable to work and care for themselves. These responsibilities are formalized, sometimes, in state "relative responsibility clauses," through which state agencies have the right to ask adult children to support dependent parents, or parents to aid the offspring of their unmarried teenage mothers. State family case law is also a basis for social service agencies demanding that families be responsible for their dependent adult members.

Women's ideologies of caring and household culture make the family more than a "functional" institution for capitalism to which the costs of social reproduction can be transferred (Humphries 1977). The family may not always be a "haven in a heartless world" (Lasch 1979) given the emotional, sexual, and physical abuse and intense conflicts that occur there. Yet the family may provide its members with much joy and pleasure, succor, and financial support, and it may buffer its members against some of the harsher, effects of capitalist rationality. In this, women's dedication to caring and tending is fundamental.

The chapters that follow show the conceptual inadequacy of considering domestic labor as "private" work or as important only for social reproduction (the reproduction of the working class, daily and generationally). Furthermore, if we abandon the fiction that only *paid* women workers directly experience the problems and contradictions of daily life in capitalist societies (Weinbaum and Bridges 1976), we may take seriously the efforts of women workers to organize around reduced services to their clients as well as loss of jobs and lowered incomes for themselves. The flip side of the coin would be efforts by women as householders (mothers, wives, and daughters frustrated by the rationing of human services and their distribution) to organize around reduced services from businesses and the state. Women's everyday struggles as shoppers, patients, clients, caretakers, and users of state-provided services may be a potential terrain for organizing with women who work for wages.

Part Two
The Retail Trade Industry

4

The Restructuring of Retailing

Between 1912 and 1960, most salesclerks in U.S. retailing were replaced by the cashier and the customer. Grocery, variety and department stores, fabric, hardware, shoe stores, and gasoline stations, serving middle-class women and men shifted from clerk-service to self-service. In general, only luxury stores for the rich and specialty shops (those selling furs, jewelry, photographic equipment, and so forth) retained customer services including an experienced, knowledgeable salesperson. In most stores, the clerk became the "order processor" or cashier, performing the few services still offered. Customers themselves began to do most locating and evaluating of goods, paying cash and carrying their merchandise home. The search for profits and lower labor costs, ideologies of privacy and choice, vertical integration in retailing, the growth of advertising, and national standards in measures, weights, and sizes made it possible for employers to reorganize the labor process. Retailers also adopted self-service and eliminated other services to overcome labor shortages, to attract low-income customers, and to exploit impulse buying. Because of the new labor process, workers lost their jobs, or their jobs were deskilled or became waged work rather than salaried or commission based, and often part-time. The gender composition of the industry workforce became predominantly women, who dominated as cashiers and clerks, but not as managers. The customer was inserted into the labor process in place of the salesclerk.

The reliance of customers on the market for commodities made it difficult for all but the rich easily to find an alternative to self-service. The development of monopoly-like conditions (through the growth of chains, mergers of stores, and the vertical integration of much retailing) allowed corporations to reorganize work in retail stores with relatively little fear that customers could shop elsewhere, seeking clerk-service. (Vertical integration means that all or nearly all the activities from the provision of raw materials through manufacturing to distribution are controlled by one corporation or a holding company.)

Full Service and Self-Service

FULL SERVICE

Prior to World War I, most food and other merchandise were sold in small, independent, family-owned, and specialized shops. For example, meats were sold in butcher shops and fabric in drygoods stores. Large food markets date back to colonial days, to the public markets such as Faneuil Hall Market (Boston) and Pike Street Market (Seattle) (Bluestone et al. 1981; Markin 1963), which were composed of small retailers or retailers–producers sharing space. By the 1870s and 1880s, there were large, diversified drygoods stores such as Filene's, Jordan Marsh (Boston), and Marshall Field (Chicago) in the central cities. Smaller, diversified drygoods stores served neighborhoods and small communities, and general stores served rural market towns.

Typically, stores ran on clerk-service, and the customer received other services too. Stores employed a staff ("Mom and Pop" stores used the unpaid labor of family members) with knowledge of goods and customer needs, who located merchandise, summed the cost, could charge the patron's account, and see that the goods were delivered to the customer's home. Orders could be left at the store by a child or housewife, to avoid waiting for the merchandise to be assembled. Credit could be used for convenience, to survive from one week's wages to the next or in times of hardship.

By the late nineteenth century, retailers were expanding into a market with increasing numbers of working-class customers as goods became cheaper and the incomes of the top stratum of the working class rose. Retailers continued clerk-service to the new market and added other services, such as monthly payments on free layaways, to suit the limited incomes of these new customers. By the turn of the century, services in large department stores for more affluent customers were often extravagant, including elegant restaurants and waiting rooms, travel agencies, and personal shoppers. Local grocers offered more modest services: cooking demonstrations, food samples, free home delivery, and some credit. By 1929, ninety-one department stores reported providing an amazing array of services, such as layaway plans without a deposit, a nurse in infant departments, public stenographers, Saturday children's theater, smoking rooms, real estate services, fashion magazines, personal shopping, a circulating library, art and needlework instruction, umbrella checking, a toy psychologist, a golf practice net, a want-ad desk, and bus and train information. Some stores also had a post office, restaurant, tour planning, and shoe-shining services (Personnel and Management Division 1929).

SELF-SERVICE

Self-service is very different from full service. The customer works in self-service. Some work must be done even before the shopping trip: for example, the customer may read advertisements and consumer reports to learn about new goods, their characteristics and quality, since the clerk is now an unlikely source of information.[1]

Shoppers do many other tasks in the self-service store that were once done by clerks. In a food store, for example, the shopper must find and collect goods without consulting a clerk and must take the goods to a cashier. At the check-out stand, the customer may be expected to unload the selections, bag the purchases, and carry them to an auto. In variety and most departments in large stores, the customer is expected to locate merchandise and assess its appropriateness, fit, durability, and so on, without clerk assistance.

Lutey's and Piggly Wiggly were two of the earliest self-service food stores. In 1912, Lutey Brothers of Butte, Montana, adapted the cafeteria (invented in the 1890s) for grocery sales, opening a self-service store adjacent to their full-service one. The Lutey Brothers had strong structural support: a mail-order business, a wholesale warehouse, a coffee blending and roasting company, and their own bakery. Their Marketeria differed a good deal from its full-service neighbor. The full-service store, where housewives shopped once a week and consulted with a Lutey clerk about their shopping lists, had "personalized" service: "To discuss quality, price, and current 'specials' was one reason they 'came to town.' It took possibly half an hour sitting at the counter with their regular clerk to settle the family order," pay the bill, and depart to await delivery (Lutey 1978: 52). Next door, the self-service customer found goods at lower prices, paid cash, and did what Lutey's euphemistically called "personal shopping," that is, self-service. Customers chose goods from among uniform packages and carried them to the check-out stand in a basket. The clerk accepted the cash and wrapped the goods, which had to be carried home by "Butte's strong and husky men" on the city's electric street railway (Lutey 1978: 52).

After visiting Lutey's Marketeria, Clarence Saunders designed his 1916 self-service stores and thus started the first chain of self-service groceries (*Sales Management* 1937). To encourage buying, the store plan forced customers to pass by all the merchandise, up and down all the aisles "in order to reach the exit turnstile beyond the cashier" (Vestal 1918: 193). His store accepted only cash (no credit and no checks), refused telephone and mail orders, and made no deliveries. Like Lutey, Saunders was a wholesaler as well as a retailer, and initially, as did Lutey, he packaged, in uniform measures, goods such as dried fruits, rice, and oatmeal, which were usually sold in bulk. Unlike Lutey, he decided to cease selling so-called private labels, denounced grocers who did, and eventually sold only nationally advertised brand-name goods (Vestal 1918). Saunders thus supported emerging trademarked nationally advertised merchandise (Murphy 1917: 17).

The Piggly Wiggly stores went bankrupt in 1924 because of Saunder's personal financial problems, not because of problems in the stores. Kroger Grocery and Baking Company, which also owned Safeway, took over Piggly Wiggly operations, discontinuing self-service (Zimmerman 1955: 22). In 1934, Kroger, which then had a chain of over forty-five hundred franchised stores, reintroduced self-service in its Piggly Wiggly stores. The results were excellent, especially for these depression years (*Business Week* 1934: 14–15).

Eventually, customers would do "personal shopping" for many different items, for clothing in Littman (Cash and Carry) (*Business Week* 1932), groceries in Keedoozle's (*Sales Management* 1937: 520), and drugstore items in Macy's Drug-O-Mat (*Business Week* 1951: 52). Today, they search for correct shoe sizes in stacks of boxes; wander through warehouse-like but full-price stores looking for furniture, computers, and VCRs; and buy expensive goods without any consultation with clerks. Often, the major form of clerk assistance is offering directions: "If we have that blouse in size fourteen, it's over there"; "wood screws are in aisle five"; "men's sweaters are on the table over there." In some one-stop-shopping supermarkets, even such sparse information as this may be hard to find, and the shopper may wander up and down aisles looking for the desired goods. In self-service gasoline stations, buyers pump their own gas, check oil levels and tire pressure, clean their windshields, and hand the payment to a clerk ensconced before a computer terminal in a warm, dry booth. Product information may be limited to the tag on the merchandise and clerk skills to operating the cash register.

Self-service was first introduced into food retailing before World War I and was adopted extensively by food chains and supermarkets in the years before the World War II.[2] Most variety and department stores switched to self-service after the war.[3] By 1970, typical stores (except those catering to the very rich or selling luxury jewelry and the like) were self-service.

Infrastructure for Self-Service

In retailing, the necessary technologies and relationships that supported self-service were national in scope: a transport system for goods, increased mechanization and centralization of production, standardization of goods, national mass media and advertising, and real gains in working-class incomes. In-store technologies and the automobile were initially insignificant and became important only as stores tried to decrease their labor force further and moved to the suburbs for new markets.

NATIONAL INFRASTRUCTURES

Although the original reason for the use of self-service by retailers was to lower labor costs and prices, and hence, to attract more customers, changes in central control (such as through chains) and in production and merchandising explain its widespread success. The integration of the production and distribution of goods through wholesale and retail outlets gave major retail stores control over prices. It allowed them to push advertised brands, appeal to local and regional tastes, and promote "forced consumption" as the underpinning of successful capitalism (Lebow 1955–1956).

THE CHAINS

Chain-store organizations, which relied on central management and buying, first became a serious competitive threat to independent retailers in the 1920s. In 1890, there were only 10 chains in the United States; by 1920, there were 808 chains, whose numbers more than doubled in eight years to 1,718 (Haas 1939).

Why independent retail grocers believed themselves so threatened by the chains is evident in the growth of the market share of chains during the first years of the Great Depression (see Table 4.1). In 1929, independents had about 89 percent of the retail stores and 78 percent of the sales. By 1933, independents had decreased their share of stores by only 1 percent but had reduced their share of sales to 71 percent. Though the chains also lost stores, they increased their share of sales from 20 percent in 1929 to 25 percent in 1933 (see Table 4.1). Total retail sales decreased dramatically, by nearly 50 percent between 1929 and 1933, from $49 to $25 million, a reflection of massive unemployment and shrinking family income.

By 1946, self-service chains dominated "grocery–combination" sales, which refers to sales of household supplies along with foods. As Table 4.2 shows, in 1946, chain stores made up only 8 percent of all retail grocery–combination stores, with 80 percent of their stores using "self-service." The chains accounted for 40 percent (Corina 1947). In contrast, the independents, which had 92 percent of all the stores, were less likely than chains to use self-service (43 percent did so), and accounted for only 60 percent of sales. Self-service sales per employee averaged $26,711 a year compared to only $20,522 an employee in full-service stores (Corina 1947).

Independent grocers tried to compete with the chains by emulating some of their strategies. The chains used quantity buying to force food

TABLE 4.1

Chains Made Disproportionate Gains during the Early Years of the Great Depression

	1929	1933
STORES	(1.5 million)	(1.5 million)
independents	89.1%	88.4%
chains	9.6	9.3
other	1.2	2.3
SALES	($49.114 million)	($25.037 million)
independents	77.3%	71.2%
chains	20.0	25.2
other	2.3	3.6

Source: Based on Harold M. Hass, *Social and Economic Aspects of the Chain Store Movement* (Minneapolis: University of Minnesota Press, 1979), 19.

wholesalers to give them sizable discounts. To gain a similar advantage, beginning in the late 1920s, some grocers joined associations such as the Independent Grocers Alliance (IGA), Red and White, and other buying groups. The associations also carried on joint advertising campaigns, which made them appear to customers to be similar to the chains. Small, local chains and independents attempted to make the larger chain and supermarket practice of lowering prices below cost illegal and brought such pricing policies to the attention of the Federal Trade Commission (FTC). "Loss leaders" were the main object of attack in the commission's investigations (Phillips 1941). The smaller, local stores urged wholesalers not to sell to supermarkets. They asked local newspapers to refuse the advertising of self-service markets, arguing that these stores were engaged in "unfair trading practices" and had eliminated jobs for working men (Peak and Peak 1977). Chains maintained their competitive advantage, however, despite the passage of the Patman-Robinson Act of 1936,[4] which set "fair pricing practices" by prohibiting wholesalers from giving chains price breaks that they denied independent retailers. The act was often evaded, and small retailers did

TABLE 4.2

Self-Service Chains Had Disproportionate Sales Compared to Self-Service and Full-Service Independents, 1946

Type of store	Percentage of Services	Sales (billions of dollars)
INDEPENDENT		12.250
self-service	43	
full-service	57	
N = 375,500 (68%)		
CHAIN		6.265
self-service	80	
full-service	20	
N = 32,000 (6%)		
GROCERY ONLY		
self-service	45	4.850
full-service	55	
N = 141,000 (25%)		

Source: John Corina, *Spotlight on Self-Service* (Manchester, England: Co-operative Union Ltd., ca. 1947).

not benefit from it (Bluestone et al. 1981). Independents also attempted unsuccessfully to control competition by seeking other legislation, such as special local taxes on the chains. Eventually, they followed the chains by adopting self-service to decrease their own labor costs.

The supermarkets that boomed in the 1930s made self-service an integral part of their organization[5] and were attacked by other grocers for eliminating jobs (Peak and Peak 1977). Supermarkets reorganized the labor process to do away with clerks even in the sale of goods, such as meats and coffee, that grocers once thought demanded clerk-service. Though clerk-service remained typical for many years, the cost advantages to retailers also forced associated grocers to adopt self-service (*Progressive Grocer* 1941: 65–66). The success of "cash and carry" self-service supermarkets encouraged chains and the associated grocers to convert to self-service and also eliminate other services, such as credit and home delivery (Peak and Peak 1977).

By 1940, with self-service widespread in food sales in the United States, the Progressive Grocers Association evaluated relative costs and other advantages in a national survey. They concluded that the self-service stores were more profitable than the full-service stores, even though expenses such as advertising to "attain and hold a large volume" and rent at a "more favorable location" were higher.

After using self-service to lower labor costs (Dipman and O'Brien 1940: 32; Murphy 1917: 20), retailers realized that higher profits resulted because customers were "impulse buying," "selling themselves" on the displayed goods (Swan 1947; Zimmerman 1955). Manufacturers of national food brands, and wholesalers who provided grocers with merchandise to sell under their own names as "private" brands, also preferred self-service. Impulse buying, shaped by national advertising campaigns, increased the sale of national food brands to 73 percent of sales in self-service stores, compared to only 44 percent in clerk-served ones (*Sales Management* 1938: 39). In the emerging "consumer society," retailers concluded that sales grew, with or without brand names, because of human nature: "The minute we see [goods], we are tempted to buy them" (Collins 1940: 100).

PRESELLING

Self-service depends on goods being successfully presold through national advertising (*Printers' Ink* 1921a, 1921b). Packaging was necessary too, eliminating the need for clerks to measure out foodstuffs, even though it also prevented customer examination of most groceries and household supplies. Except for fresh produce, itself increasingly packaged over the past three decades, and some soft goods, customer inspection has been limited largely to the external packaging.

Retailers in the 1920s could sell goods packaged by standardized weights, measures, and container sizes because of federal legislation, which both they and manufacturers resisted at first. Buyers, too, had an interest in standardization, as a remedy for adulteration and false weights and measures. Liquids, dry foods, and produce had been sold in varying containers, differing from one another in slight ways that made estimating their size difficult and could cost the customer considerably. Adulterated milk had been common, sold mixed with dangerous thinners. Unstable fillers were mixed with silk and bread contained contaminants. (In 1884, the *Ladies Home Journal* had warned against fraudulent advertising in the mail-order sale of silk—"leftover, none less than 4 or so yards." Bargain hunters found themselves with a bag of the ends of threads!) Manufacturers accepted standardization, hoping that it and trademarks might build national, as distinct from local, markets for their goods.

The Standard Container Act of 1916 specified the size of the measuring cup, the pint, bottles and caps, jars and lids, cans, and fruit boxes. By the late 1920s, bed linen and other household linens, electrical wiring, light bulbs, and fuses had been sized, and their wide variety reduced sharply. By 1929, women's and children's apparel had been only roughly standardized, and remain so today, with women's clothing in a given size being much larger in an expensive line than in a cheaper one.[6]

Product standardization allows goods to be sold in a wide geographic area with the customer able to expect the same trademarked goods in New York as in Washington, D.C., or Dayton, Ohio (Frederick 1917). For example, a twin-size sheet bought in one community fits a twin-size bed bought in another, and a 2″ × 4″ piece of lumber is always about 1-¾″ × 3-¾″.

Standardization gave large companies a competitive edge over smaller ones, making customers subject to growing monopolies in some goods, such as refrigerators. (See Cowan 1983 for a fascinating historical account of the effect of corporate power, rather than customer convenience, in determining the use of Freon-based refrigeration.)

The reliance of retailers on national brands was possible because of vertical integration (where retailers controlled the product from the raw materials to the finished goods), mergers of stores, and takeovers of family-owned, locally based stores by national chains and holding companies. This centralization made it possible for national advertising to be an effective seller of national brands.[7]

National advertising creates a homogeneous market for standardized goods and minimizes regional differences in tastes and markets. By establishing national tastes, at least for many products, retailers and independent manufacturers can depend on a ready-made customer nearly anywhere in the country. National chains can centralize purchasing and use economies of scale to improve profit margins.

Self-service began as a relatively small-scale attempt by food retailers to lower operating costs by shifting work to the customer. It succeeded as retailing in the United States changed from local to national production, sales, and control.

There has also been a shift of responsibility for many important and expensive goods from the seller to the manufacturer. Retailers at first relied on national manufacturers to provide product information and advertising. Gradually, many manufacturers took on more responsibility. Instead of asking local sellers to replace or repair products, the customer is forced into a social relationship directly with manufacturers, who may offer only limited warranties.

TECHNOLOGY IN STORES

Early changes in the workplace, that is, in the store, drew largely on the imagination of the retailer. The initial technology used to displace clerks was a labor process borrowed from the cafeteria, although the check-out clerk's work was eventually redesigned using principles borrowed from assembly-line production (U.S. Department of Commerce 1947).

No new, innovative machinery was needed for Lutey's Marketeria in Butte, Montana. The store opened in 1912 with simple changes: hand-carried baskets, a booklet (*Cutting Out the Frills*) explaining the system to customers, and the packaging of goods in uniform quantities by Lutey workers. Only fresh fruits and vegetables were not packaged (Lutey 1978). The stores that flourished in the 1910s and 1920s added other simple equipment: a one-way turnstile to prevent customers from exiting without paying, a check-out counter for collecting cash payments, and large and easy-to-read price tags attached to goods (Vestal 1918).

Over three decades, and only after simple technologies had effectively supported self-service, did new, expensive technologies begin to be used. Expensive "fixtures," meaning specially designed racks, counters, cases, tables, and drawers that gave the customer easy access, "the real purpose of self-service," became widespread (Glave 1943: 103). Other new and expensive devices included self-service coffee grinders, gravity feed (in which goods rolled down to a shelf, to replace an item removed by the shopper), and refrigerated stock cases. One-way mirrors were in wide use; employers watched for pilferage (or "leakage") while doing other tasks (*Architectural Forum* 1948; Corina 1947). Clarence Saunders, who had tried to patent the layout for his chain of franchised self-service stores, developed the Keedoozle store with its Rube Goldberg–like contraptions in display windows, metal rods, electrical feeds, and moving belts (*Business Week* 1946; *Sales Management* 1937).[8] Automatic dispensing machines were used in groceries and even drugstores tried self-service (*Business Week* 1939: 36; 1951: 52). Automatic packaging machines replaced scales and scoops, calculating machines replaced paper and pencil, price-marking machines and printed tags replaced memory and price lists, and cash registers and moving belts replaced mental calculations and the manual labor of assembling (Henksmeier 1960).

GETTING THERE

Self-service in food markets was a part of urban life before World War II, and preceded the decreased availability of public transportation and the rapid development of automobile-dependent suburbanites with moderate incomes. In Butte, Montana, the first self-service grocery customers carried their purchases home by electric streetcar. The Atlantic & Pacific chain, IGA, Red and White, and even upscale grocers such as Hillman Brothers in downtown Chicago adopted self-service in the late 1930s and early 1940s in urban communities with public transit systems. By 1940, the supermarket and smaller self-service groceries in major U.S. cities did 25 percent of all annual sales. Hence, automobiles were not necessary for the growth of self-service, since it was adopted in cities where the automobile was of no or limited use in shopping.

Nevertheless, the use of the auto did account for the higher percentage of self-service sales in the West and Southwest, where cars were more widely used than in New England and other East Coast states (Curtiss 1940). In the postwar years, the increasing use of the auto in suburbs without public transportation, but with extensive highways, made shopping-center construction a major form of investment for land developers. Retailers had a virtual captive audience of buyers: shopping centers, in which self-service food stores were the "magnet stores," were often the only stores available to suburban residents. The suburbanite reliance on the auto gave these retailers access to vast markets outside the inner city, away from public transportation (Schwartzmann 1971: 22, 144).

The "Worker Problem"

Facing labor shortages because of competition from war industries and demands by workers for wage increases, many food retailers adopted self-service during World War I (Vestal 1918: 193). Some tried a combination of self-service and clerk-service, to attract new customers by cutting prices and yet keep the old customers who wanted an array of services (Zimmerman 1955: 24). After that war, retailers were concerned about increased selling costs, but still had to improve wages so as to attract competent clerks (Jackson 1925). Wages continued to be a problem: for retailers, they were too high; for clerks, they were too low.

During the Great Depression, the Retail Code of the National Recovery Administration (NRA) regulated wages, hours, and overtime work, prompting retailers to reduce their costs by hiring more part-time salespeople and by mechanizing stock and office work (Dameron 1935). Also, while there was hardly a labor shortage, there was a decline in sales and profits. Retailers tried to compensate for their losses by using self-service. For example, Clarence Saunders, who had started the first successful self-service grocery chain in the 1920s, opened a new and equally successful chain of self-service stores in 1937 (*Sales Management* 1937). Other stores reduced free delivery (Schatz 1933), and the retailers' association debated which other services could be eliminated without reducing sales (National Retail Dry Goods Association 1939).

Self-service continued to appeal to retailers because it decreased the wage bill. The grocers' association reported that "wage expense, the biggest single item of operating costs, is, as a rule, lower in the grocery departments where customers wait on themselves . . . insofar as other services may be curtailed by self-service arrangement and operation, operating expense may be reduced" (Dipman and O'Brien 1940: 266–267). In their follow-up report of 1946, the association called self-service "labor and expense saving" and suggested that it be used to counter the postwar militancy of labor unions, which retailers feared would raise wage costs and shorten working hours (Dipman et al. 1946: 5, 8). The association concluded that "by getting consumers to do some of the work now done by employees . . . a merchant [can] make the greatest use of the fewer hours available to the store and employees" (Dipman et al. 1946: 9).

LABOR DISCIPLINE

The substitution of self-service for clerk-service before World War I may have also been a strategic reaction by employers to union activity. Changes in the labor process do not necessarily provoke resistance from workers, but when workers make gains, especially because of union actions, employers may try to reinstate control (Geschwender and Levine 1983). The major clerk union, Retail Clerks International Protective Association (RCIPA), was not notably militant or successful, though craft unions, such as the Butchers, were. Nevertheless, wages had been increasing with the growing threat of a world war, and a peak in RCIPA membership occurred in 1919, coincident with the growth of the first regional chain of self-service stores (Harrington 1962: 6–8).[9]

The years after World War I were also ones when public opinion was somewhat sympathetic to unions, and grocers formed organizations to oppose them (RCIPA 1936: 31). Associations continued to do so after the passage of the National Recovery Act (NRA) and the Wagner Labor Relations Act, Section 7a (Coulter 1936).

Unions did not appear to interpret self-service as injurious to workers. The RCIPA gave no special attention to it in its newsletter, consistent with retail unions rarely interfering with management attempts to rationalize the labor process by using self-service (Bluestone et al. 1981). Though a majority of its members worked in grocery stores, the RCIPA did not protest against self-service, though they knew of it as soon as employers began to adopt it and reduce wages (RCIPA 1919a: 14). Only the Congress of Industrial Organizations (CIO) seems to have understood that self-service would cause problems. The CIO cautioned that self-service was "slaughtering employment opportunities and carry[ing] with it greater centralization of the industry in fewer hands" (RWDSE 1941: 2) and would result in employers "relying upon less skilled labor" (RWDSE 1942: 11).

During World War II, the shortage of labor and goods hastened the spread of self-service beyond food retailing (Thompson 1942; Wingate 1942). With the unemployed finally back at work and earning good wages, and with a wartime-induced shortage of goods, stores did not need attentive clerks to attract customers (Steagall et al. 1942). Moreover, in an attempt to control the inflation that followed full employment after years of economic depression, the federal government froze both retail prices and wages. The government advised retailers to moderate the effects of the wage freeze on their ability to attract new workers by cutting services to customers, including everything from late opening hours to home delivery (Plant 1942). Distributors and advertisers already had in place displays and fixtures designed to substitute for clerks lost to the war, which gave the customer easy access to goods (Coutant 1942; Cumming 1943). Retailers eliminated even those services once considered necessary to attract wealthy customers accustomed to servants and to hold onto poorer customers who relied on credit and layaways. To compensate for the shortage of civilian consumer goods, some retailers tried to attract customers by giving lower prices to those who did not use home delivery or alterations for men's clothing (National Retail Dry Goods Association 1942). After the war, retailers continued to reduce "free" services to customers, calling those who used home delivery, layaway plans, and alteration services "freeloaders" and overlooking that they had instituted the services to attract customers (Baker 1956).

Labor shortages, the shorter workweek, and union organizing continued to be problems for retailers after World War II. Workers, used to higher wages in war industries, did not rush to jobs in retailing. *Printers' Ink* (1945: 29), the trade journal of advertisers, complained that "most workers are reluctant to accept lower salaries and seem content to live on unemployment benefits and wait for wages to go up." Macy's and Gimbels ran advertisements on "selling's attractions": liberal discounts, vitality and variety, and part-time work (*Business Week* 1946: 36). Others sought to circumvent union drives for a shorter workweek and higher wages by using self-service, which they had observed in groceries (Canfield 1948: 104).[10]

The Other Worker

Retailers adopted self-service at the same time as housekeeping was becoming less of a drain on the energy of middle- and working-class housewives because of new household appliances and public utilities (such as paved streets). In the 1920s, as self-service was being adopted, bakery bread, cleaning supplies, and toiletries, as well as canned foods, were becoming cheaper and available to more lower-income families. Self-service continued to expand during the depression, when even rural areas were electrified with federal support. In the postwar years, housewives could buy automatic washing machines and steam irons at the same time that more stores were asking their shoppers to serve themselves. By 1960, as married women with dependent children were increasingly combining paid work with domestic work, self-service was established so firmly in grocery chains, superstores, variety and department stores, and specialty shops that many readers may have no or only a faint memory of shopping any other way.

Studies of the labor process have neglected service workers in favor of industrial workers. And the customer has been nearly totally ignored. Retailers, in contrast, have long been concerned with *customer control*. In their trade journals, retailers view the clerk's time as often wasted, spent waiting for the customer to arrive. From the retailer's perspective, self-service is an advantage because it eliminates "the wasted [*sic*] time of the clerk." The customer waits for cashier services, rather than the clerk waiting for customer demands.

Along with producers and distributors, retailers tried to cope with what they called the "disorderly" marketing burden, that is, the unpredictability of customer demands. They wanted to "make maximum use of the customer's in-store-time," namely, by encouraging maximum buying (Smith and Radolf 1960: 81). By the early 1970s, retailers' concern with shoppers won a formal label, "customer management" (Sibson 1971), and soon the use of customer labor was seen as a solution to "lagging productivity" in a variety of service organizations (Lovelock and Young 1979: 66). A new term, "servuction," a parallel to production, was invented to describe the customer's participation in producing services in the ill-named service industries (Langeard et al. 1981: 2).

CONTROLLING THE CUSTOMER

From its beginning, retailers used self-service to influence where the customer went in the store, what the customer did, and how much the customer bought. As early as 1921, advertisers were urging California's markets to use self-service, albeit politely: "It is right and proper that the average [*sic*] housekeeper should pick out the things she buys. And if there is a savings she cannot object if she is asked to take them home.

But to wrap them up while the proprietor of the store talks politics with a friend—that, I think, is rubbing it in" (Castle 1921: 113).

Control over customer behavior was more subtle than the forms managers used to control workers (Edwards 1979). But the issue was similar: getting the most out of a person. The retailer wanted the highest sales with as much customer participation as possible and without driving customers to shop elsewhere. For example, check-out stand organization determines customer work. The design of the check-out counter may not give the cashier access to the shopping cart and thus requires that the customer unload goods. The *where* was brought under control by the layout of stores, just as in the factory, where the layout of production places some controls on worker movements. The store layout is designed to lead customers past as many goods as possible, tempting them to buy. For example, using only a few directional signs ("Meats," "Baking Goods," etc.) causes the customer to slow down and spend more time looking over goods and thus to do more impulse buying. Narrow aisles are favored by some retailers, who assume that slow movement by customers through the store encourages browsing and buying. Even the placement of items is considered carefully and is used to direct the customer's path through the store. For example, milk and bread (items of frequent purchase) may be placed far apart—one at the front of the store, the other at the rear—so that customers must walk by many items, and may impulse-buy along the way—"selling themselves" on the displayed goods (Zimmerman 1955). The numbers of floor helpers (stock clerks or floor managers) determines the ease with which customers can find items, and the number of cashiers and check-out stands determines how long a customer waits for the cashier. In all of this, the customer must learn to shop independent of helpers, to learn the layout of the store in order to shop quickly.

TEMPTING THE CUSTOMER

Retailers apparently did not expect impulse buying to be an outcome of self-service. Yet merchants were quick to observe that the introduction of self-service into their shops increased profits beyond any level that could be accounted for simply by the cost reduction in wages. Impulse buying became a point in favor of introducing self-service widely into the industry. The importance of the layout in controlling the behavior of the customer, including increasing impulse buying as much as possible without increasing costly customer returns, became a serious concern to marketing experts. Self-service was therefore not merely a cheaper process than using clerk labor but a way to increase consumption. Retailers in trade journals considered the best way to get the customer to move through the store, what kinds of displays would provoke the most impulse buying, and what kinds of advertising would bring customers used to clerk-service into self-service shops.

The New Service

Self-service is not necessarily a permanent strategy in retailing. Service has been reinstated by many retailers to lure back disaffected customers. Many customers want service, including the right to buy limited quantities of expensive items or items that spoil rapidly—and they may want advice too. For example, there has been a revival of food specialty shops in which clerks dispense bread, meat, fish, cheese, and delicatessen items. Self-service in such stores may be limited to complementary packaged goods such as condiments, jams and jellies, and cookies.

On occasion, customers have joined together with retailer associations to forestall self-service. In Oregon in 1989, a coalition of the American Automobile Association (AAA), veterans with physical disabilities, senior citizens, the AFL-CIO, and independent gasoline dealers convinced the state legislature not to legalize self-service gasoline stations (Mapes 1989: D1). The oil companies had instigated self-service gasoline after concluding "it can mean a higher profit margin" because "the customer serves as an unpaid employee" (Kingson 1989: 7). The stations had gone on to eliminate other services, such as repairs, oil checks, air for tires, and water, and had turned instead to selling junk food and soft drinks. The oil companies allege that customers demanded the change to self-service, but protests continue against the loss of gasoline-station services by advocacy groups for the elderly and handicapped and for disgruntled motorists who have been stranded after a breakdown (Kingson 1989).

Some retailers are aware that skilled salespeople are able to increase sales in "soft" markets, that is, those crowded with competitors. Nordstrom, with it's home base on the West Coast, prides itself on "excellent customer service" (Nordstrom ca. 1991). Significantly, Nordstrom sold only shoes until 1963, merchandise relatively infrequently sold by self-service even today. Diversifying into apparel, Nordstrom remains unusual in paying commissions to their sales staff, in addition to hourly wages or salaries, another tradition in shoe sales. Salesclerks receive cash prizes, trips, merchandise, and other awards for high rates of sales in one month, large sales to the same customer, high sales per hour, and exceptional customer service (Nordstrom ca. 1991: 6). Retirement benefits also depend on earnings as well as years of service.

Even more important, Nordstrom stores are organized on the self-service plan, except for shoes, cosmetics, jewelry, expensive leather goods and scarves, and the like. Customers *can* service themselves, as in other department stores, making selections and trying on apparel without any contact with clerks except for making the purchase, but the pressure on sales personnel is to serve.

The emphasis on service does not create ideal working conditions for clerks. "Customer service" has been narrowed from the wide range offered by the store to mostly the actions of the salesclerk. Commissions on sales and other rewards encourage clerks to compete with one another, lessen the support that women's work culture provides, and open the way for the mistreatment of salesclerks, such as requiring them to work overtime for free.

In 1989, Nordstrom expanded into the San Francisco and New York City metropolitan areas. Competitors who used self-service, such as Bloomingdale's, Macy's, and Abraham & Straus, began to reconsider the value of clerk skills and the use of commissions (Barmash 1989; Sloane 1989: 41). In the 1990s, retailers who face financial problems because of leveraged buyouts in the 1980s have also been considering the use of clerk-service to attract customers. Supermarkets, too, have returned to greater service. Some employ clerks on skates or a buzzer-call system to aid customers in their search for goods in giant, full-price stores (Burros 1989).

Self-service continues to have new uses: customers can use vending machines, the ultimate in self-service, to buy. Food vending sales grew from 23 percent in 1978 to 55 percent in 1988 as cigarettes declined from 27 percent to 8 percent. Vending-machine customers can buy Levi's (in Paris) and computer software (in Tokyo); prisoners in the United States can use debit cards to buy toothpaste and shaving cream (Steinberg 1989: 17). Some analysts insist customers will actually "pay for the privilege of doing things themselves" (Deutsch 1989: 1).

Self-service became commonplace in the United States because of changes in manufacturing and distribution. Today, only the rich receive services comparable to those enjoyed fifty years ago even by some of the working class. When service has been reinstated, it is in forms that usually have little to do with previous aids to buyers. I have sketched out the myriad repercussions for paid and unpaid workers. Next, I turn to the details of the consequences of self-service for the labor process, the job content of women retail workers, and the ideology and practice of women's unpaid domestic labor.

5

From Salesclerk to Cashier

Wanted: White male, family man preferred, for full-time, year-round employment. Requires good deportment, manners, and grooming, good English (no foreign-born, please); applicant must have several years' experience in selling women's fine apparel. Salary plus commission.

Or a similar notice in 1890 might have read "in butchering and dressing beef and poultry" or "in fabrics, notions, and tailoring." In 1890, hiring practices in most large U.S. stores implied a search for these qualifications, reproducing the gender, racial, and ethnic practices of discrimination and subordination in the United States. From 1912 onward, retailers adopted self-service, intending to solve labor shortages and reduce high wages, to counter union militancy and attract customers with cheap goods. Ideologies about gender, race, and ethnicity created the "labor shortages" and "too high" wages that self-service was supposed to solve. Over the next sixty years, the use of the work transfer—"self-service" in retailing—facilitated a decline in sales skills and in the relative earnings of retail workers and increased temporary and part-time jobs. It also facilitated a change in the gender composition of the workforce, typically from men to women and eventually, in the racial and ethnic composition, from white, native-born to foreign-born persons and those of color. By 1960, a job notice might list a new set of qualifications:

Wanted: Female, white or perhaps of color, either youngish or near retirement age, preferably looking for supplementary rather than primary income; for part-time and perhaps temporary employment. Requires learning to use cash register, check validity of credit cards, process purchases and returns. No sales experience needed.

The capitalist vision of the world was hegemonic: the pursuit of private profit as the most important criterion for organizing the workplace. It permeated understandings of everyday work culture. It was built into social relations so deftly that most workers unquestionably accepted the right of bosses to eliminate their livelihood. Despite successes in reducing hours and increasing wages, some union challenges to the loss of workers' most basic right—a job—have been minimal and unsuccessful. Only a left-wing union complained when sales jobs in retailing were eliminated by self-service. And, more profoundly, worker displacement by customers seems to have been largely invisible to workers themselves.

Self-service first displaced men, who were the majority of salesclerks in food retailing, and later women salesclerks, who predominated in department and variety stores. Women were hired into food retailing initially as salesclerks, simultaneously with the beginnings of the use there of self-service. They were hired as cashiers as self-service was extended. Women salesclerks historically worked under wretched conditions, sometimes earning wages that were so low that their employers expected them to survive by living "at home." Unions struggled and succeeded only modestly in improving hours, wages, and other working conditions. Furthermore, though it was small stores that often operated on the edge of bankruptcy, salesclerk labor was first supplanted by cashiers in large, successful food and department stores and later in smaller groceries.

Women had entered retailing initially in the drygoods stores that Jordan Marsh, Filene, Marshall Field, and similar retailers had designed to attract the carriage trade of wealthier white women and men. Retailers hired white women as salesclerks and women of color only in menial jobs. They also tried to lure customers to their stores with the myriad other services mentioned in Chapter 4.

Conditions in the early retail trade industry for women, as Benson (1986) notes, were much like those in other workplaces and were akin to private domestic service. Separate facilities for salesclerks and customers (elevators, lounges, entrances, bathrooms) "smacked of the upstairs–downstairs division of the servant's life." Time clocks regulated and spy systems monitored clerk demeanor and "leakage," mirroring factory life.

Before self-service, selling required that clerks have skills, such as knowledge about style, fit, and quality, and familiarity with "good" buys. The salesclerk also did the legwork of locating goods or finding compatible or complementary merchandise. Salesclerks also had skills in persuasion, a service to the retailer as much as to the buyer. But salesclerks were not always eager to sell their services to retailers. Wartime industries (1914–1919 and 1939–1945), and increasing numbers of clerical jobs were more attractive than sales with its long hours, class-based subservience to customers, and behavior, language, and dress codes. Being a salesclerk was so unattractive (though less so than private domestic service) that in the years between the two world wars, New York City retailers undertook campaigns in the high schools to attract workers (Smith 1928). Sales skills were introduced into some high school curriculums, and women were pressed to enter retailing, much as they had been pressed earlier to enter domestic service.

Patterns of Women's Employment in Retailing

Over the past sixty years, as self-service was becoming standard in retailing, women were becoming the majority of paid retail workers.[1] In 1930, before the spurt in self-service in food retailing, women were a minority (about 20 percent) of retail workers (see Table 5.1). Within a decade, the proportion of women workers had jumped to 40 percent. By 1981, 60 percent of retail salesclerks and 85 percent of cashiers were women (Rytina 1982).

Chain grocers, using self-service and cashiers, rather than salesclerks, and sometimes selling below cost, had captured a disproportionate amount of sales by the early 1930s (see Chapter 4). Between 1930 and 1950, other kinds of stores shifted to self-service in large numbers. In 1940, for the first time, the U.S. census included "cashiers" in retailing in its count of "salesclerks", and then in 1950 began reporting cashiers separately from salesclerks. Because of the census counts, though occupational changes took place over several preceding decades, the data in Tables 5.2 and 5.3 start with 1940.

Compared to general retailing, jobs in food stores were opened to women workers less rapidly (see Table 5.2). In 1940, women were 40 percent of all retail workers, compared to 26 percent of *food* retail workers. Until the explosion of higher-paid jobs in war industries, the strong male craft unions in the food industry meant that jobs there were attractive to men and maintained for men only through a restrictive apprentice system.

The relatively powerful Amalgamated Meat Cutters and Butchers

Workmen and Teamsters unions maintained male dominance in the food industry longer than in department and variety stores, where sales-clerk unions were weak, and where women moved rapidly into jobs. Women entered the retail industry at the same time as the overall pro-portion of cashiers was increasing relative to salesclerks. There were 50,000 cashiers in 1950, compared to 622,000 salesclerks. By 1970, a sharp shift had occurred, with a majority of workers being cashiers, 342,000 compared to 269,000 salesclerks.

In food retailing, most jobs were done initially by men. Hence, in 1940, women made up 45 percent of all cashiers and salesclerks in retail-ing but, at most, 30 percent of those in food stores. As women entered retailing, they tended to be hired for female-typed jobs—salesclerking and cashiering—rather than managing, so gender segregation replaced

TABLE 5.1
Women Workers in Retailing, 1930–1978 (in percent)

	1930	1940	1950	1960	1970	1978
All retail workers[a]	20	40	44	50	53	58
N (millions)	4.211	2.468	3.218	3.694	4.722	8.677
Managers	7[b]	13	19	22	20	29
Cashiers	n.a.	n.a.	89	79	90	86[d]
Salesclerks	29	45[c]	49	54	58	64

Sources: For 1930: Alba M. Edwards, *Population: Comparative Statistics for the United States, 1870–1940* (Washington, D.C.: U.S. Government Printing Office, 1943), 69. For 1940: U.S. Bureau of the Census, *Population: Industrial Characteristics* (Washington, D.C.: U.S. Government Printing Office, 1943), 98, 100. For 1950: U.S. Bureau of the Census, *Occupation by Industry*, P-E, no. 1C, preprint of vol. 4, pt. 1, chap. C (Washington, D.C.: U.S. Government Printing Office, 1954), 52–59. For 1960: U.S. Bureau of the Census, *Occupation by Industry*, PC(2)7C (Washington, D.C.: U.S. Government Printing Office, 1961), 97–111. For 1970: U.S. Bureau of the Census, *Occupation by Industry: Subject Reports*, PC(2)7C (Washington, D.C.: U.S. Government Printing Office, 1973), 25–28, 41–45, 57–60. For 1978: Barbara Job, "Employment and Pay Trends in the Retail Trade Industry," *Monthly Labor Review* 103, no. 3 (1980): 40–43.
[a]Excludes stockers, delivery persons, cleaners, and miscellaneous jobs.
[b]Data for 1930 include proprietors.
[c]Data not presented separately for cashiers and clerks. Because of changes in census cate-gories, 1930 to date, data are *estimates* of women in retailing.
[d]Data for 1978, "clerical," include office workers (i.e., typists, accountants, bookkeepers) as well as cashiers.

gender exclusion. Since 1940, the proportion of male salesclerks has declined, with men entering management (see Table 5.3) and a minority becoming cashiers. Women workers (after their initial growth in sales) were hired as cashiers, not managers. In 1950, 83 percent of women in retailing were salesclerks. That declined to 58 percent by 1960 and to 35 percent by 1970, when 60 percent of women were cashiers, and the remaining 5 percent were managers. Weinbaum and Bridges (1976) suggest that capitalism pits women against one another—customer against worker, shopper against cashier. The customer is the potential strikebreaker ready to take over from the cashier as new technologies shift more and more work away from paid workers.

Earlier changes in retailing were more complicated than that. Women workers were pitted against men workers, and workers of both genders against customers. Women workers were not brought into food retailing as cashiers but as salesclerks, doing jobs once open mainly to men. Until 1970, women in food retailing continued to be salesclerks more often than cashiers. As sales jobs were eliminated, women, not men, were hired for the cashier jobs. Employers brought women into *paid* employment at the same time that they were asking women customers to do self-service. The result is a new division of labor: women shop-

TABLE 5.2
Women Workers in Food Retailing, 1940–1970 (in percent)

	1940	1950	1960	1970
All food workers	26	42	46	56
Managers	6	11	7	12
Cashiers	n.a.	82	72	80
Salesclerks	30[a]	44	46	59

Sources: For 1940: U.S. Bureau of the Census, *Population: Industrial Characteristics* (Washington, D.C.: U.S. Government Printing Office, 1943), 98, 100. For 1950: U.S. Bureau of the Census, *Occupation by Industry*, P-E, no. 1C, preprint of vol. 4 pt. 1, chap. C (Washington, D.C.: U.S. Government Printing Office, 1954), 52–59. For 1960: U.S. Bureau of the Census, *Occupation by Industry*, PC(2)7C (Washington, D.C.: U.S. Government Printing Office, 1961), 97–111. For 1970: U.S. Bureau of the Census, *Occupation by Industry: Subject Reports*, PC(2)7C (Washington, D.C.: U.S. Government Printing Office, 1973), 25–28, 41–45, 57–60.
[a]Clerical and sales categorized together.

pers do *some* of the work that men once did as salesclerks; women paid workers do *some* of that work as cashiers.

Unpaid women were pitted against paid women only after paid women replaced men. Hence the work transfer involved a further division of labor in which women were hired for jobs once held by men, with women doing parts of what once was a single job. The retail food industry was one among many industries in which available female labor was substituted for male labor in a process that combined a detailed division of labor and a cheapening of wages. Wages in retailing did not drop absolutely, but over several decades, the rate of wage increases declined relative to the rate in other industries.

The same two-step change occurred in retailing as a whole. As women increased from 20 percent of all retail workers in 1930 to 44 percent of all workers by 1950, they first increased as salesclerks and continued to be salesclerks more often than cashiers until the 1970 census.

TABLE 5.3

Women Move from Sales to Cashier and Men Move to Management in Food Retailing, 1940–1970 (in percent)

	1940	*1950*	*1960*	*1970*
WOMEN (thousands)	142	327	401	454
Managers	3%	4%	3%	5%
Cashiers	n.a.	13	39	60
Salesclerks	97[a]	83	58	35
MEN (thousands)	398	458	462	350
Managers	19%	22%	28%	49%
Cashiers	n.a.	2	14	19
Salesclerks	81[a]	76	59	32

Sources: For 1940: Alba M. Edwards, *Population: Comparative Statistics for the United States, 1870–1940* (Washington, D.C.: U.S. Government Printing Office, 1943), 69. For 1950: U.S. Bureau of the Census, *Occupation by Industry*, P-E, no. 1C, preprint of vol. 4, pt. 1, chap. C (Washington, D.C.: U.S. Government Printing Office, 1954), 52–59. For 1960: U.S. Bureau of the Census, *Occupation by Industry*, PC(2)7C (Washington, D.C.: U.S. Government Printing Office, 1961), 97–111. For 1970: U.S. Bureau of the Census, *Occupation by Industry: Subject Reports*, PC(2)7C (Washington, D.C.: U.S. Government Printing Office, 1973), 25–28, 41–45, 57–60.
[a]The census reported cashiers and salesclerks in one category.

The increase in women workers in retailing parallels the general economic expansion following World War II that forced employers to turn to women for their labor force. Advertising had established the marketplace as the place for fulfilling the American dream earlier (Ewen 1976; Strasser 1989). But consumption was expanded by American economic dominance, high worker productivity, rising real wages, and easier access by workers to credit. This led to what might be called the "proletarianization" of consumption, making serious shoppers of women (and men) whose class relationships may have made them feel uneasy about being served and distrustful of salesclerks. Advertising established a marketplace that Veblen could anticipate but not imagine—as a mass market of the "magical system" where the purchase of a good is joined "with human desires to which it has no real reference" (Williams 1980: 189).

Employers continued to divide the work of selling, reorganizing it so that temporary workers could learn tasks rapidly. Even before 1929, sales work began to change from long-term, full-time employment as stores replaced workers with part-timers to reduce "slack time" and increase service during rush hours (Bloodworth 1930; Pickernell 1931).

TABLE 5.4
Women in the Retail Industry: From Salesclerk to Cashier, 1950–1978 (in percent)

	1950	1960	1970	1978
All retail workers	44	50	53	58
Managers	9	8	10	16
Cashiers	8	14	22	44
Salesclerks	83	77	68	39
N (women, in millions)	1.431	1.858	2.469	5.070

Sources: For 1950: U.S. Bureau of the Census, *Occupation by Industry*, P-E, no. 1C, preprint of vol. 4, pt. 1, chap. C (Washington, D.C.: U.S. Government Printing Office, 1954), 52–59. For 1960: U.S. Bureau of the Census, *Occupation by Industry*, PC(2)7C (Washington, D.C.: U.S. Government Printing Office, 1961), 97–111. For 1970: U.S. Bureau of the Census, *Occupation by Industry: Subject Reports*, PC(2)7C (Washington, D.C.: U.S. Government Printing Office, 1973), 25–28, 41–45, 57–60. Barbara Job, "Employment and Pay Trends in the Retail Trade Industry." *Monthly Labor Review* 103, no. 3 (1980): 40–43.

Employers had always used some part-time workers, but self-service increased their ability to reduce their labor force and keep wages down (Bluestone et al. 1981). Women workers were increasingly hired (along with youths) while more and more adult men took jobs with higher earnings in other industries.

The preselling of goods and services through advertising reduced the retailers' dependency on the selling skill of salesclerks and increased it on their own advertising and that of manufacturers. Self-service depended on national advertising to familiarize the buyer with name brands and hence substituted for the persuasiveness of the salesclerk. And the salesclerk was no longer present to direct customers to "in-house" brands, which were more profitable to grocers (Strasser 1989: 248), reducing the reliance of many retailers on these brands and increasing their dependency on manufacturers' "name brands." Therefore, most retailers no longer needed to hire salesclerks for their knowledge of products and psychology of selling, and retailers gradually ceased using commissions on sales to motivate salesclerks to increase sales. This meant that merchants now had a vastly expanded pool of cheap workers, including many who lacked product knowledge and selling skills. Major chains switched by using partial self-service to break up "the practice of serving customers unless assistance is requested," which eventually made it possible for them to hire "girls without previous selling experience" (Fletcher 1942: 25).

The Ideology of "Labor Shortages": Racism and Sexism

Labor scarcity or shortage is based partly on employers' socially constructed understanding of the appropriate age, gender, race, and ethnicity for a jobholder. In retailing, the concept of a "labor shortage" hides racism and sexism, masking how employers considered only certain categories of persons to be suitable for work as salesclerks.

Self-service was partly a strategy that retailers used to overcome labor shortages, which actually meant only a shortage of white men and, later, white women. By adopting "the cousin of the cafeteria," retailers initially switched to unskilled white men (Ohrbach 1943; Thompson 1942; Vestal 1918).

The use of self-service as a substitute for clerk-service had many advantages for employers. It relieved retailers of the fear that would-be workers could demand higher wages during periods of labor shortages (Jay 1953). Retailers could also continue sexist and racist practices and avoid improving general working conditions.

An early attempt in California to use self-service implied that Hispanics were not considered suitable salesclerks. Throughout the United States, African Americans, Hispanics, and Asian Americans (women and men) were not considered suitable workers by most retailers serving whites until well after World War II. With the exception of elevator operators and delivery persons, employers hired African Americans and Asian Americans only for backroom jobs. Furthermore, despite the mass immigrations of the previous two decades, in 1914 most salesclerks were native-born whites—83 percent of men and 88 percent of women (U.S. Bureau of Census 1914: 422–423). African American women and men each were less than 1 percent of salesclerks in stores, and foreign-born whites made up about 15 percent. Racism probably hastened the trend to self-service in the United States compared to Western Europe. The latter had a relatively more racially and ethnically homogeneous labor force, which lasted until the post–World War II wave of immigrants from once-colonized Africa and Asia. In Memphis, where Saunders started the first chain of self-service stores, African American men were 40 percent of all employed men; in the retail trade, however, only 2 percent were salesmen, but 94 percent were laborers, porters, and helpers.

In 1910, men were still 71 percent of the salesclerks in stores and women 29 percent (U.S. Bureau of Census 1914: 422–423). The early adoption of self-service exemplifies the limited concept of the "labor force." Retailers rejected white women and all African Americans as a major source of labor. Yet none wanted to raise wages sufficiently to attract white male workers from higher-paid jobs. In Montana, where Lutey started his Marketeria in 1912, men made up 76 percent of the salesworkers and women 24 percent (U.S. Bureau of Census 1914: 121). In Tennessee, where Saunders started the Piggly Wiggly self-service stores, men made up 79 percent of salesclerks and women 21 percent (U.S. Bureau of Census 1914: 148). African American women were 3.3 percent of all saleswomen, their only jobs reported in stores. Most, 78 percent, worked in domestic service as laundresses or servants (U.S. Bureau of the Census 1914: 564–565).

The racist and sexist concept of the "labor force" continued through two wars. As white men left retailing for the armed services or jobs created by war industries, retailers were left with a smaller white male workforce from which to hire salesclerks. The antagonism of employers toward African Americans and Asian Americans as salesclerks remained strong even in the more liberal northern states. For example, during World War II, retailers tried to hire white U.S. soldiers during their off-duty hours and furloughs. Some advertised in east coast cities for English-speaking fliers who were awaiting transport back to Allied countries in Europe. Only the objection of immigration authorities put a stop to these advertisements. Students and utility workers on their off-hours, and even disabled (white) veterans, were considered by retailers.

Retailers so feared adverse customer reaction to "colored help" and "Asiatics" that only a few hired them as salesclerks. According to a market analyst sympathetic to racial integration, such hiring was without problems: "Two colored girls," he reported, sold in a Fifth Avenue store without provoking criticism, and the writer urged large Manhattan stores to hire them too (Wingate 1944: 116). "Educated Asiatics" were seen by retailers as a special problem. Retailers would hire them only for nonselling jobs, such as packers and checkers, or in selling jobs as telephone order clerks and adjusters, where customers would be unaware of their race. Retailers were warned that Asian Americans with college degrees were dissatisfied with such "mechanical and routine jobs" (Wingate 1944: 116, 130).

A postwar study designed to solve the labor shortage by enhanced training for high schools students continued to marginalize African Americans, encouraging them to take jobs in retailing that involved no contact with whites, as porters, maids, and elevator operators "for whom there is no hope of progressing through the retail organization" (Hoffman 1949: 6).

Women were considered unsuitable for retail sales work until the mid-nineteenth century. It was only then that women were hired, and not without protest. In the early 1860s, "the respectable community of Saco, in the State of Maine, went into a rage, inspired by indignation that a store could so lower its business pride as to employ a woman behind the counter" (RCIPA 1920a: 34). Most retail employers refused to hire white women for selling positions until the 1860s, to hire immigrant women to serve native-born customers, and to hire women and men of color to serve whites until after World War II. When employers did hire women, it was for female-typed jobs in female departments and at lower wages than men. Retailers hired women of color only for menial and routine jobs, usually ones without customer contact, and thereby lost the economic benefits of the education, skills, and experience of these workers. White European American women supposedly were hired by the first department store because Susan B. Anthony pressured the wife of the owner of Jordan Marsh in Boston to pressure her husband to hire women (RCIPA 1920a: 34).

Women and men retail salesclerks were not such costly labor, nor had they won such excellent working conditions, that grocers switched to self-service defensively. For women salesclerks, retailing combined wage discrimination, class discrimination, and the expectation that they dress beyond their earnings and stand long hours behind counters. Stores had poor ventilation and drafts and few amenities for salesclerks.

Women's Earnings

When the oldest of the three major retailing unions, the Retail Clerks International Protective Association (RCIPA), was founded in 1890, women retail workers were already recognized as notoriously underpaid.[2] The RCIPA newsletter, *The Advocate*, traced the economic and social woes of women salesclerks, sometimes supporting and sometimes challenging prevailing beliefs about women workers and women in a union.[3]

In its early years, *The Advocate* published more articles about women than later; about 33 percent of all editorials, feature articles, and miscellaneous pieces discussed women in 1910. This declined to about 13 percent in 1918, rose to 20 percent in 1920, and then declined to 11 percent in 1922. Thereafter, through the early 1960s (by which time self-service was well established throughout retailing), very little was published on or directed to women, from 6 percent to less than 1 percent. The earlier rise in part reflected the hiring of Eva McDonald Valesh, a union organizer, to write a column that tried to woo the wives of union men to support the union and recruit women salesclerks to its ranks. After the establishment of suffrage, the union's concern about women declined, as it did in many other U.S. organizations.

In the earlier years, the union newsletter was concerned about women as workers. But in 1953, 1955, 1959, and 1961, during the postwar cult of domesticity, the handful of articles about or for women discussed cooking, fashions, household skills, home decorating, and leisure activities. Articles were addressed to "the family," and puzzles and short pieces were published for children. The portrait of women salesclerks in *The Advocate* is limited, and generalizations must be cautious, but the portrayal of their difficult life and marginal social position is consistent with other studies (Benson 1986; Brandt ca. 1978).

The RCIPA supported gender equality formally from its beginnings. Its 1893 constitution stated that membership was open "to any person regardless of sex, in any branch of retail trade," in accord with the times, "other than liquor" (RCNPA 1895: 11). The union opposed the fourteen-to-sixteen-hour day and Sunday openings and sought behind-the-counter seats for "lady salesclerks, in obedience to both state and hygienic laws." It demanded "equal pay for equal work regardless of sex." Despite the stated support for women workers, Mary Burke (1893: 1), the union's first woman vice-president, complained of discrimination in her address to delegates at the union's third annual convention: "I regret that the women of our organization have been snubbed, entirely ignored, by every speaker today."

Whatever the formal commitment in the union's constitution, women wage workers confronted considerable ambivalence in the newsletter. For example, some women and men in the 1890s viewed women wage earners as immoral. *The Advocate* defended women while faulting women's low wages as "so meager that it compels them, in many instances, to throw off the mantle of virtue and morality" (RCNPA 1899a: 6). One of its prominent women members urged union membership as the remedy (Lanphere [Lamphere] 1899: 11). But a letter writer speculated that most wage-earning women worked unnecessarily, taking wages from "their sisters, and *often time* their brothers, husbands and sons" (Lawrence 1895: 11; emphasis added). Another letter writer admitted that women might need and like paid jobs, but expressed his preference for separate spheres—for a woman to be the "home-keeper and home-beautifier" (Lind 1906: 15). Even some who wanted union protection for wage-earning women called their employment an "unnatural condition" (Kathrens 1899: 14).

Dissenting from the cult of true womanhood, the editors of the newsletter defended the right of women salesclerks to their jobs and continued to attribute women's "immorality" to low wages (RCIPA 1902: 12). In recognition of wage discrimination against women, for its first dozen years the union charged women members only half the dues paid by men while giving women full benefits, such as funeral payments

(RCIPA 1905a: 17). *The Advocate* editor argued that women were paid low wages for "specious excuses" and rejected arguments that women were in greater supply, better adapted for low-paid work, more reliable, easily controlled, and therefore accepting of a smaller wage. The editor explained women's work problems as caused by men's taking advantage of women's "native ability, their generosity, their confiding good nature, their docility and obedience [which] are imposed upon to the point of degradation." But the editor, out to recruit new members, blamed women for accepting such treatment and admonished the woman reader to "realize her *true worth* through organization with her fellow wage-workers" (RCIPA 1903: 14–15).

The Advocate repeatedly criticized employers for underpaying *all* retail salesclerks, but it especially condemned employers for paying saleswomen less than salesmen (Morris 1907a: 24, 1907b: 25, 1907c: 15, 1908a: 15, 1908b: 18, 1908c: 14, 1908d: 23), imposing wage cuts on women (1908e: 25), and paying women "bread line" wages (RCIPA 1910: 13–14). The union supported a minimum-wage scale and "the same wage paid men for equal work" (RCIPA 1905b: 52). It "argued [for] payment based on services, not needs, to undercut the notion that women deserved lower wages than men because their needs were less" (Morris 1908f: 15). Some letter writers to *The Advocate* blamed women's willingness to accept wage discrimination ("their meager wages") on a "long-established precedent" that would continue until "all women wage-earners are admitted into the unions of their craft with a fixed wage scale" (Williamson 1906: 30). Union officials urged "salesmen" to recruit to the union the "salesladies" who worked in their departments "at reduced wage(s)." Rejecting a separate organization for salesladies, union officials argued that "the only remedy we have ever been able to find for this unfairness is to place the saleslady on an equal basis with the salesmen, taking her into our locals and insisting that the merchant pay her the same wage as the male for equal work performed" (RCIPA 1906: 16–17).

The union also tried to gain women's support for other union causes. When Valesh wrote *The Advocate* column "Woman's Work" in 1902–1903, her main concern seemed to be the national campaign for the union label, which the RCIPA supported, rather than the working conditions of saleswomen. Valesh appealed to women as "home makers and bread winners" (Valesh 1902: 11). Over her short writing career, she urged women, as salesclerks and kin of salesclerks, to join the fight. She tied the benefits of the union label to the concerns of salesclerks—to opening hours and store ventilation—but she also discussed the implications of the label for child labor, homework, and improvements in manufacturing. She urged salesclerks to press their customers to boycott goods produced by homework and scab labor (Valesh 1902: 8).

Viewing women as wives and mothers as well as workers, *The Advocate* accepted protective legislation "to safeguard the future of the race," that is, women as future mothers (Morris 1908c: 14). They supported the protective legislation sought by Florence Kelly to abolish "night work for women in manufacture" and to reduce hours in laundry work. The editor of *The Advocate* noted the equally long day of women salesclerks and their sometimes round-the-clock workday during the Christmas season.

The editors—Max Morris from 1893 to 1910 and H. J. Conway from 1910 to about 1925—welcomed women members to the union. Still, women workers made little gain in wages. Though women took new and better jobs in retailing during World War I, they remained "notoriously underpaid and disadvantaged." As soon as the war ended, most women salesclerks who had joined unions during the war were fired (RCIPA 1919: 14). The union was powerless to respond on their behalf.

By 1920, only fourteen states had minimum-wage laws, and Tennessee (where self-service first boomed) was not among them (Conway 1920a: 79). The union remained skeptical about the efficacy of minimum-wage laws, which failed to prevent girls and women from working at wages "below the safety point that will enable them to live decently and comfortably" (Conway 1921: 11), wage levels that made "many employers anxious to employ girls who live at home" so that their families can support them (Conway 1924: 15). The editor also urged more than basic survival wages for the woman clerk, a "living and saving wage" to be won by collective bargaining (Conway 1920b: 9).

In 1924, *The Advocate* reprinted part of a federal report on women workers in Kentucky, noting the similarity to other women wage earners and that the report contradicted the widely held belief that married women worked only for pin money. Three-quarters of women workers in the five-and-dime stores were unmarried, mostly because they were young (half were under twenty years) (RCIPA 1924: 23).[4] (An earlier study had warned girls and women that five-and-dime stores gave them few opportunities for advancement and that managers hired young workers without experience who would work for low wages [O'Leary 1916: 27].)

How much support retail clerk local unions gave women members is unknown. During the tenures of Morris and Conway, *The Advocate* made an effort to support women salesclerks and recruit them to union membership. The first issue of *The Advocate* presented the address of union President James Morrow, which was gender inclusive and free from the generic use of masculine pronouns. He referred to the "man or woman who stands behind the counter," the union fraternity of "brothers and sisters," and the like (Morrow 1893: 3). Support extended to the newsletter's use of language, which sometimes seems surprisingly nonsexist for its times. *The Advocate* used "ladies and gentlemen" to refer to its members in 1899 (RCNPA 1899b: 1), "lady member" (RCIPA 1905a), and "salespeople" in 1905 (RCIPA 1905b: 52). In 1908, each member was urged to think "for himself or herself" (RCIPA 1908: 27), and in 1920, every member "is urged to scan carefully *his* or *her* membership book" (RCIPA 1920b: 22).[5]

The union never won equal wages for women salesclerks. Women consistently earned less than men in retail jobs. In 1949, the earnings of women managers in food stores were 52 percent of men's earnings. The earnings of women cashiers in retailing were 55 percent of men's earnings and salesclerks earned 48 percent of their male counterparts' wages (U.S. Bureau of the Census 1956: (184–185, 192–193). Among full-time white workers in New England, women age 25–34 earned 60 percent of white men's earnings; women age 35–54 earned 52 percent. In 1967, women's earnings had declined, respectively, to 38 percent (age 25–34) and 36 percent (age 35–54) (Bluestone et al. 1981: 101).[6] In 1969, compared to 1949, women's earnings increased relative to men's, to 77 percent for cashiers in retail stores. (It was 80 percent for cashiers in food stores.) But the earnings of women managers declined to about 50 percent in retail and food stores, while women salesclerks' earnings declined to 36 percent in retail stores. (It was 43 percent in food stores.) (U.S. Bureau of the Census 1973: 153–155). In 1981, the earnings of women cashiers (85 percent of the occupation) improved to 92 percent of men's, and the earnings of women salesclerks had risen to 67.4 percent. Women remained a minority among managers (38 percent) and made only 57 percent of men's earnings (Rytina 1982). Women retail sales workers earn considerably less than men, partly because of sex segregation within retailing (Rytina 1982) and the gender typing of sales. Women are segregated into the sales of less lucrative "white goods," such as clothing and general merchandise, and work in smaller retail food stores, which pay hourly wages rather than salaries. Men salesclerks dominate in "brown goods," such as motor vehicles, furniture, and home appliances, where sizable commissions on sales increase earnings. Most important, self-service, and hence low wages, characterize variety, department, and apparel stores where women made up over two-thirds of workers in 1970 (U.S. Bureau of the Census 1973: 798–800).

Supposedly, the gender division of labor in retail sales is necessary, a reflection of customer preference and gendered skills (Brandt 1978). But the sex of the buyer and the sex of the seller are not paired consistently. For example, women usually sell apparel to women and men to men. Yet furniture and household appliances (high-commission items) are sold by men, although bought and used by women even if husbands participate in this shopping more than in grocery or other household shopping. Women's dominance in household shopping was established in the late nineteenth century. By 1929, women's buying accounted for 98 percent of retail household equipment sales (Klein 1929: 36), 82 percent of groceries, 80 percent of electrical appliances, and 85 percent of all goods sold "over the retail counter" (Bane 1929: 102). Motor vehicles (another high-commission item) are still sold by men, even though women bought half of them by the late 1970s. In a lawsuit brought by the Equal Employment Opportunity Commission against Sears Roebuck for discrimination against women, a federal court affirmed continuing female typing of low-wage retail work, deciding that "society" made women timid, reluctant to work for unguaranteed commissions and afraid to sell brown goods (Kessler-Harris 1986; Rosenberg 1986).[7]

Not a large percentage of women have joined retail unions (Benson 1986). But retail unions have not been very successful with men either. By 1956, the six major retail unions together had organized only 7 percent of all U.S. retail workers.[8] Half of those workers (280,000) were food store employees in 1954 (Estey 1956: 24). Only 25 to 30 percent of food store clerks belonged to any union, and dominated in the RCIPA, where they made up 60 percent of all members (Estey 1956: 25). The Butchers and Teamsters tried to prevent the RCIPA from organizing in department stores, where women predominated and bore the brunt of union rivalries. The Butchers and Teamsters ignored RCIPA picket lines, signed "sweetheart" contracts with grocery chains (Lens 1959: 91) and broke a union drive by the RCIPA in Boston (Lens 1959: 104).

Men unionists were suspicious of women salesclerks because women worked for lower wages than men (Whitehead 1942). Women did, however, support unions that supported them. In Seattle and Oakland, "strong labor towns," women as well as men fought for union representation in department stores through long, bitter strikes.

Other characteristics than union membership contribute to women's lower wages compared to men's. Women have been more likely than men to be hired as part-time workers in food (Schwartzmann 1971) and department stores (Bluestone et al. 1981: 105). Furthermore, the earnings of all retail salesclerks have dropped substantially since the mid-1930s, compared with other occupations, and despite the modest gains salesclerks made in earlier decades (Benson 1986; Bluestone et al. 1981; Schwartzmann 1971). Previously, full-time, year-round sales workers expected to increase their earnings through commissions on their sales, which depended on worker skills (Bluestone et al. 1981: 109). Retailers blamed the Fair Labor Standards Act of the mid-1950s for the demise of commissions and the dependence of clerks on low hourly wages.

Relying on a detailed division of labor and self-service, employers ceased training salesclerks, except in such tasks as managing the sales transaction, accepting returns, and pushing higher-priced merchandise to customers who asked about quality. Few salesclerks were encouraged to learn the skills necessary for commission selling. Until the late 1980s, with some exceptions, few stores gave clerks more than perfunctory training.[9] For most sales workers, the result was that employers found no value in job experience and did not reward long-time salesclerks with high wages. Most salesclerks lost their ability to be upwardly mobile (Benson 1986: 191).

Deskilling

The tensions that once characterized relations between the working-class clerk and the wealthy customer arose from cross-class disdain and working-class resentment of employer efforts to force salesclerks to conform to middle-class, native-born ideas about manners and deference to class "betters" (Benson 1986: 128–131). Today, the tensions may be more directly linked to the structure of selling. Without systematic sales training, reasonable wages, and rewards for outstanding performance, the cashier lacks the knowledge and incentive to respond to customers' requests for help and information. Some managers recognize that "reduced store staffs, inadequate employee training . . . [and] erosion in selling quality may hurt" sales (Barmarsh 1983). Nonetheless, most employers try to keep the clerk–customer ratio high to decrease the wage bill and use cost–benefit analyses to estimate the highest ratio tolerated by customers.

Women and teenagers in retailing seem to be treated as a reserve army of labor, even though women make up over 50 percent of the labor force (Simeral 1978). They are hired as needed—on weekends, during the lunch-hour rush, at the Easter and Christmas seasons—and then they are fired. Retailing has an extremely high "turnover" rate, which includes workers quitting and employer layoffs.

Retailing offers women few opportunities for upward mobility and virtually no increase in earnings with age. In earlier decades, middle-age women could earn more than younger or older workers (Bluestone et al. 1981: 103–104). Women are more likely than men to depend solely on their low-wage sales jobs for income (56 percent of women compared to 42 percent of men), and women are more likely than men in sales to moonlight.

This chapter has discussed self-service as a new labor process that eliminated or altered jobs and service. But, in reality, self-service constituted a new social relation between sellers and the public. Salespersons remained "local" in their opportunities, though the decline in the need for sales skills made it easier for them to move from one employer to another and from one locale to another. Most retailers concluded that salesclerks needed no special training about either the merchandise or the clientele. Most goods came "presold" through local and national advertising, and the customer became a "cosmopolitan" relatively uninfluenced by salesclerks.

The work transfer had repercussions on the lives of working-class women. Women entered grocery retailing as salesclerks as that occupation was being replaced by cashiers (even if the cashier retained the title "salesclerk") and was changing from full- to part-time and from higher than average increases in wages to relatively lower rates. The work changed from that requiring extensive interpersonal skills in persuasion and knowledge of the merchandise to semiskilled clerical work—the use of the cash register or computer, which depend on easily learned skills. Experience in selling became less important to employers as the customer was seen as "selling herself" as she walked the aisles. What the customer read to acquire "self-selling" skills and to serve herself is the topic of the next chapter.

6

The Clerkless Customer:
Doing Away with "Wasteful" Labor

Attended by saleswomen trained to service and servility, wealthy women in the 1880s and 1890s shopped in "grand palaces of consumption," lavish department stores in Buffalo and Boston, Chicago and Atlanta (Benson 1986). Even then, however, Chicagoans were doing self-service, standing in lines for food at the new "cafeteria." Women of modest means who had visited across the counter with the clerks at Lutey Brothers' store in Butte, Montana, by 1912 were serving themselves next door, at Lutey's Marketeria, modeled on Chicago's cafeteria. In 1916, in Memphis, Tennessee, customers were doing self-service shopping at Piggly Wiggly, modeled on Lutey's Marketeria. And in 1918, *Scientific American* could describe the transformation of the well-served shopper into the "clerkless customer."

Retailers were gradually transferring the work of salesclerks, delivery persons, and other staff to women shoppers,[1] expecting them to do "much of the time-consuming unorderly marketing burden" and reduce the "wasted [*sic*] time of employees waiting on each customer" (Cassady 1962: 101).

The work transfer changed shopping for women, many of whom were simultaneously losing the services of hired hands, "helpers," and domestic servants. For them, self-service was innovative in degree, rather than kind, in the sense that preindustrial housework was rarely done by one woman in isolation. At the least, paid helpers, offspring (boys and girls), other relatives on extended visits, and even husbands participated in domestic chores. With the shift away from household production and toward the purchase of goods and services in the marketplace, women, even poor ones, were progressively isolated in their domestic activities. Self-service was one more step in the expansion of women's domestic *service* work as *goods* both freed women's energies from some tasks but demanded women's services.

From Being Served to Cryptoservant

In the post–Civil War period the shift toward the purchase of mass-produced goods began, exemplified in "palaces of consumption" (Benson 1986). Rich urban women shopped for furs and jewelry, French gloves and exotic perfumes, fabrics and porcelain, all under the one roof of the department stores of the 1870s and 1880s. Late-nineteenth- and early-twentieth-century production and distribution were in transition: mass production and rising wages made more goods available to many people, bringing much of the working class into the new marketplace. Affluent and middle-income women struggled through these decades, bemoaning the "servant problem" as they competed with factories, offices, and stores for women workers—and lost.[2]

In the settlement house movement, from Boston's Women's Educational and Industrial Union's (WEIU) School of Housekeeping to Portland's (Oregon) Jewish Community Center, affluent white women tried to solve the servant problem by training working-class "girls." The WEIU's vocational training program aimed at Americanizing working-class immigrants so as to make them into suitable servants. WEIU "housekeeping" classes were open only to girls who agreed to seek employment as servants; the girls went to their classes in uniforms appropriate for their future jobs, and there, girls who were literate read about housekeeping in the same magazine, *Ladies' Home Journal*, in which their mistresses-to-be read about training servants. Their future employers also took classes, on subjects such as the proper relationship with servants and the history of domestic service (WEIU Papers 1897). The WEIU helped domestic workers by trying to formalize the servant–employer relationship, urging written agreements about job descriptions, time off, and notices of leaving. The agreements were not without benefits to the employers too, for they stabilized the terms of employment. In Oregon, girls took lessons on bed making, hardly a concern of Portland's Eastern European Jewish immigrants, who shared beds without linens. The lessons were not merely instructions in modern hygiene, but training for "service."

Servants facilitated the new market-based consumption of the rich and the upper middle class. Labor for the use of marketplace purchases had to be increasingly provided by the buyers, mostly women bereft of servants. Immigrant girls and white migrants from rural areas sought jobs in factories, offices, and stores, where they earned higher wages than in domestic service and could have a personal life. Some new immigrants—among them Jewish and Italian girls—were rarely willing to be servants even in the homes of their own ethnic groups (Dudden 1983).

Manufacturers and distributors had to persuade housewives to increase their buying even when they could no longer afford servants or more than minimal household help. Housewives had to be convinced that they should increase their own labor, using it and new household technologies in the place of servants. If women would accept endless shopping as desirable, ultimately they would be persuaded to do-for-themselves. Do-it-yourself became part of the practice of homemaking among a class of women who previously would not have imagined themselves as workers, and for whom the nitty-gritty of household labor had once been passed on to servants or at least been shared with them. These women learned housekeeping skills from a variety of sources, including magazines, as they joined working-class women in doing more domestic labor themselves. Domestic labor was itself rearranged, rather than eliminated or reduced, by new goods and services from the marketplace (Cowan 1983).

Self-service in shopping, the transformation of women into "clerkless customers," was a continuation of the loss of services that many women experienced as unpaid household workers. As shoppers, women were coerced by the new stores into waiting on themselves, much as the invention of mechanized washing machines reduced their use of commercial laundries. The mass production of the automatic Bendix washer after World War II displaced the commercial laundry further and forced do-it-yourself laundering on to women (Hartmann 1974). Meanwhile, as women were doing more housework, advertising was trying to persuade them of the virtues of being "free" to make whatever choices they fancied, through self-service shopping. That the choices were constrained by manufacturers and distributors was a well-kept secret, not shared with "Mrs. Customer," en route to becoming the well-trained "consumer" in a "consumer society."

The Self-Reliant Homemaker

She knows very, very little, and there is so much that she must learn. . . . Who is going to tell her? . . . Good food, good clothing, good furnishings, good values for her household and children—these she will learn from advertising.

To teach her to want a better home and to make a better home for her children than even her mother made—that is truly shaping public opinion. That is the work of advertising. —Advertising company ad (George Batten 1921)

Women were constrained to do self-service by the reorganization of stores. But friendly persuasion abetted changes in the labor process as advertisers sought both to encourage extensive shopping and to romanticize its self-service form. The tie between images, beliefs, and social behaviors is problematic. It remains so here because the women who learned about the new market from advertising left no commentaries on their experiences, no diaries and letters revealing their feelings and actions. Some of what they were supposed to learn was central to a major women's magazine in the United States, the *Ladies' Home Journal*, and advice books and newspaper columns. These addressed women about their housewifely responsibilities and coaxed them to accept the new work of shopping. Readers in the early twentieth century may have seen the images less cynically than some of today's readers are likely to do. I do not know. Women, then as now, sought advice on homemaking, childcare, and relations with their husbands; and they read mass-circulation magazines for information. Manufacturers presumed that women took the varied portrayals of them in advertising, the admonishments and advice from writers, and their discussions of the new housekeeping seriously enough to promote their products within the pages of the magazine.

Supported by these discussions and forced by the new retailing to work while shopping, women in all urban communities gradually took for do-it-yourself and self-service for granted, seeing it as the "normal" way to shop. Few women complained, or if they did, their complaints were not published in the *Ladies' Home Journal*. In contrast, letters from earlier readers, published through World War I, had decried the lack of services in stores and the "servant problem" and had complained about shoddy merchandise and dishonest sellers.

The *Ladies' Home Journal*, founded in 1883 as *The Ladies Home Journal and Practical Housekeeper, A National Illustrated Family Journal*, was read mainly by upper-middle and middle-class white women, but it was also used in the schooling of their domestic servants in settlement house programs (North Bennet Street 1912) and eventually gained a working-class readership. Other magazines, such as *Woman's Day* or *Family Circle*, did not begin to publish until long after the events I am considering (the disappearance of servants, the adoption of self-service) were either accomplished or well under way. These magazines were also addressed to a specific audience; for example, *Woman's Day* initially was sold only in Atlantic & Pacific food stores.

The *Ladies' Home Journal* is the only continuously, long-published magazine for women readers that has a national and class-mixed readership. It shows the ideologies that manufacturers, distributors, and publishers present to women readers. These ideologies legitimate the increases in women's work of social reproduction, presenting it as natural and desirable. (Ideology here refers to widely held beliefs that people have about the rightness and wrongness of social relations, its naturalness and progressive character, their obligations, and the moral justifications for social relations of subordination and domination.)

In the Market: Shopping for Household Goods

Shopping for groceries and household goods, appliances and clothes, face soaps, and even cigarettes was women's work by the late nineteenth century, as manufactured goods replaced homegrown and homemade ones (Strasser 1982: 242–249). Throughout the 1890s, the *Ladies' Home Journal* ran articles on housekeeping, clothing styles, personal deportment, servants, and the like, but with minor references to the commercial marketplace. Such advertisements were usually small scale, more like elaborate "classified" advertisements than modern full-page ads. These early advertisements were crowded with text praising the goods in imaginative and flamboyant terms, but without many references aimed at convincing the reader that the product would transform her into a new and improved social person. Cookbooks and manuals of household advice later began to include chapters on buying food, as these tasks increasingly fell to "servantless" housewives (Parloa 1908). Social workers, home economists, and "household engineers" such as Mrs. Christine Fredericks, a home economist and doyenne of "consumerism," sought to turn "consumption" into a science. Advertisers, aware that women made most buying decisions (Strasser 1982: 245), targeted them in advertisements designed to promote "consumerism" by creating new social needs, even for happenstance inventions such as Crisco and Listerine (Strasser 1989).

The *Ladies' Home Journal* exemplifies many changes in advertising. At first, the *Journal* published housekeeping advice for the reader to use herself or convey to her paid domestic workers. Such advice ranged over many topics: buying dress fabric (Lambert 1887: 10), laundering with cream of tartar and oxalic acid and preventing flannel from shrinking ("The Practical Housekeeper" 1885: 5), staying beautiful after age forty (Knapp 1885), and managing domestic servants (Cooke 1889; Holt 1889). In 1903, in a regular column called "The Woman with No Servant," Miss Parloa explained how to do such household chores as keeping sink drains clean (Parloa 1903a: 43), reviving faded fabrics (Parloa 1903b: 32), and washing woolen garments (Parloa 1903c: 46).

By World War I, the *Journal*'s advertisements had become larger, sometimes a full page, with snappy slogans and messages directed to creating a vision of a buyer as much as of a product. Drawings and photographs alluded to some unnamed social value, mood, and ambience that supposedly could be created by the product, and to the benefits to the personality, character, and social worthiness of the buyer–reader. Practical uses for products receded, and simple information with only a touch of exaggeration gave way to wholehearted persuasion (Williams 1980).

Gradually, advice was linked to commercial products. By 1915, Christine Fredericks was interpreting the marketplace to the customer and interpreting the woman buyer to dealers and manufacturers. (Compare Fredericks 1926 in the *Hardware Dealers Magazine* with Fredericks in 1917.) She gave advice on shopping (Fredericks 1915: 45), outfitting a kitchen (Fredericks 1917), buying kitchen knives (Fredericks 1920a: 186), and do-it-yourself repairs (Fredericks 1920b: 188).

Business understood that "advertisements you booked and paid for were really old stuff; the real thing was what got through as ordinary news" or as articles whose authors' fees came, ultimately, from the advertisers (cited in Williams 1980: 183). Fredericks exemplified this in her magazine and syndicated newspaper articles, which promoted the products of specific manufacturers.

Customers were able to do without knowledgeable salesclerks because national and local advertising informed them about mass-produced, standardized goods. Standardization reduced the range of products, making it possible for a customer in New Jersey or Illinois to buy the same goods as someone in Tennessee and California. Standardization reflected and supported centralized manufacturing and increasingly centralized distribution, which made it feasible for manufacturers to use national advertising campaigns to persuade shoppers to buy their products and to see the marketplace as offering an alternative to home production. In the 1920s, retailers began to peddle self-service, relying on brand-name products manufactured for the national market.

In the mid-1950s, a retailer captured the core of the new consumerism in the term "forced draft consumption": "Our rate of production," he wrote, "requires the consumer to use, destroy, waste, burn things, discard them at an ever-increasing rate" for the well-being of U.S. capitalism (Lebow 1955–1956: 166).

In 1929, the same year that Piggly Wiggly self-service stores first advertised nationally in it, the *Ladies' Home Journal* joined in the process of persuasion by establishing the Clearing House of Consumer Information. This supplemented its advertising and the many articles that directed readers on the use of the market (*LHJ* 1929: 84). Upper-middle-class white women could read about their importance as customers because they did an estimated 85 percent of the buying in the United States (Bane 1929), even of automobiles (Klein 1929) and men's ties and hose.

Learning to buy finished goods was portrayed as new and complicated, with women "growing more and more interested in buying." The middle-class customer could choose from a very large selection of goods. Product standardization and quality control were new to customers, and the *Journal* discussed it approvingly. "Electric-light plugs," the number of sizes of "bed blankets," "house construction" (which cities were starting to regulate with plumbing, lighting, and ventilation)—all were noted appreciatively (Edwards 1929: 86). The many sizes of refrigerators, bedsprings, mattresses, and towels were reduced to a few standard ones. Brass lavatory and sink taps went from 1,114 to 72 sizes. Sterling silver flatware went from 192 to 62 sizes. During World War I, produce, butter, eggs, meat, and even honey were graded, and the practice continued in the postwar years. Sewing-machine needles, oven thermostats, and the volume of cups, spoons, and pans for baking and cooking were still being standardized in 1929 (Edwards 1929).

The *Journal* quizzed readers on the new facts of marketing with 129 questions, to encourage readers to face up to "the new food products appearing on the market, and [the] old ones appearing in new forms"

(Parrish 1929: 118). Some questions were about products: was cold-storage food inferior to others? (*answer*: once upon a time, but not in 1929); should bananas be put in the refrigerator? (*answer*: never); and were Oregon prunes sweeter than those from California? (*answer*: no, the second were sweeter). Others questions promoted thrift—in chain stores: what was the relative cost of shopping at large independent stores compared to chains? (*answer*: one-fifth more at first). Still others taught about standardization: how many slices of pineapple in a standard Number 2½ can? (*answer*: eight); and about federal regulations: were well-advertised brands of meat products packed under federal inspection? (*answer*: yes, for those shipped interstate) (Parrish 1929 118).

From Mistress with Maid to Do-It-Yourselfer

To track the change in the organization of work of the housewife–reader as suggested in the advertising in the *Ladies' Home Journal*, I categorized its content according to whether the maid or housewife was portrayed and the implied expectation of the housekeeping responsibilities of the woman of the home (giving advice or supervising others versus doing the work herself) for 1903, 1908, 1913, and 1929. This selection samples the earliest year (1929) for which the *Journal* carried advertisements for self-service.

LOSING SERVICE

During the nineteenth century, the "servant problem" was a major concern of bourgeois and upper-middle-class women.[3] Few advertisements pictured people, but the text focused on the use of household products by servants. Articles in the *Journal* did consider how women could run their households without "reliable" paid household help, published letters from "correspondents" lamenting the unwillingness of immigrant girls to enter domestic service and criticizing native-born girls for preferring jobs in factories, stores, and offices to domestic service (Jewett 1899: 10). The "lady" readers got advice on how to find servants and interact with them and how to get them to work properly and remain in their jobs (McConaught 1885: 4). Readers were advised to learn housework themselves so that they could supervise their servants adequately. They were advised to train servants just as employers in factories and offices trained their workers. The major complaints of servants were minimized: the lack of a personal life because of the twenty-four-hour day and seven-day week, the absence of privacy, the loss of family life, and the difficulty servants had in meeting marriage prospects and escaping from domestic service (Katzman 1978). The *Journal* dismissed the drudgery, loss of privacy, and subservience as more than balanced by benefits to servants: access to the culture of their "betters," Americanization, living in luxurious homes, and eating good food. Articles advised the very rich on finding, training, and maintaining a large staff; they urged fair treatment of servants in more modest households with one or perhaps two servants, and advised wives and mothers on running their homes without household help (*LHJ* 1886a: 3).

IDENTIFYING STATUS

In 1903 and 1908, illustrated advertisements showed maids in the conventional servant "uniform," aprons and small caps. A cap did not keep the hair dust free, as some housewife gear did, but symbolized a distinct social position. Housewives did *not* wear aprons and caps, or are identified by the text as the "mistress" or housewife. Sometimes advertisements showed a housewife, but the text suggested that the work being discussed was for maids. For example, an advertisement for Ivory Flakes showed three lounging girls; the text read: "She will tell the launderers just how she wants [dresses] washed" (Ivory Flakes 1908a: 2). Another Ivory advertisement showed a woman washing dishes and a man drying; the text identified them: "Sunday evening; and the maid is out. So Helen and Tom and Helen's sister do the dishes!" (Ivory Flakes 1908b: 4). By 1913, I found it was more difficult to distinguish maids from housewives. The text addressed "homemakers" and the women pictured wore aprons, but no caps. By 1929, homemakers wore the same clothing and jewelry in advertisements for household cleaning products that other advertisements urged readers to buy.

WORK RESPONSIBILITIES

From its beginnings in 1883, *Journal* advertisements and articles discussed the importance of the housewife's gaining control over the work done in her home. Advertisements encouraged readers to learn housework so that they could supervise servants adequately and their lives would not be disrupted unnecessarily if servants departed. Readers were advised about details of dress, cooking, and infant care, but the clear expectation was that servants would do the actual work.

The relationship between the mistress and household workers

could be difficult. For example, one writer said that she worried about the overdependence of young mothers on their nursemaids, fearing that allowing servants to run the house would make them the mistress of their "true mistress" (*LHJ* 1886b: 7). Servants were portrayed as dominating their employers, breeding overdependence on servants by the mistress (*LHJ* 1886c: 3). In a monthly column, readers could read practical household hints and cooking suggestions. Ivory Flakes advertisements in early issues of the magazine showed the lady of the house explaining to a visitor her *maid's* use of the soap. Newlywed women received advice to help them avoid being taken advantage of by shopkeepers (*LHJ* 1886b: 7).

Table 6.1 shows the frequency of portrayals of housewives and maids as responsible for domestic duties between 1903 and 1929. In accord with the trend toward "self-service," over twenty-five years the maid virtually disappears from ads showing housework and childcare, from a high of 57 percent to a mere 8 percent by 1929. In 1903, maids in advertising copy served Jello, made beds, cleaned, and did the laundry. But the mistress of the household also worked. About one-third of the ads showed the housewife working, and a few showed both maid and housewife using a product (e.g., a nursemaid and a housewife each wearing rubber gloves [Agnota 1903: 33]).

TABLE 6.1

Housework and Childcare: From the Maid to the Housewife in Ladies' Home Journal Advertisements[a]

Worker	1903	1908	1913	1929
Maid	57%	26%	18%	8%
Housewife	27	41	44	92
Ambiguous[b]	16	33	38	—
Total ads (N)	(70)	(46)	(77)	(52)
Issues (N)	(12)	(6)	(9)	(6)

[a]Issues examined: 1903, 12 issues; 1913, Feb., April, June, Aug., Oct., Dec.; 1908, Jan., Mar., May, July, Aug., Sept., Oct., Nov., Dec.; 1929, Jan., March, May, July, Sept., Nov. Figures do not measure trends in the yearly quantity of advertising.

[b]"Ambiguous ads" were of people refinishing and enameling furniture, or women without caps and aprons, but also without jewelry or luxurious dresses that would have suggested a housewife position.

By 1908, portrayals of maids declined to 26 percent, and in 1913 to 18 percent. Ambiguity increased. In 1908 advertisements, dust cap and apron sets declined, and more women were shown wearing plain skirts and blouses, a small string tie, and perhaps a small apron. For example, one woman wearing a cap and apron is shown baking, and another is shown polishing a table (Washburn-Crosby 1908: 61; Liquid Veneer 1908: 78). But other women, apparently housewives, feed babies (Pillsbury 1908) or pose using Old Dutch Cleanser (Old Dutch Cleanser 1908: 47). A Minute Tapioca advertisement (*LHJ* 1908: 56) even suggests that the housewife requires a "working costume," for she can cook the pudding in her "afternoon dress" after her "heavier cooking" is done. Finally, ads also recognize types of women, those who are served and those who do-it-themselves. The Ideal Vacuum Cleaner (*LHJ* 1913: 63) uses this theme, and it reappears in 1913 in an advertisement directed both to "the woman of wealth" and women who do their own work, "the housewife" (Simplex Ironer 1913: 81). But advertisements were suggesting that the housewife could replace her servant with mass-produced goods. Proctor and Gamble lauded its White Naphtha soap as "her laundress [who] had done all the hard work" (Proctor and Gamble 1913: 29).

By 1929, the worker was unambiguously the housewife. Articles on housekeeping no longer discussed how to cope with servants or the "servant problem." The magazine text now focused on how the housewife best do the work herself. For example, the Savage Clothes Washer "does all the work" (Savage 1929: 216). Women could lounge over coffee because the Hotpoint Automatic Electric Range "frees the modern mother" while meals "cook themselves" (Hotpoint 1929: 133).

These changes in advertising are interwoven with a real decline in the availability of servants, a rise in purchasing power, and the development of the domestic science movement, which admonished middle-class housewives to Taylorize housekeeping and childcare. The domestic science movement hoped to make homemaking a "science" by using the "scientific" principles of Taylor for running a household that businesses supposedly used for manufacture and finance. Domestic life was also being reshaped by a new understanding that the prevention of disease required cleanliness and improved nutrition.

By the turn of the century, readers saw a new image of the housewife in the *Ladies' Home Journal* (Wright 1980). The "servantless house" became a fashionable design. Women who once read about large homes run by staffs of servants (or at least a few servants) now read about "cottages." The *Journal* reader could study houses and floor plans, room decorations, and kitchen equipment designed specifically for her to do all or much of the housework. Nevertheless, maids still predominated in advertising for cleaning products, household appliances, and foods. The only advertisement I found of a housewife using a household product shows her with a child, playing at bathing dolls (Standard Porcelain 1903: 42).

By 1915, there was a war in Europe. For upper-middle-class and middle-class U.S. women, this meant fewer servants because the flow of immigrants slowed and because war industries were offering jobs to women. (The Canadians actually set up a special system in which farmers and women willing to work as domestic servants were allowed special passage to Ontario.) During the war, the *Ladies Home Journal* began to portray a servantless household in articles and advertisements.

The *Journal* dealt with the servant shortage with a raft of articles about the war and about women's duty to be supportive housewives. The magazine ceased showing household duties as unsuitable for its readers, whose social class appears to remain upper middle and middle. (Working-class women would not become readers until after World War II.) In 1916, articles discussed such topics as training girls for careers in teaching and social work, and a new monthly column was begun on photography as a hobby, although hardly one for low-income families. Housework was portrayed as an exemplar of control and self-reliance, fun and easy to do, not a necessity but a "convenient social virtue." By 1916, in less than a generation, housewives from classes that once depended on servants, did much of their own work. A beringed young woman with an angelic expression cleans her little cottage (Old Dutch Cleanser 1916: 82), and a report from a university explains how to make doing dishes "fun" (*LHJ* 1916a: 40). Product advertisements show women refinishing and polishing furniture, caring for children, doing laundry, sewing, dressmaking, and making slipcovers for furniture. They are told how to make quick meals for their families in order to make up for time lost in doing other household jobs.

In 1916, only two advertisements show women wearing caps as well as aprons, probably indicating that they were servants. One advertisement shows a maid serving coffee to six well-dressed women seated around a table (Barrington 1916: 66). There are only three discussions of domestic service: two attempt to make it palatable to young female readers, college girls, and other girls who do not have to work to help support their families. One reports the hired-help experiences of a young woman aspiring to college who worked as a maid. As a maid, she (virtuously) refused to be "one of the family," used her earnings to go to college and her domestic service experience to start a tearoom (Carson 1916: 36). Another writer makes a case for girls staying at home to help their mothers with domestic work or taking jobs as "domestic helpers" or "hired girls." She implores the young daughters from farm families to stay home to help their mothers or siblings, rather than teach, and argues that servants' wages are not really low because laundry and room and board are free (Sprague 1916: 54). An editorial admonishes *Journal* readers not to be inconsiderate by giving gifts of silver to the bride in a young couple of modest means, for she will be without help in cleaning it (*LHJ* 1916b: 7).

Over about thirty years, the materials presented to affluent readers in a major magazine changed from how women could cope with the servant problem to how women could learn about household technologies that would enable them to be housekeepers themselves. The next change was to get women to accept "self-service."

The Promise of "Control"

"Ten to twenty percent savings!" Benefits in "time, energy and patience!" Piggly Wiggly, the most prominent chain of self-service stores, thus advertised in 1921 in Denver for its eighteen Colorado stores, lauding self-service for long opening hours and freedom from clerks. Presumably there were also "health benefits" because self-service used packaging guaranteed to keep food clean and rapid turnover assured that goods were always fresh (*Printers' Ink* 1921).

Most important, Piggly Wiggly began to run advertisements in the *Ladies' Home Journal* that portrayed self-service as the quintessential example of U.S. values, personal control and free choice. These were used as key selling points by its three thousand franchises. In 1929, Piggly Wiggly advertisements ran against the current: in that same year, the Atlantic and Pacific chain stores (the A & P) portrayed clerk-service (A & P 1929a: 129). An Ivory Flakes ad advised customers to "ask the saleswoman" how to wash fabrics (Ivory Flakes 1929: 64). Another A & P ad extolled the courtesy of its salesclerks and showed a clerk loading the rumble seat of a two-door convertible, while the shopper and her child waited smilingly (A & P 1929c: 66).

In Piggly Wiggly ads, there were no clerks; instead, well-dressed, youngish women, woven baskets over their arms, collected packaged goods and "dainty" fresh produce. Triangular metal tags hung from the store shelves, the "famous price tags" of their stores (Piggly Wiggly 1929a: 170). "Personal control," the advertisements implied, meant freedom from clerks, who would interfere with choices and would try to persuade the shopper to select a product against her own interests, rush her, and make her wait unduly long. The advertisements emphasized that in self-service stores, women were "free to make their own *decisions*" (Piggly Wiggly 1929b: 114) and "to make [them] leisurely" (Piggly Wiggly 1929a: 170). Shopping was to be, not a duty or drudge work, but "a real adventure" (Piggly Wiggly 1929d: 185), "a delightful way [to shop]" (Piggly Wiggly 1929a: 170), a "delightful and sensible" custom, and a "fascinating way to cut costs" (Piggly Wiggly 1929b: 114). Shoppers and shopping were now glamorous, the additional work transformed into personal and financial benefits, compatible with the home economics movement, and concerns about health and nutrition. (Piggly Wiggly advertisements described "tempting meals" and "useful ideas for your menus.")

With the adoption of self-service, the shopper could carry out her task and limit her interaction to dealing with check-out cashiers. What was omitted from this construction was the new work required of the customer: travel to the store and collecting items from personal knowledge of the array of name-brand national products. More important, access to quality products, to variety at a specific price, were constructed in a language that hid the changing political economy of food production: the consolidation of agriculture, the centralization of distribution, and the development of conglomerates such as General Foods or distributors such as Kroger and Safeway. The advertising implied, instead, that the ill-mannered, interfering retail service worker was at fault for the shift from clerk-service to self-service.

SELF-SERVICE

With lessons in the intricacies of the merchandise offered in the marketplace, women were well prepared for self-serving. From the 1920s on, marketing specialists used elaborate rationales to make self-service attractive and did so while making women appear rather dimwitted.

For example, in calling self-service shopping an "adventure," advertisers blurred the distinction between work and leisure. They presented self-service as socializing for the housewife, rather than as work or both. One market analyst even turned shopping into maintenance for the family car and instructed women how best to use their leisure time.

> The consumer-buyer with available time for various activities might prefer shopping to attending a tea, say, and even if food buying were recognized as a task instead of a form of socializing, she may not be able to use the time any more profitably [*sic*] in another activity. Moreover, if not used in connection with shopping, the expensive automobile purchased for pleasure might sit in the garage with only the saving of the marginal cost of this operation (the cost of one gallon of motor fuel, say), and in time might indeed deteriorate even more than if utilized for shopping. (Cassady 1962: 262)

Advertising played on themes of choice, control, and freedom. One historian of supermarkets posited "a 'shopping instinct' in the average homemaker's make-up which can be satisfied only by introducing her to the great variety of foods and goods which the present Super Market displays," as if gendered instinct determined buying behavior (Zimmerman 1955: 145). Advertising's construction of mass tastes and "social" needs, and women's preoccupation with shopping, was ignored (Ewen 1976).

Advertisers and retailers thus treated self-service as gendered work, calling the shopper "Mrs. Customer" and "Mrs. Housewife" and using illustrations of women in pictures of self-service shopping. Almost all self-service customers were so portrayed in the early marketing literature, sometimes with condescension. In 1939, an economist attributed women's use of self-service to a pathetic search for self-assertion: "There is one type of shopper whose importance is magnified by the feeling that she makes her own selections, serves herself, and gets the most for her money" (Haas 1939: 98–99). While explaining how grocers push their own brands for high-profit margins, one advertiser poked fun at the middle-class woman shopper, a naive captive of advertisements, and the machinations of the self-service retailer:

> Comes the Lady Shopper, timidly at first because she had a funny idea that going to self-service stores savored a bit of slumming . . . she grows bolder . . . she gets nearly as much delight out of looking over the dozens of shelves leisurely and making new discoveries . . . as she gets shopping a department store. She does not sense that some of her "choices" are

as involuntary as the card you pick out of a magician's deck. (Coutant 1942: 56)

OTHER NEW SERVICES

Self-service retailers claimed to trade self-service work for lower prices and "convenience." Yet self-service did not inevitably lower prices to customers. When self-service was introduced, some reduction in labor costs was passed on to the customers in the form of lower prices (Corina 1947: 11; Haas 1939; Sylbert 1942). But even the rejuvenated pioneering Piggly Wiggly stores used a pricing policy that, "aside from occasional 'specials' [is] no better than those of local competitors, while . . . overhead is lower because fewer clerks are needed" (*Business Week* 1934: 14). Since World War II, self-service retailers have replaced price competition (which cuts down on profit margins) with alternatives that do not. Loss leaders, for example, are used to attract customers and "to create an impression of low prices" without the need to lower prices evenly (Phillips 1941: 386). Because of the thousands of items stocked in markets, customers are unable to comparison shop for more than a few (Markin 1963: 82).[4]

Though retailers eliminated the services of clerks, they argued that they were providing customers with a whole range of new services. Yet the main convenience appeared to be one-stop shopping and a large number of items that differ hardly at all. The supermarket carried an average nine thousand items in 1973 (Quelch and Takeuchi 1981). Other features that retailers considered services were wide aisles, in comparison with the narrower ones that allowed them to display more goods and slow down the customer, along with "kiddie corrals" and clearly marked prices. By 1947, a self-service retailer concluded that "directions, labeling, pricing, variety and convenience" were *more* service than ever given in full-service stores (Corina ca. 1947: 27). Most of the "services" supplied by self-service retailers were necessary or desirable, however, only because clerk-service had been eliminated. Kiddie corrals became "service" because self-service meant that the customer with young children could not telephone an order and expect a clerk to assemble the goods, but had to do the work herself.

Retailers using self-service portrayed the customers' opportunity to examine goods, and standardized sizes and measures, as "services." Yet prepackaging, as used by grocers to prevent pilfering and ease checkout, and as used by manufacturers to spread a brand name, made most products invisible. Some services were subject to interpretation: it might not be accurate to see "convenient" quantities as a service if this meant that customers got the amount the manufacturer wanted to sell. Foods are packaged in sizes standardized by the manufacturers and fit customer needs only accidentally.[5] And low-income customers who buy small quantities can be at a particular disadvantage insofar as cost per unit may decline with increase in the amount bought.

Class Differences

Self-service cannot automatically be interpreted as either good or bad for customers. Certain aspects of self-service may be a convenience to the customer; others may be an annoyance or may set unsuspected limits, but the insertion of the customer into the labor process varies by social class. Retailers have not been able to cut services across class lines (except during World War II [Coutant 1942]). Stores may require low- and middle-income customers to substitute their own time and labor for once-waged workers, but have had less success with the rich and more affluent, except in grocery retailing. Until the recent entry of stores promoting themselves as providing "customer service" (e.g., Nordstrom from 1963 onward), retailers in the past two decades have typically provided only the wealthy with salesclerks, locally available guarantees, free delivery, and special orders. Department stores tried less costly tactics to attract customers, by creating special images, such as expensive, elaborate consumption for the Neiman-Marcus customer, reliability for Marshall Field, high style for Bonwit Teller, in the hope of cultivating customer loyalty (Bluestone et al. 1981).

Ironically, service has declined as more women with family responsibilities have gone into the labor force. Employed women, including working-class women, have been advised by the mass media to turn to the marketplace for services, to substitute for their own now-absent work in the household. Women's low earnings prevent this from becoming an easy solution to overwork. Working-class women, especially those who are the heads of families, are unlikely to have sufficient income to buy services or shop where services are available (Glazer 1980).

Nothing may seem more incongruous than women as household members losing services as the United States supposedly shifted to a service economy. The much vaunted "service society" is an illusion for most women with household responsibilities. High productivity in manufacturing has freed them from producing goods in the household, but not from producing services for themselves and their families. It has given them more work to do in the stores from which they buy these energy-saving goods.

The mass media has encouraged women to believe that information casually acquired from magazines would enable them to be the equals of cartels of manufacturers and chains of distributors in battles over safety, quality, and social needs. Their use of the term "consumer" was brilliant. Merchants cultivated "impulse buying," in which the moment of acquisition, not the use or effect of the object, was the most seductive to the buyer. "Consumption" implied endless buying and using up, discarding, replacing with "improved" versions that would make their *buyer* (maybe more than their user) better wives and mothers, more attractive and more satisfied with daily life. The widespread caricature of the new "consumer" was the displacement of frustration onto consumption—the unhappy woman shopping for a hat to drive away her blues.

The concept of "consumer" papered over the centralization of manufacturing and agricultural production, and growing control over distribution. It obscured the wage relationship and conditions of employment under which wages were earned for spending by the "consumer." Indeed, by separating the wage relation from income, the term "consumer" displaced an older vocabulary (e.g., worker, wage earner, breadwinner) that suggested class relations, conflict and struggle, and capitalist production. The new language avoided the implication of "owners, managers, workers" and, hence, of inequality, power, subordination and domination. At first, small farmers, cannery workers, and farm laborers "disappeared" from what the buyer consumed as groceries. Later, agri-business and multinational corporations with overseas workers could disappear from TVs and autos.

"Consumer" evokes the innocence, impersonality, and fairness of a "free" marketplace in which buyers are the equals of "sellers" (growers, manufacturers, and wholesalers). Issues are considered within the assumed naturalness of capitalism. Are prices reasonable, products safe, measures fair, manufacturers reliable, chain stores engaging in unfair competition and sellers in fraudulent advertising? The questions reaffirm the vulnerability of the *individual* customer confronting innumerable products but lacking personal relations with their makers and few guarantees that the products will be as advertised. Trademarks help somewhat because the maker has a brand name to protect in a market that encourages continuous consumption.

Finally, another responsibility shifted. Selecting became the responsibility of the self-service shopper; she had only herself to blame for a wrong choice. Retailers' advertisements hinted that the self-service customer was relieved from clerk "interference," not that clerk expertise was being lost. The buyer was now in an individual struggle in the marketplace, herself to blame for useless and inappropriate purchases.

Over the course of some forty years, customer behavior was vastly altered to reflect changes in the organization of the work of clerks, cashiers, and other retail workers. Customers changed from recipients of a vast array of services designed to make shopping relatively easy to a system that coerced and persuaded them to do new varieties of work and to see the work as natural, if not enjoyable, and that encouraged an appetite for unending buying.

Changes in the U.S. health care system parallel the changes in the retail trade industry. The following chapters show how health care underwent changes in the delivery infrastructure that led to the reorganizaiton of the labor process in hospitals and home health services. Under pressure from third-party payers and, to a lesser degree, sick people themselves, and with support from nursing and other health professionals, self-service for the very sick (i.e., home health services) was vastly increased. In changing the labor of service workers, patients and their family caretakers had their work changed greatly.

Part Three
The Health Services Industry

7

Capital and Labor: Restructuring Health Services

For-profit institutions, well, we will transform ourselves into a chain of jewelry stores. —*George W., hospital administrator*

Health care is obviously important to consumers, but not as primal as food, clothing, shelter, and jobs. Why don't we demand "universal access" to these necessities? Are they not "sine qua non *to a civilized society"?*
—*J. Bruce Johnston, vice-president, USX Corporation*

J. Bruce Johnston was not proposing universal access to food, clothing, shelter, or jobs. He was opposing guaranteed access to health care in the United States (Johnston and Reinhardt 1989: 19). Along with leaders of other U.S. corporations who had organized lobbies to curb health care costs, Johnston was deploring government support of health care and rising corporate costs of employee health insurance and he was urging health planners "to deal hard-headedly with cost containment" (1989: 8–9). Corporations in the United States have long criticized inefficiency, overconsumption, and low productivity in health care delivery. According to Walter B. Maher, director of federal relations for the taxpayer-salvaged Chrysler Corporation, health care costs were partly responsible for the "deteriorating national infrastructure, an inferior education system, and many other indicators of a government strapped for funds," and near to making "citizens [pay] the supreme price of losing a job" (Maher 1990: 169–170).

Since the early 1970s, the federal government has tried a long list of cost-containment measures aimed at patients, physicians, and hospitals. To cut patient use of health care services, equipment, and supplies, user contributions to health premiums were increased, coverage was narrowed, and deductibles were raised. To cut physician use, peer review, second opinions on proposed surgeries, and a freeze on physician fees were tried. The American Medical Association (AMA) and the American Hospital Association (AHA) even proposed voluntary cost containment. To accomplish this, hospitals adopted centralized purchasing, provided cafeterias rather than meal-room delivery for ambulatory patients, and increased part-time staffing. To prevent unneeded hospital construction and the duplication of expensive high-technology equipment, the federal government began to require that regional oversight agencies issue Certificates of Need (CON). None of these actions slowed the rise in health care costs.

In the Omnibus Budget Reconciliation Act of 1980 (OBRA), Congress authorized changes that made home health services more readily available and an attractive alternative to expensive hospitalization. It eliminated prior hospitalization as an eligibility criterion, dropped co-payments, and allowed for-profit agencies to serve Medicare and Medicaid patients without state licensure. Through the Tax Equity and Fiscal Responsibility Act of 1982, Congress authorized a prospective payment system for hospitals that cared for Medicare and Medicaid patients. As a result, hospitals today keep patients for shorter periods and refer more patients to outpatient departments and free-standing clinics for diagnosis and treatment.

Most important for my thesis about the work transfer and the blurred boundary between the public and private domains, home care has been increased. The new prospective payment system, the diagnosis-related groups (DRGs) based on diagnosis rather than fees for services, has encouraged less hospital use and more home care.

Diagnosis-Related Groups (DRGs)

In 1975, the New Jersey Department of Public Health began using the Standard Hospital Account and Rate Evaluation reimbursement system. From 1983 to 1985, through congressional amendments to the Social Security Act, a modified version of New Jersey's system became the national one for reimbursing acute-care hospitals for treatment of Medicare patients. The retrospective, fee-for-service reimbursement system, in which the insurer pays charges for a patient's room and meals, drugs and supplies, nursing services, and so on, was eliminated. With retrospective payments, hospitals had an incentive to keep patients for long stays; provide many services, use expensive equipment, and lots of supplies; and readmit patients casually. Under diagnosis-related groups (DRGs), hospitals receive prospective payments, which are flat fees assigned to each of over 460 diagnoses. The DRG fee recognizes differences in average amounts of nursing time allotted to patients on the basis of demographics. For example, a patient 0–17 years of age (DRG 396P) with "red blood cell disorder" is allotted higher nursing costs ($335.37) than a patient who is eighteen or older (DRG 395, $285.69). But the DRGs distinguish diagnoses with standardized measures based on race, and age, not individual need, edging medical and nursing work towards being factory-like.

Because the DRG system means the same fee regardless of patient use, the sooner patients are discharged, the more money the hospital keeps. Hospitals have an incentive to do as much treatment and care as possible in outpatient clinics or in the patient's home, which are excluded from the DRG fee and paid for separately. (In 1991, Congress passed legislation that was to pay flat fees based on diagnosis to outpatient clinics.)

The DRG reimbursement system applies business practices to human services, bringing together assumptions from manufacturing about the standardization of products with those from the service sector about the use of buyer labor. Hospital services are conceptualized as if treatments for diseases and injuries are identical because sick people are interchangeable, with the same needs and responses to treatments. The new cost-containment regulations conceptualize patients as physical diseases and ailments, using a medical model that ignores social needs, a model that consumer advocates criticized sharply during the 1960s and 1970s.

Legislators recognized that some patients would need longer hospital stays and more costly treatments than others. Still, they concluded that "hospitals would make a few dollars on some patients and . . . lose a few dollars on others" (Committee on Aging 1984: 47). The National Association for Home Care reports that home health costs to insurers are "one-half to one-third (and sometimes as little as one-tenth) of costs of comparable hospital care" (Employee Benefit Plan 1988b: 13). This assessment of savings ignores the hidden cost of the transfer of work to family members.[1] According to federal estimates, "for every $120 of taxpayer money spent by home care agencies, an estimated $287 worth of unpaid services is provided by the homebound person's family and friends" (U.S. Department of Commerce 1978: 490). The industry estimates a $10 billion savings in wages because of unpaid family work (Paringer 1985).

DRGs were intended to make hospitals "more efficient," but hospital administrators translated this into "dehospitalization." Dehospitalization results in the work transfer. More patients rely on a combination of self-care, family caregivers, and home health service agencies. (They also rely on nursing homes, but this is beyond my immediate concern.) In the home, women as family members, sometimes supervised by RNs and helped by other paid health workers, do work once done in hospitals by paid professionals and ancillary staff.

Women as Caregivers

Women's labor in nursing is a "traditional" familial obligation. Its integration into the delivery of complex medical–nursing care in the home extends a practice borrowed from retailing, banking, and bill paying: the use of the labor of the customer to reduce employer costs.

Women are the unpaid family workers who are essential to these savings. Both women and men seem to assume that the responsibility for care belongs to women (Anderson and Elfert 1989). As caregivers, women enable the family to be a health services "provider" unit (Jones and Vetter 1984; Littman 1974) and help prevent rehospitalization (Pesznecker et al. 1987). Women make up from two-thirds to three-quarters of all unpaid providers (Stone et al. 1987). They are the usual primary caregiver (Archbold 1982; Brody, E. 1985), even when family members ostensibly "share" and men "help" to care (Employee Benefit Plan Review 1988; Haber 1986; Matthews 1987). Women do most of the caregiving when spouses are unable to do so (Brody and Shoonover 1986) even when they are employed (Stoller and Stoller 1983). Men are likely to be primary caregivers when patients have no daughters living close to them or when sons are their only children (Horowitz 1985). The price for women may be the disruption of their personal lives (Finch and Groves 1983; Haber 1986). In contrast, men caregivers are more likely than women to use support networks to relieve them of full-time responsibilities (Miller 1990).

Shifting Concepts of Care

Historically, women have nursed family members at home, and for good reasons. Until the early years of this century, American hospitals were a cross between punishment and health care for the poor and were avoided by middle- and upper-class patients, who paid private-duty nurses to care for them in their homes. The modern hospital and scientific medicine encouraged hospital use from the 1910s through the Great Depression. But both post—World War II "high-technology" medicine and the peculiar U.S. health insurance system supported hospitalization over health maintenance and home care and discouraged outpatient care (Rosenberg 1987). The home was displaced as a site for most complex medical—nursing care.

Eased restrictions on access to home care services and the DRGs have helped reverse the decline in home care. But the shift away from the hospital to more self-care and home care occurred with the increasing corporatization of the health services industry (Bergthold 1987). It occurred, too, in the context of U.S. capitalism, with its class-based contests over social entitlement to health care. Furthermore, the shift assumed traditional practices of sexism and racism (taken to include ethnicity). Programs were enacted by policymakers without regard for the special consequences for women. They simply assumed that women family members would take on new responsiblities that would be a spin-off of "cost containment" (for example, more hours in the home caring for sick family members) and they assumed that the family would pay any additional financial costs of having a very sick member in the household. Nor were the consequences for paid women service workers considered. "Efficiency" for hospitals would mean the loss of jobs. This too would affect women more than men, women of color more than white women, and low-waged more than well-paid women. The context also includes a continuing, if low-key, battle over public health and preventive care versus treatment for illness.

Until the depression of 1929, both poor and rich received a good deal of medical and nursing care in their homes. Physicians made house calls. The rich used private-duty nurses; the poor were seen in their homes by nurses from the public health service, which was started at the turn of the century. The public health nurse, the precursor of today's home health nurse, treated the sick poor in the home while educating families (especially women) in good health practices. The service also sought to understand the social sources of illness, especially among the poor, and to prevent disease through social measures, such as a pure municipal water supply, unadulterated foods, good ventilation in housing, a safer workplace, and higher wages and hence a better standard of living. By the 1920s, public health nursing had declined as infectious diseases were controlled, while degenerative diseases increased (Buhler-Wilkinson 1983).

The rejection of illness as socially shaped and the acceptance of an individualistic medical model supported the decline in public health and an intensified concern with individual responsibility for health and health care. This model sees illness as an individual experience, shaped by an interaction between genetic characteristics and personal lifestyle choices. Hence prevention and treatment are presumed to be individual, not social (Krieger and Bassett 1986). Our contemporary legacy is also self-responsibility and the "lifestyle" approach that disregards social factors, such as the social stresses of daily life in capitalism and downplays industrial pollutants and toxic chemicals in the food supply. It underpins corporate arguments that workers have a "genetic predisposition" to become ill from workplace conditions. For Johnson Controls, the possiblity of pregnancy was such a "predisposition," and the company fought for the right to refuse to hire fertile women for certain jobs. The Supreme Court in 1991 denied Johnson the right to do so.

As practiced in the United States, home health care is a variant of health self-responsibility. Home care, rather than hospital care, is not inherently undesirable; actually it may be better medical practice than nursing-home care or hospitalization. Although hospitals have improved, they are still unpleasant and sometimes dangerous places. Many sick people prefer to remain in their homes. Home health care is a problem today because of how it is organized. People are commonly released from the hospital without an adequate support system to meet their medical, social, and psychological needs. The financial and emotional cost to patients and their caregivers can be high. The problem is that home care is used to cut costs, not because health care experts know it is better for patients than other care. Thus home care has not been expanded to meet patient needs but to reduce the insurer's costs. Unfortunately, there are few data on the quality of home care, but there is considerable concern that relatively untrained persons are doing care "requiring substantial skills" (Kramer et al. 1990: 414).

Paying for Care

No country wants to spend unnecessarily on health care. But in the United States, corporations and small businesses, not just citizens and government, have an unusual interest in national expenditures on health care. The health care delivery system in the United States is unique among developed capitalist societies. Until the Great Depression, health insurance programs were rare, and prepaid health care programs were unusual. Union-organized programs were attacked by the American Medical Association (*Fortune* 1958).

Limited health care is distributed through government-sponsored, means-tested insurance for the poor and universal insurance for the elderly, which nevertheless covers only about half the costs. Employed people may have access to health care through workplace-based insurance for themselves and their dependents, insurance won largely through union struggles. Corporations have expressed many misgivings about rising costs and have implied that they have a special right to be concerned because insurance is workplace based.

Insurance costs and coverage also affect workers. They may have to pay part of their insurance premiums and some co-payments for treatments, drugs, and equipment. The newest contribution of the insured is the invisible one that results from the work transfer, by which the family assumes the work of a good deal of after-treatment care. The family also assumes certain costs that go with it, such as a leave of absence from work and additional housekeeping or childcare help.

Corporate views on public and private spending on health care are not uniform. While all firms want federal and state policies designed to maximize accumulation, raise profit levels, and ensure a cooperative and compliant workforce, their views differ on strategies. The major division among American corporations is between those who buy and those who sell health-related goods and services. Some corporations and small businesses buy health insurance for their workers. Some may purchase insurance from themselves, running health maintenance organizations (HMOs) for their employees. Others sell health insurance. Still others profit by selling goods and services used in health care: pharmaceuticals, computers, medical supplies, contract nursing, medical emergency care, and laboratory services. Others may sell goods and services to and buy insurance from these same providers (Waitzkin 1983).

Such divisions and multiple interests in capitalism are not unique to health services. As noted in Part Two, between 1915 and 1960, U.S. retailers were in conflict over state policies as they fought each other for markets. Some retailers eliminated clerk-service, while others organized boycotts and sought local laws to prevent self-service. Some fought against product standardization, brand names, minimum-price setting, and labor organizing; others saw these things as the key to predictable markets and labor peace.

Few businesses gave much attention to the cost of health care until unions won insurance as a worker benefit and the federal government began to subsidize care for the poor and the elderly. Until World War II, the high cost of health care was an issue only for people who could not afford adequate care (Committee on the Costs of Medical Care 1932; Embree 1933; Falk et al. 1933). After the war, some social commentators considered health care as an unmet social need (Dewhurst et al. 1955). In *Fortune* magazine, writers told corporate leaders that rising health care costs signaled American prosperity (Burck and May 1959; Silberman 1959). Yet some managers were already concerned about corporate "overinvestment" in social wages, that is, benefits for their workers (*Management Review* 1958, 1960). By 1960, employer purchases of health insurance covered over 60 percent of employed women and men, mostly for "major medical," that is, the costs of hospitalization (Skolnick 1962). Five years later, Congress established Medicaid to pay for the care of the indigent and extended Medicare to cover part of the health care costs of the elderly. Within three years of the start-up of Medicaid and Medicare, however, President Lyndon Johnson was already asking Congress to control costs. The Nixon administration tried to cut costs by capping physician fees. It also tried to attract private capital, assuming that for-profit firms would be more cost effective than their nonprofit counterparts and that profits could be made in health services (Faltermayer 1970). During subsequent administrations, health services became an important area of corporate investment.

Corporate Costs and Profitability

Before the oil crisis of 1973, rising wages and increased worker benefits contributed to the accumulation process so that corporations gained from increased working-class consumption, including health services. Yet, as early as 1970, corporations were attacking health care costs, arguing that health care faced a "cost crisis" (Caplan 1981). This corporate interpretation is accepted widely: the major crisis in health services is seen as too-high expenditures by corporations on corporate-provided health care, and too much social spending on federally funded health insurance. Other issues, for example the lack of health insurance for poor Americans, inadequate prenatal care, childhood malnutrition, in-adequate preventive care, and the high rates of female breast cancer, are not "crises" (Schlesinger et al. 1987). Only AIDS is an exception and is considered a "crisis," partly because many AIDS cases are young and employed men whom insurers had expected to need very little care and now draw heavily on health insurance. National health insurance is only now being considered by some major corporations as a serious alterna-tive to a fragmented system, unsatisfying to the public as well as to the corporations.

Interestingly, not one administrator, manager, educator, or nursing worker I interviewed dissented from the view that "cost" is the crisis in health services. Even those who expressed support for national health insurance or socialized medicine believed that too much money was being spent on health care in the United States. As Navarro (1987) notes, this complements the view, accepted unreflectively by many so-cial scientists, that the dismantling of social programs, cuts in funding for health care, and proposed schemes for rationing care for the poor reflect a "popular mandate." It also overlooks the possibility that service prices rise more rapidly than commodity prices in a "mature" economy and that health services have grown more in work hours and have a lower unemployment rate than the overall economy although in low-wage jobs (Waldo et al. 1986).

What is significantly ignored in cost-containment efforts is the profitability of the health industry to corporations. The focus of cutting costs has been on users (patients) and providers of services (physicians and hospitals), but producers of equipment and pharmaceuticals have been largely ignored as sources of rising costs. Americans take for granted the right of corporations to earn a profit, even in providing the means of surviving life-threatening ailments. Indeed, most corporate in-volvement in developing health policy has been like "sending the foxes to guard the chickens." Corporations have invested billions in health industries—in pharmaceuticals, equipment, supplies, and services; in hospitals, nursing homes, and home health agencies. Growth in corpo-rate sales has been impressive: home care sales of services and products rose from $10 billion in 1983 to $15 billion in 1987 with anticipated sales by 1993 at $35 billion (Souhrada 1988: 51). Costs for two widely used home care treatments (enteral and parenteral nutrition) more than tri-pled between 1983 and 1985, from $180 million to $554.3 million (Roe and Schneider 1985: 52). Thus, major American corporations have complementary, even if sometimes conflicting, interests: they want to reduce their costs for health insurance, but to maintain high levels of profits from their investments in health technology, services, hospitals, and so on (Salmon 1975; Waitzkin 1979; Zink 1976). No corporation has yet proposed a cap on profits from drugs and equipment that would be comparable to caps on charges for hospital, nursing home, and health service use.

How Much of a Burden?

Even modest forms of access to health care in the United States are contested and have been contested virtually since their establishment. After World War II, as employer-sponsored health insurance plans increased, many major corporations and businesses began to complain about health care costs. After 1965, when the federal government began extensive support of health care, businesses complained about public spending on health care for the elderly and the poor.

Corporate concerns with high health insurance costs fueled federal attempts to curb costs (Herzlinger 1986; Herzlinger and Schwartz 1985) and produced "business circles" or "business health coalitions" organized by the U.S. Chamber of Commerce. To some analysts, these groups were seeking rational solutions to the falling rate of profit that plagued the manufacturing and service industries in the United States beginning in the early 1970s and continued until the mid-1980s (Economic Report of the President 1991).

Whether or not the federal government is overburdened (and in turn overburdens corporations with taxes) depends on one's views on social entitlement. Canada, with its national health insurance system, makes an interesting comparison to the United States. In 1960, Canada spent 5.5 percent of its gross domestic product (GDP) on health care, compared to 5.3 percent by the United States. Canada's public expenditure for health was 2.4 percent of GDP compared to 1.3 percent in the United States. Compared to Canada, the U.S. government consistently pays a smaller percentage of health care costs. In 1983, total expenditures in Canada had risen to 8.5 percent of GDP with public expenditures at 6.2 percent. In the United States, total expenditures were 10.8 percent of GDP, with health costs higher than in Canada, but the U.S. government spent less, only 4.5 percent of GDP (Iglehart 1986: 205).

PUBLIC VERSUS PRIVATE ASSESSMENTS

The effort of private corporations to reduce costs and entitlements suggests that they have complementary agendas for pursuing profits: to
undercut the gains that the poor, the elderly, and workers have made in
entitlements and to rationalize an attractive investment area. In newspapers, magazines, and business journals, corporate managers worry
about rising health costs, calling them a threat to profits and to the
international economic position of the United States. Many small or
marginal businesses in the secondary and tertiary sectors of the economy find insurance costs burdensome. Insurers charge small businesses
very high rates and refuse to insure many businesses that have higher-
than-average use of health services.

Business analysts sympathetic to corporate needs have exaggerated
employer health care costs and their impact on profits. For example, a
much-quoted allegation of the mid-1970s was that a $5,500 auto in-
cluded $2,000 in health benefit costs. I traced this cost estimate to testi-
mony before the President's Council on Wage and Price Stability that
"health insurance was a larger component of the cost of building an
automobile than steel" (Congressional Hearings 1977: 636). Supporters
of health insurance for workers responded that a more accurate figure
was $150 to $300 (Sapolsky et al. 1981). In 1989, over a decade later,
Walter Maher of the Chrysler Corporation informed the nation that
health insurance increased the cost of an automobile by $300 to $500, a
figure far more modest than the earlier one, which was 36 percent of the
cost of a car (Maher 1989: 3). In addition, the contention that the rate
of increase in health costs will wipe out profits is based on the odd
comparison of the percentage that health insurance is of costs with the
net of *after*-tax corporate profit (Herzlinger 1985). This comparison ne-
glects to mention that virtually any cost, such as wages or materials, will
be larger than returns on investments. Health benefits cost about 7 percent, while labor costs run about 40 percent. Respectable rates of return
on investment range between 5 and 8 percent.

Corporate cost-containment proposals are not consistent with other
analyses of the affect of insurance costs on profits. *Fortune* 500 companies employ about one-third of the U.S. workforce and give their
workers a higher benefit package than do most other firms. Despite
allegations that health insurance costs "erode" corporate profits, major
American corporations in the *Fortune* 500 have not privately expressed

concerns about the cost of health insurance for their own workers or retirees (Sapolsky et al. 1981). Health insurance is presented as one among many costs of doing business and keeping a stable workforce. Rising disability costs and pension benefit levels, rather than health insurance costs, figured as serious problems. Corporations proposed reductions in the size of the workforce, a shift to new products and activities and a move to rural areas or abroad for lower labor costs to fight falling profits. In their annual reports for 1978 through 1985, Xerox (active in business circles on health costs), Goodyear (a self-insurer, rather than a buyer of insurance), and Ford (with a large and well-insured labor force) attributed falling profits to worldwide inflation, increased competition from abroad, unstable world economies, the too-high value of the dollar, an increase in the price of raw materials, high interest rates, and excessive government regulation.[2] No report mentioned health insurance.

CORPORATE COSTS VERSUS SOCIAL ENTITLEMENT

The attempt in the late 1980s by a major health maintenance organization (HMO) to reduce health benefits to their part-time workers illustrates the distinction between corporate concern about costs and attempts to reduce corporate responsibility for the health care of their workers. Given its prepaid health delivery system, this HMO's additional costs for insuring its part-time employees are mainly for drugs and supplies. The cost of preventive care, the treatment of routine ailments, and other care is minimal. In negotiations with the union, the HMO managers justified their attempt to take these benefits away from part-timers by arguing that "no other employer in town has such a benefit package [for part-time workers] and neither will they" (SEIU 1988).

While access to health care is contested, some believe that it is a social entitlement. Corporations, for example, have begun to accept some form of national health insurance as they have moved to divest themselves of responsblity for their workers' health insurance. At least corporations may cease being an obstacle to universal care. U.S. business has had a long history of blocking such a system, as well as only recently tolerating HMOs and their prepaid programs.

Comparing housing costs with health costs supports the view that the basic issue is social entitlement and corporate costs, not the prices themselves. For fifteen years, housing prices rose more rapidly than the cost of health services. To mask this increase, the government actually recomputed housing costs in the Consumer Price Index, substituting an estimated rental cost in place of homeowners' actual monthly mortgage payments.[3] Housing is rarely considered a public or corporate cost of social reproduction, yet it is certainly a serious issue. Public investment in housing has declined substantially, despite growing homelessness, the need for low-income housing, and the struggles of low- and middle-income households to buy houses. Few Americans believe that they have a "claim" to housing, and corporations share this belief, rarely helping workers (except for high-level executives) with housing costs. Rising housing costs have not been called a "cost crisis" by corporate capitalism or the housing industry. The U.S. Chamber of Commerce has not established business roundtables, circles, or coalitions to curb the rise in the percentage of family income that Americans spend on housing. Instead, housing has been seen by business as an attractive area of capital speculation at the local level, just as the health services industries have been at national and international levels.

Rationalizing for Profits

The lack of economic rationality in the health services industry compared to other industries may be more the issue to corporations than actual employer costs (Faltermayer 1970). Capital investment has flowed at increasing rates into the health services industry since 1965, and investors expect high rates of return. As health services have become increasingly "corporatized," competing industries and investors demand that the same criteria apply to human services as to durable goods industries (Bergthold 1987). Health services can no longer be insulated from market conditions by government subsidies because it is an investment area, not a "human service."

In reality, health insurance costs were burdensome to *unfettered* accumulation by corporations. Foreign competition, corporate success in saturating domestic markets, and the deindustrialization of northern states forced down the rate of profits. In turn, declining profits prompted diversification, so corporations such as American Cyanamid, Dow, and Greyhound expanded into health services; they found lucrative rates of return on investments and easy capital accumulation (Waitzkin 1983). Diversification by large American corporations into medical technologies, pharmaceuticals, proprietary hospitals, and nursing homes was followed by companies forming their own HMOs to serve their employees and generate a profit for themselves and their investors.

In the mid-1980s, home health care remained exempt, temporarily, from the more stringent cost-containment regulations, such as capping. The result was that major hospital corporations and subsidiaries, such as medical supply companies, invested in home health agencies. They moved into home care through mergers with visiting nurse associations and by contracting for the services of home health registered nurses. (Other companies, such as Baxter Travenol, had anticipated the expansion into home care, investing much earlier.)

Despite the ideologies that suggest individual responsibility for health and claims of the medical and moral benefits of family care, the increase in home care is embedded in a straightforward cost-cutting agenda. For example, professional nurses were not asked to testify before Congress in the hearings on the DRGs (Halloran and Kiley 1987), though it is they who must manage home care. Patients still ask RNs for information that physicians have not provided about medications, self-care, alternative treatments and costs, prognosis, and the limits of medical practice—all concerns raised by the self-help movement. The decision to go home is, of course, still made by the physician, not the patient, who alone may grasp the social consequences of the early discharge.

The Infrastructure for Home Health Care

Home health care rests on many things: the shift of control over health care delivery from physicians and other providers and private buyers to Congress and third-party payers, and on the corporatization of health services and supplies. It rests also on the absence of a belief that workers have the right to jobs at reasonable wages with adequate benefits, and the view of women as a surplus population whose labor can be used in the home as needed by capitalism and the state.

THE RISE OF THIRD-PARTY PAYERS

A third-party payer is a nonprofit insurer such as Blue Cross or an HMO that contracts with employers to serve their workforce. Third-party payers are also "financial intermediaries," agencies that review bills sent to the federal government for the care of Medicare and Medicaid patients and decide which bills should be paid. In 1929, most spending on health care (86 percent) was by private users, that is, by sick people and their families, who paid physicians, private-duty nurses, hospitals and nursing homes, and so on directly. Federal, state, and local governments spent relatively modestly (14 percent).

Private spending decreased slowly over the next twenty years. In 1950, private funds (including insurers) had declined only slightly (from 86 to 73 percent) with most payments (89 percent in 1948) coming directly from users to providers (Brewster 1958). But by 1960, shortly before Medicare expanded from covering members of the armed services to cover the elderly, direct payments had declined substantially. Insurance coverage had increased for health care, but largely to reimburse hospitals, which expanded through federal subsidies for construction (the Hill-Burton Bill) and medical technologies too costly for physicians in solo practice but not for large, urban hospitals (Ehrenreich and Ehrenreich 1971; Starr 1982). Private payments had decreased to 55 percent while spending by private insurers and government had increased by 21 percent each. By 1970, government spending was in the ascendancy, 34 percent compared to 23 percent from private insurers. In 1984, as DRGs were being phased in, 40 percent of all spending was by the goverment (U.S. Public Health Service 1985: 136).

Third-party payers are now large and powerful. The federal government is the broadest in geographical scope, and able to regulate the delivery of care to the elderly in considerable detail. Medicaid combines federal and state regulations, while Blue Cross and other insurers may have rules that apply to narrower populations, such as particular corporation's or government agency's workforce or within particular states. But, as national, regional, and state agents, these organizations have been able to require standardized categories of medical and nursing treatments, diagnostic techniques, and other services for purposes of reimbursement. They have been able to force practicing physicians to think about patient care using those categories, since the categories are fundamental to the billing systems of health service facilities.

HEALTH AS AN INVESTMENT

Since 1965, the security of third-party payment by the federal government has attracted investors. In turn, these investors have sought to apply business standards to human services that were exempt from "bottom line" considerations until after World War II. Social services, health care, schools, and recreation only gradually gained features (such as high government expenditures) that made them attractive to corporate investors and subject to regular scrutiny.

The *U.S. Industrial Outlook* illustrates the tangle of corporate interests. Published since 1960 by the Department of Commerce, it addresses investors, advising them on potential growth areas for the upcoming year.[4] The *Outlook* did not even consider health and medical services as an area of investment until 1969, four years after Medicare and Medicaid were expanded. It noted diversification by "nonhealth" corporations, as the computer industry and motel chains entered nursing-home management, group-care organizations bought up clinics, pharmaceutical companies bought clinical laboratories, and catering services substituted for in-hospital food preparation (U.S. Department of Commerce 1968: 316). From 1960 to 1968, pharmaceuticals were the only health-related product considered as an area of investment. Medical and surgical instruments and medical and health services were added in 1969 (U.S. Department of Commerce 1968: 247, 316).

In 1973, home care was discussed as an additional investment area, along with hospitals and nursing homes, and proposed as a way of lowering costs (U.S. Department of Commerce 1973: 362). From the mid-1970s on, the cost to the business community for health insurance has been described as a serious problem (U.S. Department of Commerce 1975: 399–404; 1976: 422, 472; 1977: 438–439; 1980: 489).

Earlier I said that the health services industry had multiple sectors, with inconsistent and contradictory interests, and this is reflected in the discussions in the *Outlook*. Would-be investors are advised of prospects for the coming year, but are also warned of the burden of these social expenditures on medical-nursing services and on supplies for corporations. For other sectors, where businesses have no obligation to their workers, "more spending" means "more profit." The conflicts between social entitlements and corporate costs, between the gains of some corporations (the sellers of services and supplies) and the losses of others (the buyers of insurance and services) makes the health services industries a complex terrain of struggle over social rights.

HOME HEALTH AGENCIES

Home health agencies mediate between the hospital and the unpaid homeworker, and their growth reflects an increasing reliance on the home. Before 1980, home health services were delivered by visiting nurses associations and public health agencies; there were only a small number of hospital-affiliated and for-profit agencies. In 1980, Congress allowed for-profit agencies to participate in Medicare without licensure by the states, as previously required, and earnings stood at less than $1 billion. By the third quarter of 1983, earnings had grown to $3 billion and revenues to nearly $30 billion (Kleinfield 1983: D1). Given an opportunity, in anticipation of changing eligibility standards (July 1981) and possibilities for profit, home health agency affiliations with hospitals nearly doubled between 1979 and 1982, from 450 to 720 (Office of Technology Assessment 1984: 185). Certified home health agencies participating in Medicare grew slowly to 2,858 in 1980, but jumped to 5,769 in 1986 with the DRG phase-in. Perhaps another 6,000 agencies did not participate (Health Care Financing Administration 1988a: 16; National Association for Home Care 1986: 37–38). In Chicago alone, for-profit agencies increased by 90 percent during the 1983–1986 DRG phase-in (Kilbane and Blacksin 1988: 438).

Supplies and equipment sold through health service agencies or through specialized supplies became a lucrative investment with the Health Care Financing Administration neither certifiying suppliers nor regulating acquisitions and prices. Baxter Travenol Laboratories, for example, acquired Caremark, which sells about 40 percent of home drugs. Home health technology and supplies boomed: electronic infusion pump sales rose from $210 million in 1987 to $306 million in 1990, ventilator sales rose from $100 million to $128 million, and apnea monitoring machines went from $22 million to $26 million (Meier 1989: 32). The net revenues of the sellers of intravenous drugs for home care use rose from about $40 million in 1983 to nearly $1.5 billion in 1988 (Freudenheim 1988).

WOMEN AS A FLEXIBLE LABOR FORCE

Women are the basic unpaid labor force that takes up the work discarded by hospitals and increasingly discarded by home health agencies, which were supposed to provide the services lost from the decline in hospital use. A low-waged female labor force is a critical underpinning of DRGs, as is the free labor of women. The unpaid and paid service labor of women is crucial to profits in health care. Hospital administrators responded to demands by owners–investors for lower expenditures and higher profits, as health services were increasingly corporatized by rationalizing the use of labor (e.g., using more part-time workers and contracting out). They were well aware of demands by corporate employers for lower insurance costs. The 1983–1985 reimbursement policies for Medicare, Medicaid, and private prospective payment systems led some hospitals and agencies to fear bankruptcy. In turn, nurse managers in hospitals responded to administrator demands for "cost-effective" uses of nursing labor by cooperating in trying new labor processes to reduce wage costs. Some faced worker objections and resistance to new labor processes. Registered nurses responded in various ways to the new labor process, at times grumbling about and rejecting the new assignments made by nursing managers. Sometimes they rejected the view of nursing leaders and managers that professionalization required primary care with an all-RN staff (where RNs function with minimum support from other staff). Yet RNs also continued to demand higher-quality patient care, increased wages, and more staff.

HOSPITAL VERSUS HOME CARE: DRGs

Until 1983, federally funded programs for the elderly and the poor supported the use of hospitals for most care, even though access to home health service was eased by legislation in 1980. DRGs discouraged hospitalization and long hospital stays (see Table 7.1). Hospital admissions steadily increased for Medicare patients, from 302 per 1,000 enrollees in 1970 to 330 in 1975, peaking at 381 in 1984. Hospital use declined following the introduction of DRGs, falling to 352 per 1,000 enrollees in 1985 and 330 in 1987. Average length of hospital stays, however, had begun to decline before the DRGs. Stays fell from 13 days in 1970 to 8.61 in 1985, after the phase-in of the DRGs. Average length of hospital stays then rose slightly to 8.8 in 1987, as only very sick patients entered hospitals. When case mix is considered, between 1983 and 1985, the average length of stay for Medicare patients actually rose by 5.8 percent, indicating that more seriously ill patients were being hospitalized (Farley 1988: 6). Between 1983 and 1987, the average length of stay increased from 10.8 to 15.3 for older persons in "poor health," while hospital stays for others age sixty-five and over declined (Moss and Moien 1987: 8).

Between 1965 and 1983, the use of home health services by Medicare and Medicaid patients expanded fivefold, even though it was limited to certain medical treatments: dialysis, parenteral nutrition, apnea monitoring, and phototherapy. (Yet, most families in the United States with chronically ill, acutely infected, but otherwise able-bodied members rarely got financial support for home health care from either federal or private insurers.)

Medicare patients and other older Americans who are hospitalized spend considerably less time currently recovering in the hospital than at home. Under the supervision of their physicians, about 3 percent of patients are discharged to home health care services directly from hospitals and another 6–7 percent receive home care after nursing-home

TABLE 7.1

Where Medicare Users[a] Over Age 65 Get Health Care, 1970–1987

Care site	1970	1975	1980	1983	1985	1987
HOSPITAL						
Admissions per 1,000						
Medicare patients	302	330	369	381[b]	352	330
ALOS Medicare						
patients[c]	13.0	11.2	10.77	9.79	8.61	8.8
HOME CARE						
Use per 1,000						
Medicare members	8	16.2	34	45	51	50
Average visits per						
home-care user	n.a.	20.6	21.7	27.3	24.0[d]	n.a.

Sources: U.S. Bureau of the Census, *Statistical Abstract of the United States, 1988* (Washington, D.C.: U.S. Government Printing Office, 1987), table 577, p. 348; Health Care Financing Administration, *Medicare: Use of Short-Stay Hospitals by Aged and Disabled Patients, 1978* (Washington, D.C.: U.S. Government Printing Office, 1970–1975), table 1, p. 5; Dean Farley, "Trends in Hospital Average Length of Stay, Casemix and Discharge Rates 1980–1985," *Hospital Studies Program Research Note no. 11* (Rockville, Md.: National Center for Health Services Research, 1980, 1983, 1985), table 3, p. 8; Health Care Financing Administration, *Use and Cost of Home Health Agency Services Under Medicare: Selected Calendar Years 1974–86*, Research Brief no. 88–4 (Washington, D.C.: U.S. Government Printing Office, 1988), table 1, p. 4; U.S. Bureau of the Census, *Statistical Abstract of the United States, 1986* (Washington, D.C.: U.S. Government Printing Office, 1985), table 623, p. 371; U.S. Bureau of the Census, *Statistical Abstract of the United States, 1988* (Washington, D.C.: U.S. Government Printing Office, 1987), table 576, p. 347; Health Care Financing Administration, *1988 HCFA Statistics*, HCFA Pub. no. 03271 (Dec.) (Washington, D.C.: U.S. Government Printing Office, 1988), p. 28; Based on data from Health Care Financing Administration, "Home Health and Long Term Care." *Contemporary Long Term Care* 8, no. 9 (Sept. 1989): upper table, p. 30.
[a]Excludes disabled persons under 65 and those with end-stage renal disease otherwise not elegible for Medicare.
[b]Figure is for 1984.
[c]ALOS = average length of stay, in days.
[d]Figure is for 1986.

stays. Other Medicare patients—80 percent—go home to self-care and family care (*Homecare News* 1985). From 1970 to 1980, Medicare users of home care services per 1,000 enrollees increased steadily, especially between 1980 and 1983 after the Omnibus Reconciliation Act of 1980. Use per 1,000 enrollees rose from 27 in 1980 to 45 in 1983. Average visits per person served by home health agencies rose from 21.7 to 27.3 in 1983. By 1986, however, the growth of home health services had slowed. In part this was because of the increased use of outpatient clinics for a new array of treatments. Some clinics assumed that since patients were ambulatory, they needed no or minimal home health services. Patients receiving home health care after outpatient clinic services rose from .07 per 1,000 Medicare enrollees to .09 during the phase-in of the DRGs (see Table 7.3).

The Health Care Financing Agency (HCFA) began to use a narrow interpretation of eligibility. For example, the agency refused to reimburse home health agencies for patients who received home care on five consecutive days, though an RN may have been present only for two to three hours. HCFA interpreted the five days of visits to be "continuous" rather than "intermittent," and therefore argued that the patient should have remained in the hospital (where the DRG fee would have had to cover the cost of care). Their interpretations of congressional legislation were so restrictive that a consortium of fourteen members of the Congress, representatives of home care patients, home health agencies, and the national trade association of home care providers sued HCFA. In 1988, a federal judge estimated that thousands of patients may have been wrongly denied Medicare coverage and ordered the agency to reconsider all claims it had denied home health agencies for the previous eighteen months (Boffey 1988: 24).

In addition to controlling costs directly, Medicare encouraged a moderate use of home health services as a cost-containment measure from 1966 to the 1970s (Health Care Financing Administration 1988b). Home health use grew between 1966 and 1969 to 8.5 million visits. In 1970–1971, funds were reduced, and visits declined by an average of 25 percent, to 4.8 million. In 1972, Congress reinstated funding for home health, and the number of visits increased to 13.5 million by 1976. The rate of increase declined from 1977 to 1980, though it continued to grow at 10–17 percent a year. In 1980, Congress increased access to home health services by eliminating the deductible, the hundred-visit cap, and the three-day prior hospitalization requirement for Medicare patients.

For-profit agencies were allowed to operate in states without licensure laws. The numbers of visits per patient rose to 27 one year after the DRG phase-in, with a rate of growth of 15.9 from 1980 to 1983. In 1985, visits per 1,000 enrollees began to decline as access was curtailed by restrictive enforcements of regulations (National Association for Home Care 1986). DRGs resulted in less hospital use, more outpatient care, and more home care services through Medicare and supplementary health insurance. But, there was a much greater decline in hospital use than increase in Medicare-provided home health care, leaving families with new work.

TABLE 7.2
Home-Care Use by Medicare Enrollees, 1970–1986

	Visits (in thousands)	Per 1,000 enrollees	Percentage change	Visits per person
1970	6,000	8.0	−29.4	
1974	8,200	16.0	29.3	21
1976	113,500	24.4	23.8	23
1978	17,100	28.0	9.6	23
1980	22,600	34.0	13.0	23
OBRA[a]				
1982	30,800	40.0	17.5	26
DRG phase-in[b]				
1983	36,844	45.0	19.6	27
1984	40,337	50.0	9.4	27
1985	39,742	51.0	−1.47	25
DRG period				
1986	38,359	50.0	−3.47	24
Annual rate of growth:				
1980–1983		9.8		15.9
1983–1986		3.9		−.5

Sources: For 1969–1982: U.S. Department of Health and Human Services, *Health Care Financing Program Statistics 1986*, HCFA Pub. no. 03247 (Washington, D.C.: U.S. Government Printing Office, 1987), table 2.14, p. 29. For 1983–1986: Health Care Financing Administration, *Use and Cost of Home Health Agency Services Under Medicare: Selected Calendar Years 1974–86*, Research Brief no. 88-4. (Washington, D.C.: U.S. Government Printing Office, 1988), table 2, p. 6.
[a]Omnibus Budget Reconciliation Act.
[b]1983 to 1985.

"QUICKER AND SICKER"

After DRGs were adopted, hospitalization declined, and so did length of stay before transfer to home health care. RNs label the trend "quicker and sicker." The numbers of Medicare patients discharged to home health from a sample of 467 hospitals doubled after DRGs, rising from 2.47 in 1983 to 6.24 in 1985 (see Table 7.4). The evidence for patients going home from hospitals "quicker" is substantial: length of stays dropped from 17.7 days in 1980 to 12.9 in 1985. The evidence for patients going home "sicker" has been inferred from reports of home health service agencies and a study of release forms of nearly five hundred hospitals (Morrisey et al. 1988). While data suggest that those discharged to home health agencies are sicker than before, there is no doubt that those sent directly home are. The posthospital dependency

TABLE 7.3
Home Health Care for Medicare Enrollees[a] Before and After DRGs, 1967–1984

Service	Persons Served Per 1,000 Enrollees			
	Early use 1967	Pre-DRGs 1982	Phase-in 1984	Percentage Change 1982–1984
HOSPITAL				
Inpatient[b]	184.7	242.7	228.5	− 6.2
Outpatient[c]	77.4	290.4	326.7	11.1
HOME HEALTH				
After hospital[d]	6.5	41.1	51.6	20.3
Outpatient[e]	6.6	.07	.09	22.2

Source: Health Care Financing Administration, "Medicare Utilization, 1984," *Annual Medicare Program Statistics*, HCFA Pub. no. 03250 (Baltimore, Md.: Bureau of Data Management and Strategy, 1987), table B, pp. 3–5; definitions *b–e*, pp. 253–255.
[a]Excludes disabled persons.
[b]Room, board, nursing services, drugs and biologicals, and other usual hospital services.
[c]Services obtained through hospitals and clinics, such as diagnostic tests; diagnostic x-rays; x-ray, radium and radioactive isotope therapy; splints, casts, prosthetic devices; ambulance service; speech, occupational, and physical therapy.
[d]Under the Social Security Act, sec. 1833(d), home health services are now paid as "after-hospital services."
[e]Does not require prior hospitalization.

of patients in 1981–1983 (pre-DRGs) was less than in 1984–1985 (post-DRGs) for five frequent diagnoses. Patients recovering from hip-replacement surgery, heart failure, and pneumonia needed more help at discharge time *after* than *before* DRGs. Those with strokes and major joint surgery were the same (Coe et al. 1986: 153). Comparisons of hospital releases for patients before and after DRGs show a marked increase in discharges to subacute facilities (i.e., nursing homes), but by modest levels of 70–85 percent, while those to home health care increased by 153 percent. Medicare patients discharged to nursing homes and home health agencies were about equally sick, which "may be a reflection of the availability of a caregiver at home when home health services are recommended" (Morrisey et al. 1988: 59). Rehabilitation hospitals reported changes, too. Their patients were sicker (as measured by how well they could care for themselves) *after* compared to *before* DRGs. By 1986, when patient acuity level declined, the rehabilitation hospitals had already increased the ratio of RNs to licensed nurses and nursing assistants to care for their sicker patients (Hickey 1987).

TABLE 7.4

Medicare Patients Discharged from Hospital Before and After DRGs, 1980–1985[a]

	Pre-DRGs		Post-DRGs	
Discharged to:	*1980*	*1983*	*1984*	*1985*
Home health (%)	2.39	2.47	3.56	6.24
ALOS[b] before discharge to home health	17.7	15.4	12.8	12.9
Case-mix index[c] for discharge to:				
home health	1.31	1.31	1.29	1.36
home	1.07	1.10	1.12	1.17

Source: Michael Morrisey et al., "Shifting Medicare Patients Out of the Hospital," *Health Affairs* 7 (Winter 1988): 56, 59, 60.
[a]467 hospitals surveyed.
[b]ALOS = average length of stay, in days.
[c]Excludes hospitals not covered by DRGs.

Benefits of Home Care

Until 1980, most physicians and RNs not in HMOs, and Medicare and Medicaid reimbursement policies supported hospital care over home care for patients with acute as distinct from chronic problems. ("Chronic" problems are those in which no marked change is expected, such as insulin-treated diabetes or a stabilized heart condition.) Health service workers in hospitals and home health agencies expressed support for patient recovery or death at home as a patient's right. Some workers said that recovery was faster and death less upsetting at home than elsewhere. Also, patient advocacy groups fought for the right to recover or die at home, seeking—with limited success—federally funded long-term care. Home health agencies can provide short-term care only to Medicare and Medicaid patients. Long-term care would enable many people to live independently: the elderly who need some assistance with the tasks of daily living and those with chronic illnesses who may need more extensive assistance. Only a few groups, such as some nursing-home owners, still argue against home care.

Critiques of home health care therefore come mainly from its supporters. The concerns of workers about the provision of care in the home are voiced in Chapters 8, 9, and 10. Workers want to make home care work: to continue their jobs without burnout that makes them leave the health services industry; to meet patient needs; to reorganize and help lighten the burden on unpaid caregivers.

Home health care is problematic because its use has been driven by costs to insurers and providers, rather than by an attempt to improve the quality of care and the patient's life. Changes in home-care delivery have been designed to reduce labor costs—to get as much work as possible from home health RNs and aides, and to shift as much of the financial cost as possible—in the interests of reducing costs to insurers and providers. An adequately supportive home health care system is not likely to be inexpensive or cost effective. A review of the cost of home care before it became more accessible concluded that it is cost effective only for patients who have been stabilized before discharge from hospitals or nursing homes (Hammond 1979). Two reviews (which included pre-DRG experiences) also concluded that home care was not cost effective (Government Accounting Office 1982; Office of Technology Assessment 1984). Home health care becomes cost effective when costs can be shifted to patients and their relatives.

Changes in health services are thus motivated by political decisions designed to save federal, state, and corporate funds by shifting costs increasingly to patients and caregivers. But the invisible cost to patients is shorter hospital stays and more outpatient diagnoses and treatments, with the free domestic labor of women becoming crucial to the new health care labor process.

A wide array of domestic labor must be done in the home. Cost containment visibly shifts the direct costs of caring for the sick to the user. And it shifts both financial and psychological costs to women as family members and friends of the infirm.

Capital and the state use women's unpaid domestic labor for health services by changes in the labor of paid women health service workers in both professional and lower-grade jobs.[5] Changes in the labor process in the health services industry (in hospitals, clinics, nursing homes and home health care agencies) result in some essential paid labor being decommodified, making it less available to patients and requiring more unpaid domestic labor from family members. For wage workers, the use of the free domestic labor of family members to complete health care delivery may mean a change in their jobs or a job loss.

This chapter has focused on examining the political economy of health services delivery and the pressures for cost containment that resulted in DRGs. Business firms with varied and conflicting interests vastly expanded their interests in the health services industry as it became an attractive area of investment. Ironically, that very attractiveness led to higher national expenditures on health care, including expenditures by other business firms, which viewed health costs as socially or economically problematic.

Women workers, paid and unpaid, link capitalism and family life. Through the work transfer, women as family members have their labor increased, a consequence of DRGs, which increased the use of home care. I consider this in detail in Chapter 10. The next two chapters discuss the changing labor process for nursing personnel in the hospital and in home health care, examining what new work has been assigned paid workers and which aspects of their work have been transferred to family members.

8
Changing
Hospital Work

Planners, legislators, and corporations critical of insurance costs and government spending on the poor and elderly sought to limit the cost of health care. DRGs were supposed to force hospitals to be more efficient. "Efficiency" translated into rationalizing the labor process in the hospital by eliminating paid workers, consolidating jobs, or a work speed-up. Most important, work that was no longer done in hospitals did not disappear; it was shifted to the home. Thus, paid health service workers and unpaid women family members together form a new labor force. The work of paid workers forms a seamless web of caring and tending with the work women do as wives, mothers, and friends. Thus, changes in the labor process in one work site, the hospital, rebound on the labor process in another, the home.

DRGs are the immediate cause of decreased hospital admissions, shorter hospital stays, more outpatient care, sicker patients in the hospital, and sicker patients going home. The context for changes in the labor process and the transfer of work between paid workers and unpaid family members includes the long-standing occupational rivalries among nursing personnel. Workers are differentiated by schooling and along racial, ethnic, and class lines. The labor process for nursing personnel, an overwhelmingly female labor force, changed under DRGs. Workers now include top-grade registered nurses (RNs) and home health RNs (HH-RNs), middle-grade licensed practical nurses (LPNs) in hospital and home care, and lower-grade home health aides (HHAs).

Women have been unable to influence state and corporate policies. All social policies minimize women's needs as earners and as family members, and policymakers respond to demands for reductions in health service costs within narrow limits. Changes in the labor process reflect the rules and values of a "free market economy." This means that workers have no right to employment, and decisions about jobs are made without much consideration of the impact on workers (except, perhaps, when there are labor shortages). Women unpaid family care-givers are the most ignored, their care taken for granted. (Their work is discussed in Chapter 9.) Deliberately and inadvertently, the state and major corporations shift a major portion of the burden of containment in health care to low-waged workers, especially women.

Work in Hospital Services

The following analysis draws from interviews with health service workers, including administrators and RN managers, practicing RNs, and aides. Their statements give some sense of the multiple meanings of work and the varying interpretations that people have of recent changes in the health care delivery system. The women and men I interviewed were largely in agreement about *what* was happening, but they differed sharply on the causes and consequences for the health services and equipment industry, for health care facilities, and for themselves person-ally and professionally. And they differed on what they believed the consequences were for patients and their family caregivers. (See the Ap-pendix for a discussion of methods and for a description of fifty-nine workers in hospital and home health services whom I interviewed.)

FULL-SERVICE CARE

Before DRGs, most hospital patients received an array of services and stayed in the hospital until they were walking, with any wounds nearly healed, functioning as much as possible as they did before their illness. As described in Chapter 6, even before DRGs, the acuity of hospital patients (a measure of how "sick" they are) was rising, while the aver-age length of hospital stay was steadily declining. Patients lost some services with the decline. Patients had been admitted for medical emer-gencies, such as a heart attack or stroke. Some reentered for treatments for chronic rather than acute conditions. Others needed "elective" treat-ments, such as gallbladder or knee surgery or cataract removal. Except for emergencies, patients were likely to be admitted one or two days before surgery for evaluation, that is, for laboratory tests to assess their condition, and for them to rest and ready themselves for treatment.

After the procedures, patients rested and recovered. They were tested and retested, assessed and reassessed to monitor their condition, protect against malpractice lawsuits, and make money for the hospitals. Nursing care, not medical care, was the backbone of care. Typically, care was given by a "team." Nursing aides delivered meals, changed bed linen, brought patients magazines and fresh water, and wheeled them to the various specialized departments for tests and therapies. Licensed practical nurses did a bit more nursing. They measured blood pressures, changed dry dressings, helped patients exercise, got them to the toilet, and talked with them about their pains and mental state. RNs did some of the latter but also worked out care plans, distributed medications, assessed the overall status of the patient, and wrote up the assessment for physicians. They assisted physicians on their daily rounds, called them for emergency back-up, and cleaned up after them. RNs also changed complex dressings, gave intravenous medications, and monitored patients after invasive diagnostic procedures. They supervised LPNs and aides; some also supervised other RNs.

Sick patients ran the gamut from the very sick in intensive-care units to patients who needed little care. Patients stayed in the hospital until self-care at home was easy. Before being discharged, most walked, had recovered bowel and bladder functions, ate some solid foods, and were nearly healed and certainly free of infection. Indeed, some hospitalized patients were well enough to help sicker ones, bringing fresh water for flower vases or magazines and books to the bedridden.

SELF-CARE AND FAMILY CARE

Mainly to reduce costs, but also to improve care, hospitals began experimenting with "minimal care units" more than thirty years ago (Tunstall 1960). For example, at the University of Florida hospital (1960), New York University cooperative-care unit (1979), and Vanderbilt University (1987), patient and family caregiver shared a hotel-like room. Since no meals were served in the sleeping rooms, people cooked their own meals or ate in the hospital cafeteria or a special dining room. Patients purchased medications from the pharmacy and took them on their own. Physicians, nurses, and aides attended patients on request, rather than making regular rounds (*American Nurse* 1979; Blitzer 1981). "Care partners" attended patients, changed dressings, monitored vital signs, regulated fluid intake, and so on. Care-by-parent wards, for mildly to severely ill children, were intended to save money and help children psychologically (Evans and Robinson 1983).

In 1979, New York University opened a model cooperative-care unit for adults, anticipating that patients would save 40 percent on their bills (*American Nurse* 1979). Patients shared rooms with family members or a two-room unit with a hired caregiver who would later go home with the patient. All medical and nursing services were on one floor, away from patient rooms. Wards were limited to brief stays for patients recuperating from invasive diagnostic procedures before being sent to a cooperative-care room. Another floor contained a cafeteria, with attractive small tables (unlike the usual hospital cafeteria) where patients selected their meals under the watchful eye of a dietician. Patients and caregivers also socialized, including at a nonalcoholic, low-calorie "cocktail" hour. In the educational programs, patients and caregivers learned the routines of posthospital care and daily life. The savings the hospital gained through cooperative care were not passed on to patients, but the hospital averaged the costs of this unit with more expensive full-service wards and charged all patients (in reality, usually third-party payers) the same room fee (Blitzer 1981).

Between 1960 and 1975, only a minority of hospitals (never more than 8 percent) experimented with minimal-care units. The units saved hospitals from 10 to 25 percent on new construction and some on wages. Insurers such as Blue Cross were usually reluctant to reimburse hospitals for this care (Glass and Warshaw 1978). Few hospitals today run minimal-care units, while most patients who could have been in such units are no longer in the hospital but have been discharged home or transferred to nursing homes.

CARE AFTER DRGs

In the 1980s, hospitals tried to economize by lowering their wage bill. Most important, the nursing team of RN, LPN, aide, and ancillary staff vanished, to be replaced by primary-care nursing with an "all-RN staff." Today, RNs cope with more varied and serious work for very sick patients and do so with little or no help from LPNs, aides, and other ancillary workers. Many of the latter lost their jobs during the budget crises in the early 1980s or after the introduction of DRGs. In 1985, RNs I interviewed brought bedpans to patients, changed bed linen, brought meals from the central kitchen to the wards, supervised therapies, and did tasks once done by social workers. They transported patients to X-ray units and laboratories and checked that discharge plans have been made for patients. This work was added to the usual professional responsibilities of RNs. (The all-RN staff did not save money. Hospital managers continue to seek the optimal mix of nursing personnel.)

Patients now enter hospitals sicker than before the adoption of DRGs; patients who are less sick are diverted from hospitals to other health care sites. Hence, patients needing cataract removal, knee surgery, or some kinds of chemotherapy are likely to be treated in outpatient clinics or "day" surgeries. Outpatient and short-stay cancer patients will go home to self-care and family care. A minority will be guided by a home health RN, instructed by a therapist, and helped with personal care and housekeeping by an aide. Others will go home with written instructions and a telephone number to call for emergency help, and will receive supervision on the telephone from a hospital RN checking on their condition and by office visits to their physician.

Very sick patients may be discharged from the hospital to their homes too. Patients will be sent home sicker than before and with a greater chance than before DRGs that they will be readmitted. Fewer will walk out of the hospital and have recovered basic bodily functions. Some will have wounds that are "wet" and need careful tending. Some will take home high-technology equipment for continuing treatments. But all are likely to be gone from the hospital or nursing home long before they need worry about fresh water for their flower vases. In their homes, they may have care from an RN and from some of the ancillary staff who lost their hospital jobs—licensed practical nurses, nursing aides, and specialist therapists.

Hierarchies in Nursing

Ideologies about gender and race are underpinnings of the adaptation of health care managers to DRGs. First, nursing, the backbone of the hospital labor force, is a female-typed occupation, and white women or women and men of color hold the lower grades of nursing and other ancillary jobs. These workers are most affected by changes in the labor process, including the work transfer. Changes include job consolidation and speed-ups without any increase in wages, layoffs, and loss of benefits as more health care facilities use part-time and temporary workers. Women of color, in particular, are disproportionately likely to do much of the poorly paid work in home care. Second, physicians (still mostly white men) have been insulated from the cost-containment effects of DRGs. Their only experience with cost containment was in the early

1970s and late 1980s, when their fees were capped briefly. Third, and most important, hospital administrators rely on the work transfer, deliberately or inadvertently, to reduce spending from their DRG-based flat fee. The shorter the hospital stay, the more of the prospective payment remains with the hospital. But the work of nursing remains. Gerontologists and nurse providers (see Chapter 10) recognize the burdens of family caregiving, including new work and new responsibilities, the invasion of family privacy, and the unreimbursed or "out-of-pocket" costs (Haddad 1987: 6). Health planners and evaluators rarely admit, however, that women's family work and the family's financial costs increase with home care, though such estimates have long been available (Rushmer 1976; Russell 1989). Business analysts are usually either unaware or mute, though over a decade ago, the value of family labor and care was estimated at twice that of home-care agency costs (U.S. Department of Commerce 1979: 490).

Since the adoption of DRGs, the work of home-care nursing personnel has become more technical and more demanding and has broadened in scope as hospitals seek to reduce their labor costs. More training in administration, public health, and the ambiguous area of "nursing theory" are distinctive features of the baccalaureate degree (BSN), a formal requirement for working in home health agencies. In practice, RNs with other training have been "grandfathered" in because of the shortage of BSNs. Ancillary staff positions have been eliminated or reduced in hospitals, especially for licensed practical nurses, who may have trouble finding new jobs, and for technical workers whose tasks have been consolidated into RN jobs. The shortage of RNs and the increased acuity level of hospitalized patients could have led administrators to hire more ancillary workers. But hospital administrators, along with government agencies and physicians, have pursued two contradictory strategies: on the grounds that they lack needed skills, lower-grade and ancillary workers have been eliminated as *permanent* hospital staff and then hired back as temporary and part-time workers. And a new stratum of workers, "physician assistants," who do work similar to that of RNs, has been created (against the wishes of organizations representing RNs). "Physician extenders" earn lower incomes than RNs and physicians. The goal of Congress is also "to shift the burden of providing health care and maintaining health to a greater extent to the patient" (*Congressional Hearings* 1977: 631), which implies, to *untrained* women family members. Women of color are the most likely to train for jobs in the lower grades and to do much of the paid work in home care. Poor women and women of color are more likely than other women to do a good deal of home care because they have less money to hire others.

Changes in care site reflect most directly the impact of DRGs, but long-standing distinctions and rivalries among nursing personnel have made it easy for most hospitals to change health care without prolonged protest by nursing workers (Glazer 1991). Nursing personnel are stratified into grades based on schooling and skills, and the grades are distinct in racial and ethnic composition. It is the work of nursing personnel that has been especially changed, upgraded and degraded, reskilled and deskilled, and decommodified. Technical–medical tasks for which considerable training, as much as four years, is required, have been transferred to family caregivers with minimal training for doing them.

In an ironic twist, some of the professional issues that have divided RNs and set RNs against other nursing personnel have been resolved de facto by insurers who assume that nursing work is easy to learn. Nurse educators have battled to increase training, arguing that more schooling is the key to improved patient care and to higher status for RNs. This theme runs through the quarrels over which level of RN and which other nursing personnel ought to do what work, and it prevents most coalitions among nursing personnel on issues of working conditions and the quality of patient care. Views are sharply different. The director of ambulatory care at "Teaching Hospital North" explains the need for training:

> If we RNs are going to hold ourselves out as a profession, we have to demand the level [of education] that other professions demand. Technicians, that's exactly what diploma schools were training. If nurses want to be professionals, they have to have a standard of education that is at least equal to lawyers, physical therapists, occupational therapists, dieticians, social workers.

Wendy Carr, with a BSN degree, worked in home health care for a decade, but left to return to hospital work after she failed to unionize nursing personnel at her agency. She has a different view on the baccalaureate degree:

> Bullshit. I learned the major part of my technical skills from my colleagues. I don't care what you say about theory; you have to put it into practice.

The RNs from two- and three-year programs knew everything I knew and more from practice. RNs and LPNs used the same theory that I used. It involves nursing theory to assess, to look at the social and the physical.

This contrast runs through the approach to training, job assignments, and upward mobility. Nursing is very hard work. Physical labor, coping with contagious diseases and toxic chemicals, emotional stability in the face of trauma and death, and technical competence are the mixed demands of nursing. The levels of skill and performance required vary between the different grades. Nevertheless, the LPN and the nursing aide do demanding physical work, too, and take many of the same risks as the RN. Yet they get lower pay, less respect from administrators and RNs, and have less job security and lower benefits.

JOBS AND RACE

The job differences and training in nursing work closely follow race, ethnicity, and class lines (Butter, Carpenter, and Simmons 1985). Usually, whites are likely to be RNs, while African Americans and Hispanics are disproportionately in the lower grades. Asians born outside the United States are also often RNs. Educational differences among RNs create and reflect rivalries, and varied earnings and opportunities.

Following the Brown report (1948), the American Nurses Association (ANA) supported the bachelor of science in nursing (BSN) for all entry-level nurses. The ANA and some nursing managers consider only RNs with a BSN to be "professional" nurses. Other RNs, those with diplomas earned in schools of nursing or the associate degree in nursing (ADN) earned in community colleges, are designated "technical" nurses by the ANA and in need of supervision by BSNs.

Training has not, however, been upgraded uniformly. Between 1963 and 1983, the number of BSNs rose from 13 percent to 30 percent of new RN graduates. Yet RNs with associate degrees increased more rapidly than BSNs, growing from a small minority of 4.4 percent in 1963 to over half of RNs, 54.1 percent, in 1983 (see Table 8.1). For women of color, women on welfare, and less affluent white women, the associate degree was a much more likely training route to nursing than the longer and more expensive BSN. Other opportunities for poor women, waxing and waning with federal support, included training as licensed nurses in an eighteen-month community college program or as aides (for jobs in nursing homes as well as in home health services) in a 180-hour course at a skill center (Glass and Eisner 1981).

Jobholders in the different nursing grades have always varied by race and ethnicity. Asian and white women have made up most of the RNs. Foreign-trained Asian women are more likely than whites to be upper-grade nursing workers. African American women fare the worst, disproportionately holding the lowest-grade aide jobs. Hispanic women also work mostly as aides, except in a few major U.S. cities (Glazer 1987).

JOBS AND GRADES

Most nursing educators support improving the quality of patient care and upgrading the status of RNs by encouraging a sharp distinction between nurses with a diploma or an associate degree in nursing and

TABLE 8.1

Trends in RN Schooling in the United States, 1963–1983

	BSN[a] (4 years)	Diploma (3 years)	AA (2 years)	(N)
1983	30.8	15.1	54.1	(77,408)
1982	32.5	15.8	51.7	(74,052)
1981	32.9	17.4	49.6	(73,985)
1980	33.1	19.2	47.9	(75,523)
1979	32.5	20.5	47.0	(77,132)
1978	31.1	22.0	46.4	(77,874)
1977	30.2	23.2	46.7	(77,755)
1976	29.2	25.8	44.9	(77,065)
1975	28.5	30.6	40.9	(62,056)
1972	22.0	40.5	37.5	(49,525)
1971	21.2	47.5	31.3	(46,455)
1969	19.0	60.8	20.2	(39,089)
1966	14.8	75.7	9.5	(34,713)
1963	13.3	82.3	4.4	(31,863)

Sources: For 1971, 1976–1983: U.S. Department of Health and Human Services, *Fifth Report to the President and Congress on the Status of Health Personnel in the U.S.*, Pub. no. HRS-P-OD-86-1 (Washington, D.C.: U.S. Government Printing Office, 1986). For 1972, 1963–1975: U.S. Department of Health and Human Services, *Minorities and Women in the Health Fields, 1984 Edition*, DHHS no. (HRSA) HRS-DV 84–5 (Washington, D.C.: U.S. Government Printing Office, 1984), table 35.
[a]Includes bachelors', masters', and doctoral program students.

those with a BSN. Nursing educators have waged a state-by-state battle to recognize this difference, and have won in nearly all states, though the recognition has not yet driven RNs with the first two types of training from "professional" to "technical" status. Winona Sanders, a white BSN with training in public administration, has worked in health care

TABLE 8.2
Job Ranks among Women in Nursing, by Race and Ethnicity, 1960–1980

	Job rank	1960	1970	1980
White	RN	57%	54%	49%
	LPN	19	13	15
	NA[a]	24	34	36
(N)		(945,015)	(1,396,046)	(2,192,223)
Black	RN	24%	23%	18%
	LPN	25	19	15
	NA	51	59	66
(N)		(134,562)	(273,774)	(487,693)
Asian	RN	[b]	74%	65%
	LPN	[b]	8	9
	NA	[b]	18	26
(N)		[b]	(14,244)	(63,386)
Hispanic	RN	[b]	33%	25%
	LPN	[b]	18	14
	NA	[b]	50	61
		[b]	(49,039)	(99,690)
TOTAL[c]	RN	53%	48%	43%
	LPN	19	14	15
	NA	28	38	42
(N)		(1,079,577)	(1,684,064)	(2,743,302)

Sources: Detailed Occupation and Years of School Completed by Age for the Civilian Labor Force by Sex, Race and Spanish Origin: 1980, SR PC(80-S1-8) (Washington, D.C.: U.S. Government Printing Office, 1980); U.S. Bureau of the Census, *1970 Census of Population, Occupational Characteristics*, PC(2)-719 (Washington, D.C.: U.S. Government Printing Office, 1973); U.S. Bureau of the Census, *1960 Census of Population, Occupational Characteristics*, PC(2)-7A (Washington, D.C.: U.S. Government Printing Office, 1963).
[a]Nursing aide
[b]Not reported
[c]Excludes Hispanics

for over twenty-five years and is currently director of ambulatory care at "District Hospital." She represents the opinion of the nursing managers interviewed, in contrast to nursing educators:

> The nursing schools are not producing nurses to work in the hospital. . . . Nursing educators took over nursing schools from the hospitals but don't know how to deal with patients. They turn out 7 A.M. to 3 P.M. [day] nurses, and don't know about evening or night nursing because educators do not want to work nights. The new graduates start on the night shift and cannot cope—it's scary and quiet, and they don't have the experience or benefit of close contact with patients. The National League of Nursing has a pie-in-the-sky world, not the reality of seven patients.

Most nursing workers are women, but gender is not a sufficient basis for shared goals. On the contrary, the division of labor in health services is embedded in a hierarchy of authority, rewards, differential opportunities for upward mobility, and so on. This makes conflict among women across grades inevitable. (See the Appendix for a typical organizational line of command.)[1] The educators of white RNs with the baccalaureate, who themselves certainly have done some graduate work, have tried to improve the position of these RNs.[2] Their efforts have sometimes been at the expense of less-trained nursing workers, including other RNs with diplomas or associate degrees and less-trained LPNs and aides—frequently working-class women of a different race or ethnic group (Hines 1989). Educators have tended to support a restricted educational ladder that limits upward mobility to those with more schooling and makes upward mobility through more training difficult for diploma and ADN RNs and for LPNs. Nursing leaders (RN educators), modeling themselves on physicians, have striven for "professionalization" and supported the upgrading of RNs at a cost to other nursing personnel.[3] The basic hands-on care and patient education that some nursing leaders and many RNs see as the core of nursing has been lost or diminished as RNs have become managers.[4]

The distinct class perspective of nursing leaders in professional associations and of educators influenced the labor process in nursing work in two different directions, toward specialization and toward general practice. Changes in the labor process of RN work fit the principle that the detailed division of labor is used even in professional occupations. During the Great Depression, RNs went from being quasi-entrepreneurial, home-based generalists to having hospital-based jobs that increasingly required administrative skills. During and after World War II, work once done by RNs was divided into tasks and redistributed among specialized and hierarchically ordered workers (licensed practical nurses, aides, attendants, specialist therapists, ward clerks, etc.). Simultaneously, with the support of many nursing leaders, managers assigned more supervisory and less hands-on care to RNs. Many RNs also learned to use "high-tech equipment" for the care of acutely ill patients in intensive-care units.

More LPNs and aides were trained. These acted, in part, as assistants to RNs, doing routine tasks like bed making and feeding. Sometimes they dispensed nonprescription drugs, charted incoming patients, and did other tasks that blurred the formal boundaries between ranks. By the mid-1970s, LPNs and aides did a mix of tasks that once had been done by RNs. This change made RNs more "professional" by reducing their "scut work" and was appreciated by nursing leaders. Nursing leaders were less sanguine about shifts in tasks that implied that less-trained personnel could do RN tasks such as patient assessment, irrigating and changing dressings on wet wounds, giving medication, and admission assessment. The skills of LPNs were not necessarily their main concern. It was an open secret that in emergencies, specialized units such as pediatric intensive-care units were staffed by LPNs. Night, but not day, shifts were also sometimes staffed by LPNs, without salary increases.

Nursing leaders struggled with physicians and others who wanted to create a cheaper labor force. RNs were controlled, limited, and exploited by physicians who treated them as "handmaidens," incapable of autonomous caring (Melosh 1982). Many nursing educators of BSN RNs tried to distance this stratum from other nursing personnel by claiming a distinctive nursing theory and mandating a four-year university-training program. In practice, the differences among the three RNs, and between themselves and LPNs, have often been blurred. Like other professionals employed in bureaucraticized organizations, RNs were never able to establish control over the labor process and had only weak control over credentials. Administrators and nursing managers have been able to use these rivalries to change the labor process without worrying that workers would join together to resist. They could play on the hopes of all nursing workers, who wanted to be considered professional, to be respected, and to be able to give patients quality care.

Hospital Care and Home Care

Hospital administrators organized a new labor process to cope with the rising acuity level of hospital patients, which was accelerated by DRGs, and to lower labor costs. Many replaced team nursing with primary care and an all-RN staff. Nursing managers may use primary care and the move to the all-RN staff to justify increased work for RNs. Primary nursing care (PNC) assigns the same three RNs (day, evening, night shifts) to patients for their entire hospital stay. The day-shift RN coordinates a work plan for which all three RNs do most of the direct care. In team nursing, a "charge nurse" coordinates the work of other RNs, LPNs, and aides. Ancillary staff, such as therapists, ward clerks, and housekeepers, may assist RNs, but much less so in primary care than in team nursing. In all-RN units, RNs fill as many staff positions as possible, which allows hospitals to reduce therapy, clerical, and housekeeping staff and RNs are expected to "rise to the moment." In the ideal model of primary care, though not often in practice, lower-grade workers give extensive support to RNs, but do not do direct patient care.

Nurse educators and managers have argued that an all-RN staff is more "professional" than team nursing. In the latter, an RN supervises lower-grade workers, LPNs, aides, and others. RNs do a minimum of direct patient care. Primary care reassigns all responsibility for patient care, even "scut work," to the RN. This broad spectrum of work is interpreted by administrators and managers as showing RN "autonomy"! No one would dare make a similar argument about physicians and "scut work," that physicians ought to weigh patients and do blood-pressure readings, let alone clean up after themselves, to demonstrate their ability to function autonomously. That work is passed on to underlings.

DRGs and new regulations regarding outpatient surgery have resulted in site specialization too. Site specialization means that the range of how sick patients are within each site is narrow and that the workforce in each is more homogeneous. Only very sick people now get care in hospitals, while the less sick are in nursing homes or receive care in outpatient clinics. Housebound, seriously ill, but recovering patients get some health services in the home.

Before DRGs, the hospital was the care site for a range of patients, from the very sick to the nearly recovered. Since DRGs, hospitals have delivered a narrower range of services to their patients. If possible, diagnoses and all pretreatment surgical procedures and tests are done in outpatient clinics or brief hospital stays, some of less than twenty-four hours. After procedures, as few services as possible are given in the hospital, and as many as possible are done in outpatient clinics and at home. More services are given in settings with fewer highly paid workers, and more delivery is shared with amateurs in the home.

Site specialization means that some workers do tasks in one rather than another place, but also that work done by those in lower grades in one site may be done by workers in higher grades in another. Hence, intensive-care monitoring continues to be done in acute-care hospitals. But the acute-care hospital is no longer used for long-term recovery. Medicaid patients must do their long-term recovery in nursing homes or at home. Poststroke treatment is no longer done in most hospitals, but in rehabilitation hospitals or, more likely, at home. Cataract surgery is done in outpatient clinics.

The level of skill of workers varies across sites. RNs do most of the nursing in acute care. LPNs and aides predominate in nursing homes, where federal law requires only supervisory RNs. BSN nurses, some LPNs, and many aides work in home care. Nursing work is done in the home by a peculiar combination of the most highly trained of staff RNs, the minimally trained nursing aide, and the unschooled family caregiver.

By the mid-1980s, the organization of nursing work had shifted away from steadily increasing occupational differentiation within the hospital. Most hospitals hired more RNs and allowed the numbers of ancillary staff to drop. Recently the shortage of experienced RNs has led some hospital managers to rehire lower-grade workers to relieve RNs of routine tasks.

Other reasons have been given by managers for cutting hospital staffing. The new reimbursement policies encourage outpatient ("ambulatory") treatment and home and nursing-home care, rather than hospitalization, and this results in empty hospital beds and less need for hospital labor. The ongoing decline in hospital occupancy rates for acute care accelerated sharply from 1983 to 1985 as the prospective payment system was phased in: the rate of occupancy fell by 2.6 percent from 1980 to 1982, but by 12.9 percent between 1983 and 1985 (Farley 1988: 6). Nonetheless, the use of RNs as generalists, responsible for the work once done by ancillary workers, is an unexpected reversal of earlier labor processes in which RNs were trained to supervise and do only specialized care.

Nancy Stover, a white director of patient care at a small medical center, moved her staff from team to primary nursing and to an all-RN staff. She explained the hospital's decision in ways similar to managers' describing their blue-collar workers and retailers their salesclerks: "We save about $26,000 a year in nursing costs. Nursing with a mixed staff means too much 'down-time.' We cannot afford to keep [RN] nurses on down-time. They must draw blood, do pulmonary therapy, bed-make and other activities."

Professionalism or "Speed-Up"?

RN leaders and nurse managers described the shift to primary care as reducing hospital costs, but also as professionalization. The director of patient care, Nancy Stover, expected great financial savings from using the all-RN staff. She believed that RNs could be separated into the "task-oriented, those who can do medications, make beds, get patients to walk" and the "patient-oriented" RNs who assess, document, create a relationship with the patient, and coordinate all complex services. (Given short stays, the kind of relationship that this manager hoped for is probably rare.) Enhancing the status of RNs, according to Stover, requires that

> nurses have to become professionals and take responsibility. Patients are in hospitals for nursing care, not for surgery. Nurses must learn to be totally accountable. Often all of the nurses say everyone [RNs, LPNs, aides] is doing the same thing. Actually, it is the [RN] who signs off for the LPN and whose education allows her to make an assessment that others cannot. In the face of the DRGs, the professionalism will either rise or fall. We could take people off the street and train them to do basics and use RNs to supervise, but I think patient care would suffer.

Stover's hospital also hires from a national registry of RNs, including the Flying Nurses, who are flown in temporarily when more nurses are needed in wards or intensive-care units. Regular staff nurses object to the temporaries; they say they lack knowledge of hospital and ward procedures and are difficult to integrate into existing staff.

Some RNs view the loss of other staff as "overwork" and a cause of "burnout." Some complain that with the primary system, they no longer can eat lunch and at times even go to the toilet. The pressure to give quality care to very sick patients makes them sacrifice meeting their own needs. They also resent seeing lower-grade staff lose their jobs and fear that a glut of physicians threatens their own jobs.

Greta Edwards, a white charge nurse, sees primary care as a "speed-up." She says that lower-grade workers are laid off, then hired back to do irregular work as "floaters": "We are not really doing primary care, we [RNs] are just doing more work. You cannot do primary care without a stable staff, and with licensed practical nurses as floaters, you do not have the stable staff you need."

Managers and staff RNs explain staff responses to the changed labor process in a contrasting way. One nursing manager, who interrupted an interview with me to quell a "revolt" of nurses she had just switched to primary care, said, "Nurses are scared of being responsible for a patient. It's not that they don't want to do new tasks but are unfamiliar with and afraid that they are not competent to do primary care. I temporarily suspended primary care for today, and tomorrow I will educate my nurses to take on the new responsibilities."

Nursing leaders had hoped that hospital administrators would adopt primary care because they recognized the professionalism of RNs, their ability to perform autonomously, to manage cases, and to provide patients with continuity of care. But administrators have used primary care to save money. RNs have more responsibility for patients, but have lost the help of other nursing personnel and ancillary health service workers. Hence, instead of professionalization and increased specialization, RNs in hospitals now do sharply contrasting tasks, the most technical work requiring extensive training and the least technical unskilled work.

This is by no means to suggest that RNs do not continue to be responsible for the most exacting nursing but that attempts to contain labor costs have produced *job consolidation* in hospitals and upgrading in home care, where RNs do more specialized work, but LPNs and even aides do work once done only by RNs. And, of course, unschooled family caregivers must also learn the work of RNs.

Legitimating Changes

Changes in the labor process are not talked about on hospital floors as helping to increase profits or lower health insurance premiums. Nor are the changes seen as a corporate attempt to attack social entitlements.

Instead, administrators and managers discuss "cost containment" and the new reimbursement policies as a reaction by Congress and the public to hospital greed, patient overuse, inefficiency in hospital administration, and the like. Managers describe hospitals as having abused federal and private insurers by overusing hospitalization, acquiring expensive equipment that duplicated what was already available in the community, requiring too many laboratory tests, performing unnecessary surgery, and overusing medications. Few administrators, managers, or caregivers discuss patient overuse, though most new reimbursement policies try to "contain costs" by increasing the percentage that patients must pay while decreasing reimbursements to hospitals. Consider the shift to part-time and temporary workers and to primary nursing. George Adams, chief administrator at a major medical center, explained: "It is cheaper than keeping people on staff year-round without work. That costs over $1 million compared to $16,000 for nine days paid to a recent national temporary agency including airfare, boarding the RNs in an empty ward and giving them meal tickets for our cafeteria. They worked twelve-hour shifts for seven out of nine days." But RNs believe that temporary workers do not know hospital routine and regulations and that staff RNs must spend time training them.

Whatever the financial and medical reasons for changing the organization of the nursing staff, discharged nursing workers resent their loss of regular jobs and their reassignment as part-timers. Racism is seen in management's actions too, but not only African Americans were fired. Many aides who had worked in their country of origin as RNs had helped at one hospital with patients who spoke no English; these aides also lost their jobs without much warning.

Barbara Morton is an African American who trained as an LPN in 1980 in a federally funded job-training program for women on Aid to Families with Dependent Children (AFDC). While in training, she decided to become an RN and in 1985 took the state boards for RNs. In the early 1980s, she had been hired at a major community hospital as a part-time worker with health and other benefits. Two years later, she was fired with one week's notice. Since her layoff, she has been working about twenty hours a week "on-call" for the same hospital. She has lost her health benefits and receives Medicaid for her children. Because her earnings are low, she gets food stamps for herself and her family and lives in subsidized housing. She also works as a psychology technician at another hospital on a per diem basis and works ten hours each week at a facility for the developmentally disabled.

Despite working three jobs, she considers herself "unemployed" and is likely to remain so until she can take the examination that will license her as an RN. She says, "The hospital laid off forty LPNs five months ago, giving us one week's notice. They then hired nineteen new RN graduates. The administration said they were switching to primary care, but I went to a seminar on primary care and the instructor described [it] as including and needing LPNs, aides, and all other support workers."

Morton found a study of San Francisco General Hospital with "facts and figures on the cost effectiveness of licensed practical nurses." She gave the report to the president of the hospital board, who responded by explaining that the hospital wanted to attract new patients by having an all-RN staff.

As Table 8.2 shows, women of color are more likely to be in the lower grades of nursing workers than to be RNs. Morton says the belief among many workers of color is that the all-RN policy is

> an attempt to get an all-white staff and to cut costs for LPNs by eliminating our benefits. About 70 percent of the LPNs who were laid off were minority women. All of the RNs hired after the layoffs were white. Though the census [occupancy of beds] had gone down for a few months before we were laid off, we were shortly hired back as "casuals" working as much now as before but without benefits. We are compensated with 50 cents more per hour in lieu of those benefits [up to $20 per week]. We also get no holidays or vacations.

The hospital gets around the union contract by carefully regulating assignments for LPNs, which would force them to rehire. Says Morton:

> Our contract [with SEIU] is that anyone who works twenty hours a week on a *predetermined* schedule for ninety days automatically becomes a "regular" employee. In our new contract, the word "predetermined" was eliminated, but the hospital simply manipulates the schedule to keep from reclassifying us as permanent. It sees to it that we don't work twenty hours per week within sixty days.

Neither of the unions to which hospital workers belong, SEIU 250 for LPNs and the state Nurses Association for RNs, are viewed by many workers as especially helpful. At Morton's hospital, when the patient census shot up immediately after the LPNs were laid off, the Nurses Association did not protest against the hospital's flying in RNs from out of state. The association did force these temporary RNs to become union members, but it did not support the LPNs who tried to get rehired as regular staff.

The elimination of LPNs "translates into speed-ups for RNs," said another RN. The association actually filed a grievance on the increased workload after an ad hoc committee of "radicals" protested. Three RNs and three LPNs organized Nurses for Democracy after the layoffs: "We had to pressure the association to file," says one member of this group. But the "compromise" was a two-tier system for aides, dietary workers, and housekeepers, which the union did not fight. Morton says,

> It did not affect people on the job, so they breathed a sigh of relief. They do not realize what this will mean down the line and the conflict it will create between workers. You'll be working next to someone who knows they get a lot less pay than you; you'll ask them for help, and they can tell you to do it yourself because you are getting twice as much as they are.

In other two-tier systems, those hired after the new contract was negotiated receive lower wages and fewer benefits than those hired earlier. The pharmacists at this major medical center were already on a two-tier system. Subcontracting is another system that reduces hospital costs and creates a two-tier system with the small number of workers remaining as regular staff being paid better than the temporaries. For example, skilled nursing has been subcontracted to a large corporation, which provides LPNs whom they pay $5.50 an hour. The medical center pays $9.50. Aides also earn less as contract workers then as regulars.

Workers in this hospital have formed a small but vocal alternative to the existing union, as well as the ad hoc committee mentioned earlier. In the union, the Committee for a Democratic Union (CDU) ran an alternate slate for two offices. The caucus lost the election for officers but won six seats on the union board. After the election, the union old guard "did some cosmetic clean-up, firing the worst business agents and hiring new ones who do not know the health industry. The committee was red-baited during the election, and when the [CDU] members [on the board] voted against a no-sympathy strike clause in the new contract, they were again red-baited."

Morton sees the administration of the hospital as "out to bust the union" and as using retrenchment because of DRGs to do so. Her suspicions were heightened when she saw the book *How to Make Unions Unnecessary* on an administrator's desk. When the administrator refused to lend the book to her, she borrowed it from the library; after reading it, she concluded that all three of her employers are following its advice and making life as difficult as possible for hospital workers.

Hospitals now seem to many workers to be a place of harder work with less support, more very sick patients, fewer chances to get to know and be supportive of patients, more like a factory or "a jewelry chain," and overall an increasingly unsatisfactory workplace.

The preceding analysis shows how the origin of the work transfer in health care is found in changes in the labor process. In health services, this means changes in the work of RNs, LPNs, and aides in hospitals. Nursing personnel report experiencing speed-ups, more job-related stress, distress over perceived declines in the quality of patient care, and even job loss. This chapter has described how the work of nurses has been altered by the efforts of hospital administrators and managers to encourage physicians to shorten the hospital stay of their patients and refer patients to outpatient care. Managerial concern with reduced earnings because of DRGs increased the shift from hospitalization. Some hospital nursing personnel found themselves with a broad range of tasks and very sick patients, while others found their jobs eliminated. A task mix from the earlier jobs of these workers became the responsibility of women in the family.

The next chapter discusses home health workers. In contrast to hospital workers, they seem less harried, though under pressure to do more work. They are anxious about their patients, worried that patients lack sufficient services, always conscious of the need to secure reimbursements for their agency. Yet home workers on all levels seem pleased with their increasing professionalization and are often happy to be out of the hospital, away from direct supervision, and on their own.

9

Changing Home Care

Changes in reimbursement policies have prompted managers to organize a new division of labor between hospital service workers, home-care workers, and patients and their unpaid caregivers. Before DRGs, hospital workers typically performed a wide array of tasks for patients who ranged from very seriously ill and totally dependent to nearly completely recovered and able to help other patients. But by the mid-1980s, typically only the seriously ill were hospitalized. This changed the composition of patients receiving home health care services or relying on self-care.

In the home, patients vary widely in the seriousness of their illness and in their dependence on others for basic care (meals, clean clothes and bed linen, baths, etc.) and for nursing (medications and exercise, nutrition through tube feeding, access to oxygen, regulation of breathing, etc.). Who does the work? Much of it is has been redistributed among home health agency workers and between them and patients and their unpaid caregivers. To be sure, and this is a central problem, some of the work that could hasten recovery, prevent hospital readmission, lessen family burnout, or even forestall disaster does not get done or gets done badly.

Changes in Home Health Care

We were products of the 1950s and we did what we were told. We never thought of teaching the family or telling the patient anything that the physician had not told us to say. We made so many visits because this increased the reimbursement to the local VNA [visiting nurses association] from the March of Dimes and other agencies. There was a lot of emphasis on making as many visits as possible and doing everything that could be done for the patient.

—*Home health care administrator, HMO*

The new slogan, "patient self-reliance," makes home care a money-maker. Nurses [RNs] have to change from being a caring person to a business person. They have to do more charting and writing, to put a charge slip through for every item because the insurance companies reimburse for supplies. . . . It is hard on the nurses to think care and think about business. Since there are only two of us [specialists], we continue to give quality care but as [the agency] grows I do not know if we will be able to.

—*Raye Knight, RN infusion specialist*

Between 1965 and 1985, home health services went from a "graveyard" for nurses who were burned out and waiting to retire to a challenge for nurses with high levels of training and willing to practice complex caring with considerably more autonomy than in a hospital. In hospitals, there is always back-up: other RNs, physicians, an array of equipment and supplies. To nursing personnel, jobs in home health have improved greatly. Registered nurses and home health aides have been released from immediate supervisions—for RNs, from that of physicians, and for aides, that of RNs. Nursing personnel have learned new skills, including new techniques of care and complex case management. Perhaps, or so they hope, they have gained more respect: RNs want respect, especially from physicians and nursing managers, and aides want respect, especially from RNs.

But there are problems. Changes in home health care over the past two decades, especially from 1983 to 1985, led to sicker patients and more complex treatments and more responsibilities, especially for RNs. Some felt undertrained or lacking in experience for the new responsibilities. Under more stringent reimbursement standards, budget cuts, cost containment, and the large numbers of new for-profit agencies, home health workers had to become more "businesslike"; they had to pay more attention to "bookkeeping," tracking supplies and equipment, and documenting their work. Documentation also became a method of informal patient advocacy, an attempt to reverse aspects of the work transfer. Documents addressed the "fiscal intermediaries" who decided whether patients were entitled to home health services and the agencies to reimbursement. Finally, nursing workers had to be more "productive," to do more work in less time, for more seriously ill patients. This could mean unpaid overtime and, for some RNs, doing semilegal unpaid work for needy patients.

Problems of financial solvency plague both nonprofit and for-profit home health agencies. Previously, without federal subsidies for the poor, nurses from nonprofit agencies made many home visits because the agencies received funding on a per-visit basis. Today there are fewer nonprofits, and few can afford to give free care. For-profit agencies may trade the quality of patient care for investors' satisfaction by pushing RNs and home health aides to work overtime for free and may expect more skills of all workers. RNs who move from hospital to home health services often lose income, since the latter pay less than hospitals. Many RNs lose union protection when mergers, organized between hospitals or hospitals and independent agencies, are designed to eliminate collective bargaining.

THE SICK AND HOME HEALTH

In the early years of Medicare and Medicaid, as in the preceding period of public health practice, patients usually went home from the hospital ambulatory—that is, they could walk and had recovered other bodily functions. Very sick patients (on ventilators, for example) or dying patients rarely were discharged to home health agencies. Most home-care patients were recovering from heart problems or were being treated for diabetes and its complications. Others were recovering from surgery and needed wound care. Still others had impacted bowels from lengthy bed rest.

Many procedures once done in a hospital, such as simple knee surgeries and cataract removals, are now done in an outpatient or "come and go" clinic. For example, federal guidelines require that cataract surgery be done on an outpatient basis except for persons with serious medical conditions. Most surgeries, including all cosmetic, tonsillectomy, urinary sphincter, cyst removal, and hernia repair are also done on an outpatient basis. For home health workers, this increases the dependency of their patients, who once would have been hospitalized until able to care for themselves.

Patients too have changed. Ten diagnoses accounted for one-quarter of all persons using home health services and for 26 percent of all federal payments. In 1986, 23 percent of home health patients had strokes (cerebrovascular disease), 19 percent had congestive heart failure, and 10 percent had hip fractures and joint replacements. The remaining seven diagnoses, with each accounting for less than 10 percent of the top ten, included hypertension, diabetes, pneumonia, bronchus and lung problems, acute myocardial infarction, and incontinence (Ruther and Helbing 1988).

Twice as many patients were discharged to the care of home health agencies after the introduction of DRGs, with a rate of increase of 153 percent in 1985 compared to the preceding three years, and after shorter hospital stays (Morrisey, Sloan, and Valvona 1988: 56–57).

There was no difference in how sick patients were who went to home health and those who went to nursing homes; the difference seemed only that those discharged to home health had a family caregiver (Morrisey, Sloan, and Valvona 1988: 59). Home health RNs cannot treat the patient by themselves and must try to train family caregivers or others, and to find social service agencies to support the families.

Medicare billings for five DRGs (stroke, pulmonary disease, heart failure and shock, major joint procedures, and hip and femur procedures) show a similar increase in discharges to home care. (Pneumonia and pleurisy are excluded from the following conclusions.) The diagnoses listed above are for about one-eighth of Medicare patients discharged from hospitals and more than one-quarter of those receiving after-hospital care. In 1985, the five were the most common diagnoses (41.8 percent) for Medicare patients sent to nursing homes, for sizable numbers (22.2 percent) of those sent to home health services, and for more than half (53.1 percent) of Medicare patients sent to rehabilitation hospitals (Neu, Harrison, and Heilbrun 1989: 6).

While the quality of hospital care may have improved since DRGs (Rubenstein et al. 1991), shorter hospital stays have resulted in more patients being discharged to their homes who are medically unstable, and the death rate among such patients is higher than among those discharged in a stable condition: 16 percent of unstable Medicare patients died within ninety days of discharge, compared to 10 percent of the stable patients (Kosecoff et al. 1991). Also, more patients with the five diagnoses were readmitted to the hospital after being discharged to a home health agency rather than to a nursing home or a rehabilitation hospital. Yet the patients readmitted from home health services were similar as measured by "case mix" to those sent elsewhere. Hence, home health patients need skilled nursing care, and where they go after hospitalization is based on judgments of physicians and discharge planners, including judgments about the adequacy of family care. The home health RN is faced with ensuring that care is provided by training relatives or friends, who do work once done by paid caregivers in acute and rehabilitation hospitals and nursing home. (Only about 5 percent of patients in these five DRGs used after-hospital care in more than one setting [Neu, Harrison, and Heilbrun 1989: 67, note 6].)

Stroke patients and those with joint procedures who receive after-hospital care are most likely to be discharged to home health, just as home care is the most likely discharge for all Medicare–Medicaid patients. Most, 82.5 percent, get no posthospital care. Those who do, 14.6 percent, get home care (Neu, Harrison, and Heilbrun 1989: 9). Among patients in these five DRGs, home health patients are more likely than others to be readmitted to hospitals, suggesting that patients are quite sick and have more problems after discharge than those sent elsewhere. Within ninety days of hospital discharge, 36.8 percent of home health care patients in these five DRGs have returned to hospitals; within six months, 52.7 percent have been readmitted, usually with secondary illnesses. A sizable percentage of patients in these DRGs have returned to hospitals within three months: 27 percent from nursing homes, 28 percent from rehabilitation hospitals, and 29 percent from among those who received no posthospital care. Home health patients start out with the highest return rates and continue to have them through the first six months after hospitalization (Neu, Harrison, and Heilbrun 1989). This supports the contention that patients are sent to home care from hospitals too hastily.

SCOPE OF SERVICES: FROM FAMILY TO PATIENT

Traditionally, home health agencies have provided the entire family with considerable help with daily activities. Today's care is limited to patients and their needs; technical care has grown, while social care has declined. For example, as recently as 1970, if a patient's children were drug or alcohol abusers, the RN treated them and was allowed to make several visits a day to the home to monitor the family. By 1985, nurses could be responsible for only the patient and "concerned with the children insofar as it upset and hindered the patient from becoming independent and stable" (Home Health Agency Coordinator). Twenty-five years ago, RNs did a wide variety of nontechnical work, such as foot soaks, baths, and nail cutting, now done by aides or student podiatrists. The home health RN does less hands-on care. She observes, assesses, and teaches.

Workers View the Changes

Troublemakers in the hospital are the ones who often do the best at home because they are independent and don't conform to hospital routine. Our nurses are like that, too. Home health nurses are wavemakers in the hospital, troublemakers, who do really well in home care because they are so independent.

—Betty Clarke, coordinator, home health care agency

The entrance of "for-profit" home health agencies into health services makes good delivery impossible. . . . [It] means a deterioration in quality. Proprietory agencies don't have as their goal to provide best care. Their objective is to make money. Maybe I'm old-fashioned, but bedside care was what I learned to stress.

—Sally Neil, discharge planner, for-profit medical center

Health service workers spoke with both pride and concern about the new mix in home care of autonomy, complexity, rising status, and circumvention of what they viewed as harmful regulations. Work has become more technical, more dangerous, and life-threatening. Workers expressed pride in doing the complicated technical work without the presence of a physician or the back-up of a hospital staff. Aides were pleased to do less personal care and housekeeping and more nursing tasks.

Home health agency coordinator Priscilla Green sums up two decades of experience. When she began her work in the late 1960s, most home visits were to cardiac and diabetic patients or for wound care and impacted bowels. There were few cancer patients, either dying from the disease or undergoing chemotherapy. Today, home-care nursing is much more technical than it was earlier. RNs do hyperalimentation, intravenous procedures for administering antibiotics, chemotherapy, and transfusions. They treat infected patients and dying patients, particularly those with cancer and AIDS. Four complex procedures, major money-makers for suppliers of medical equipment, were once done in the hospital but are now also done in the home (Roe and Schneider 1985): intravenous antibiotics administration; intravenous chemotherapy, the administration of highly toxic chemicals as therapy to cancer patients; parenteral nutrition, feeding that bypasses the patient's digestive system and is infused directly into arteries; and enteral nutrition, feeding that bypasses only part of the alimentary system and is administered by a nasogastric tube.

Home Therapies

Nurses use skills in intravenous (IV) therapies that they fought physicians for the right to learn. Hospital nurses battled for the right to set up and start intravenous treatments. Following a change in the technology that made it easier to administer, hospitals began to train RNs to do IVs, and physicians went on to newer procedures. Today, in many home health agencies, RNs do a variety of intravenous treatments. Home health RNs also now make judgments about drawing blood samples for analysis, rather than wait for an order from the physician, and report the findings.

RNs clean lines (Hickman lines) inserted into the chest wall and irrigate or clean catheters that give access to the lines that allow infusions near the heart. After training by hospital RNs, home health RNs then teach their patients, in the hospital and later in the home, and teach family caregivers how to use these technologies.

CHEMOTHERAPY

The contrast in the use of home chemotherapy before and after the expansion of home health services is sharp; for example, chemotherapy patients used to enter a major teaching hospital for ten or twelve days at prescribed intervals, such as every three months. A director of ambulatory care reported that by 1985 "patients got their chemotherapy infusion on an outpatient basis, coming back to the hospital every single day for a week, or three times a week or every week for six months."

Chemotherapy was one of the major services given by home RNs with support from major medical-supply companies. In 1980, nurses from Priscilla Green's unit mixed chemicals in the home and infused them to patients. But RNs were fearful. By arguing that state guidelines required special equipment and training for nurses, neither of which the agency was providing, Green succeeded in getting chemotherapy treatment dropped from her HMO agency. Except for this reversal, home-care nursing has become increasingly technical over the past twenty years in this HMO.

Dying cancer patients, who once would have been in the hospital or a nursing home, are now supported in home care. Toxic drugs may be infused automatically to ease the patients' pain. Dying patients require a twenty-four-hour on-call system and a small number of patients for each RN, to enable the nurse to spend many hours with each patient. Thus Betty Clarke, who coordinates a home health agency in an HMO, believes that her group does not have a hospice because it is "so labor intensive." Her department assigns "a large caseload, between forty and fifty patients" to a home health RN who manages her own cases. She sees some patients twice a week or more and others only once a month, according to physicians' orders. This is very different from five years ago, when a closer watch would have been kept on patients.

The change from hospital to home for care does not seem to be the result of new medical treatments or detailed treatment instructions. Instead, new reimbursement policies allow hospitals and free-standing home health agencies to train special home service oncology nurses to administer toxic chemicals and monitor and assess patients. (By 1990, premixed containers for chemotherapy were widely used, eliminating concerns about workplace safety.)

ANTIBIOTICS

Intravenous antibiotic treatment is the most common IV therapy. It is used in the home for a variety of problems including postsurgical infections, pneumonia, infections in the lining of the heart, and osteomylitis (an infection of the bone in otherwise healthy persons). All these problems had once been treated in the hospital because home applications were not reimbursed. Rachel Brown, director of ambulatory care at a medical center, explained her preference for home care over hospitalization with an enthusiasm typical of home health RNs. Her comments underscore the importance of reimbursement policy:

> Jeepers-creepers, should they be sitting in this [hospital] bed for six weeks? We call the visiting nurses association, who sends somebody twice a day to administer the antibiotics. And in fact, if it takes two or three hours, it is very costly from the visiting nurse's perspective. From the business perspective, you have a critical mass of patients to support this kind of service, and there is reimbursement for it.

NUTRITION

Enteral and parenteral nutrition can be used temporarily or while patients recover from disease and surgery, or permanently for those with untreatable conditions. At regular intervals, fluids are infused that bypass some organs, going directly into a vein or through a tube inserted in the nose. Care must be taken to keep the lines clean because in parenteral therapy, infusion is into a vein. Instructions used in home health care by RNs for the specific purpose of teaching patients and their family caregiver to do parenteral nutrition illustrate the complexity of work that the latter are expected to learn to do:

> *Purpose.* To maintain catheter patency [*sic*] and optimum site condition, keep the site free of contaminants, wetness (including leakage), infection, and infiltration (due to improper anchoring/taping stability).
>
> *Equipment and supplies.* Gather the following supplies on a clean, dry surface: (1) hydrogen peroxide. . . . (5) ointment as ordered.
>
> *Procedure.* (1) Wash hands thoroughly with an antibiotic soap. (2) Remove old dressing and dispose of in a controlled manner to prevent contamination. (3) Inspect IV insertion site area for infiltration (blanching, swelling, coldness); phlebitis (redness, warmth, palpable vein cord); and infection (tenderness, drainage, inflammation). (4) Clear insertion site outward. . . . (5) If ointment is to be applied, do so at the insertion site with a sterile cotton tip applicator. . . . (6) Loop the catheter and tape securely against the body (to avoid dislodging the needle by a direct pull on the tubing). (7) Document dressing change in nursing notes and treatment sheet. Mark the dressing and date (optional). Be aware that the dressing should be changed every 48 to 72 hours. Change immediately if the dressing becomes wet, dirty, or loose. (Bontempo and Eggland 1987: 16–17)

I do not know if a glossary for patients and their relatives came with the instructions! The home health RN also has to teach the patient or caregiver other instructions for cleaning the home parenteral equipment and for preparing and administering medication as well as the nutritional solution. Separate instructions are also given to the family caregivers on "documentation, precautions and safety measures, prevention and recognition of complications, side effects and considerations applicable to activities of daily living" (Bontempo and Eggland 1987).

TRANSFUSION

RNs may do home-transfusion therapy for "the physical, financial and emotional benefits to the patient" with a capable caregiver in the home. The RN brings the blood components to the patient's home in a special container, rechecks the patient's name and blood type, and checks the blood for "compatability, product unit number, expiration date, color and appearance" (Marek and McVan 1987). She has an emergency drug kit to use during each transfusion that includes cards imprinted with the transfusion reaction protocols, and she follows the patient for the next six months for signs of infectious disease or other adverse reactions.

OTHER FUNCTIONS

Home health RNs once did work that other professionals now do, for example, medical social work and physical, respiratory, and occupational therapy. Some nurses saw this as being displaced "unfairly and unnecessarily" by specialists and were ready to do the work again. In one agency, RNs suggested a reversal—that medical social workers be eliminated to save the agency money and that nurses coordinate social services. These reactions are examples of the persistent struggle of RNs to define the content of "nursing" and establish an exclusive domain of practice.

For the home health nurse, the new labor process mixes old and new work, some of which reflects the difficulties that nonprofit home health agencies have had with cost containment. To some RNs, their professionalism seems violated by the demand of insurers that family amateurs do RN work. Informal caregivers are expected to use complex medical technologies and to monitor patients receiving complicated therapies. Teaching patients is a traditional home health nursing responsibility, but much of the content used to emphasize wellness. Today, what is taught is far closer to professional nursing than before. The content of what must be taught to patients and their caregivers is so complex that home health RNs take special courses. Specialists are brought into home health agencies from the hospital to teach the new techniques: intravenous chemotherapy, the use of catheters and lines, and apnea monitoring. Home health RNs may become nurse specialists themselves—in wound care, colostomy care, respiratory treatments, oncology, and intravenous care, or may spend their time exclusively teaching patients and family caregivers how to do this work.

Professionalism may also be undercut by RNs having to pay close attention to reimbursement guidelines, drawing their attention and energy from patient care. The change of home health to a for-profit business and stricter reimbursement standards have given the RN new tasks: she must keep detailed records on supplies used in home care and must document in detail the patient's progress and need for home-care services. Agencies have been forced to be preoccupied with teaching their staff to write documentation that is acceptable to insurers. An RN describes her reactions: "I was congratulated by my supervisor on my charting finally being up to [how] she wants it. She said she could use me as an example of how to do good charting. She was thrilled to death because a year ago, I was having a terrible time. I just had to snicker when she said that. I said, 'That's wonderful. I have become a professional liar.'"

This nurse also said that she felt that the statements she had to write to ensure Medicare and Medicaid reimbursement demeaned her nursing skills. For example, sometimes no relative or neighbor was available to change dressings or a catheter. The home health agency supervisor told her to write the following: "I could not find anyone in the home who was willing to learn to do this." To the nurse, this implied that any layperson could acquire nursing skills. The same manner of documentation is required when RNs visit patients who need intramuscular injections, such as an antibiotic, twice a day because no relative or neighbor is willing to learn how to do this. The RN is expected to write an apology on the patient's chart: "I am going out twice a day because no family member is able to learn injection technique."

Work may mix together what the federal government defines as legal and quasi-legal tasks, that is, work that nurses do because they believe it is in accord with nursing ethics. Nurses may take on these tasks on their own or be urged to do them by their supervisors. The work arises largely from the federal funding cuts of health services for hospital care and home care. When DRGs cut reimbursement to hospitals, many health service workers, both managers and staff, assumed that home health services would be expanded. They anticipated not only more patients but more visits to each patient, longer visits, and more home help from ancillary workers. But the Department of Health and Human Services decided that it could have it both ways: it would not pay for hospitalization or for home-care visits (Cooper 1987).

RNs worry that their patients are released from hospitals too soon and that the work needed to help them recover may be cut off inappropriately early. To continue the RN's part in the new division of labor, RNs may use documentation as a new form of *patient advocacy*, a weapon against the efforts of HCFA to cut Medicare spending on home health services. It is also advocacy for their agency, another new element of work that emerges with the reorganized labor process. One result is that RNs do "creative writing" (their label) in clinical reports. They can no longer write reports solely to inform medical decisions but must craft ones to convince reimbursers to pay their agencies. "Recharting," an illegal action in virtually all states, may be done to increase the chances that the agency will be reimbursed. This recharting does not change data on the nurse's technical observations, assessment, and medication, but revises the language used to summarize the patient's overall medical condition. Hence, "patient is better" may be expanded to "than at last visit" to prevent the reimbursement agency from interpreting "better" to mean recovered completely and therefore ineligible for further home health services. Patient activities, such as churchgoing, visiting offsprings' homes, or, for those living in single rooms without cooking facilities, going out to a restaurant, cannot be "charted" because they may be interpreted by HCFA to mean that the patient is not "housebound."

Careful phrasing and omissions are not new to health care or unique to RNs. Physicians use "silence" to cover their errors (Paget 1987). Physicians doing industrial accident work must use language carefully in writing insurance claims and continuances of work leaves. What is new for RNs is the burden of integrating their reports into the daily practice of patient care, making sure to use a language that will forestall an additional work transfer and get fees for their agencies. In the past, health care agencies may have given unneeded services so as to increase their earnings (as VNAs reportedly have done), but today, RNs and coordinators in home health care talk about underserving patients. The nearly hundred-year-old nonprofit VNA of Chicago ceased providing free care visits in 1986 after having been used as a dumping ground when the for-profits took over the market. The VNA was providing nearly half of all free home care—about 50,000 visits (Kilbane and Blacksin 1988).

Patients with chronic illnesses treated by home health agencies after an acute illness represent another area of quasi-legal service. (Long-term care for "stable" medical conditions is outside the jurisdiction of home health agencies, according to current federal reimbursement guidelines.) RNs must cope with diabetic patients who have lost home health services before they have managed to get help with insulin preparations or home tests. One RN made unpaid visits after her working hours to help a woman with syringes. This nurse would have a legal problem if the patient or her family were to sue her for malpractice, such as a mistake in preparing the syringes or negligence in training a neighbor, because the agency's malpractice insurance would not cover such "Good Samaritan" acts.

Home-care RNs have also become case managers for very sick patients. In the absence of hospital social workers, discharge planners, or a family caregiver who will do the work of drawing on community resources, the RN contacts neighbors, friends, attendants, libraries, Meals on Wheels, and community agencies. While coordinating social services has always been part of the work of the home health RN, the work is now crucial, exacerbated by federal cuts. Thus, some RNs complained that they spent long hours telephoning community agencies to find meal service and transportation for the isolated and poor elderly and respite for family caregivers.

Other sociocultural skills have become necessary for home health nurses. Coping with language barriers and ethnic differences is more important in the home than in the hospital, where if a nurse does not know a particular language or understand a patient's wishes, another health care worker or patient will. In home care, the RN must try to make the work transfer function in families in which only one member may speak English, though the RN must teach several members to care for the patient. The nurse must recognize how the work transfer is limited by poverty. For example, costs that she may view as trivial, such as for a tub bar to help an elderly patient bathe, may be beyond the income of a poor family.

Home Health Aides

It's like a three-legged chair. We are the leg that keeps the stool from falling over.
—Olive Deere, home health aide

Aides have the least training and get the least respect from other nursing workers, but have the most continual contact with patients (Donavan 1989). Under medical guidelines, their job content too has changed over the past twenty-five years, mostly for the better. According to home health aide educators, agency coordinators, and aides, the changes have "professionalized" aide work. Before 1965, aides did personal care and a wide variety of housekeeping tasks, often during visits as long as four or five hours. Sometimes they made bank deposits and paid bills. Patients also may have pressured them to serve others, such as by changing bed linens or ironing clothing for a healthy relative. With the entrance of the federal government into home health care, visit lengths have been gradually cut, and housekeeping and personal assistance have been curtailed. Laundry is done only in the home, and shopping is restricted to stores within a few blocks of the patient's home. The shortened visit time automatically eliminated some house-keeping because federal guidelines mandated that "personal" care be given priority.

Patty Gleason has worked as an aide in home health agencies for twenty years, since completing six weeks in a community college course. Her work has changed considerably from her initial patient load of two visits per day, four hours in each home. In 1968 (after the establishment of Medicare and Medicaid), the agency increased her patient load to three per day, about two and one-half hours per patient. In 1970, Medicare adopted new "Taylorized" standards based on observations of the time it took to do personal care in hospitals. This reduced the time Gleason was allowed to care for a patient to about one and one-half hours, and she was given four patients per day, with thirty minutes' travel time between each patient.

Because of the current patient load at Patty Gleason's agency, aides who travel a good deal by bus (aides are less likely than RNs to have cars) may go without lunch, eat on the bus, or work unpaid overtime. Since her agency has recently unionized, Gleason will now be paid for her overtime. Because today's sicker patients often cannot be left without care for two days, the aide workweek has changed to include weekends. Moreover, the agency refuses to give aides two consecutive days off (i.e., a Monday when they are not working on Sunday, or a Friday when they are not on Saturday duty). Aides have been told that they must "be available" and must use a middle-of-the-week day to do their own routine chores.

Alice Dale, a sixty-year-old African American, has worked intermittently for fifteen years in home health after six weeks of training funded by her employer. In the early years, she was bonded so that she could write checks and pay bills with cash. She made appointments for her patients and took them to the doctor in special transport.

Sandra Green, a sixty-year-old African American, began in health care services eighteen years ago, after a six-week training course at a home for Adventist elderly. She saw her job as "keeping people out of rest homes." She shopped, did laundry, cleaned house or "tidied up," cooked and prepared meals for weekends and holidays. She bathed patients and ironed their clothes. She is relieved that she no longer has to "clean homes with years of garbage, sometimes dry and sometimes greasy and dirty. Once my previous agency sent four or five aides out together because the place was so dirty that no aide would ever be able to clean it up. I had to do heavy cleaning at my other [home health agency] job, everything except moving furniture and washing walls."

Aide work has been "upgraded" as personal tasks have been cut and tasks once done by RNs and LPNs have been assigned to aides. They still continue to do some food preparation, cleaning, clothing care, and shopping. The low status of such "women's work" is reflected in the low wages of aides, a speed-up (not compensated with higher wages), an unreasonable workweek (e.g., the refusal to allow two days off in a row), and unpaid overtime. Despite the upgrading of their work, aides continue to earn between $4.50 and $5 an hour (1988), which may help to explain their shortage (Koska 1988: 63). Some campaigns to change the conditions of employment of aides are under way; in Boston, for example, aides have begun a Home Health Workers Campaign on issues of wage equity, travel time, and cuts in hours (*Progress* 1990).

As the numbers of home health agencies have increased, hospitals have started their own departments, and corporations (such as Upjohn) have entered the market. The competition among home health agencies has forced many to upgrade the work of aides.

Because of increasing competition between agencies, Grace Lowry, a white woman who is the director of a visiting nurses association, decided to try to attract aides by assigning them work that only LPNs and RNs had been doing. Her agency allowed aides to check for "vital signs" (e.g., do blood pressure readings) and do skin care. Because RNs were no longer allowed by Medicare and Medicaid to make three visits a day (necessary for some wound care), aides would now do the care if family caregivers were unavailable. This was not unusual. At a major HMO, aides had been caring for bed sores resulting from patient immobility, improper diet, or lying in urine. Observes Deena Rattner, a white woman who supervises many African American aides: "They have their own elitism; they want to be seen as doing 'health care.' The director of our Visiting Nurse Association told them he wants to expand the homemaking service. They were aghast, upset and threatened. They thought they would be back to being maids and see themselves as falling backward."

Aides have also been taught to change dressings on amputee sites, postsurgical wounds, extrusions of cancerous tissue, and on wet wounds that require technical care called irrigation. None of these activities may seem complex or esoteric. Until recently, however, and in many states still, these were defined as the province of RNs. In Rattner's agency, RNs demonstrate the techniques to aides and leave written instructions on wound care in the home to guide the work of the aide, the patient, and any family caregivers. In some agencies, an aide, rather than an RN, may even teach the family caregiver to do simple wound care. Aide Olive Deere, an African American who has worked in home care for twenty years, is pleased by her new assignments: "It's better on my morale. People know I can do more than clean shit. It's better for patients that aides do [it] because it means that nurses can do other things."

Aides, like RNs, ignore or circumvent the new guidelines, though it means that they must work harder and faster to do so. Based on her observations of what patients need, Olive Deere has continued to do housekeeping tasks that the new federal guidelines for home health aides prohibit: "We go by the rules but also you do a bit of housekeeping. It is hard for me to see people breathe the dust and lie in bed and look at a messy house. I'll also feed an elderly man, even if he is not the patient."

More and more restrictions have been placed on aide work, as patients in the home have become sicker and more dependent. About a year ago, the agency for which Sandra Green works merged with a VNA. Her work changed considerably; she sees more patients and for less time, doing only light housekeeping. Mainly, she does "personal care": bathing, linen changes, shampoos, dental care, and some exercise, and prefers being called a "health worker, not a homemaker."

Aides may be undervalued by others, but they recognize their importance nonetheless. Summing up what aides do, I said in a halting fashion, "The home health aide—." Before I could finish, Olive Deere interrupted me with "does all the work!" And she laughed.

> Home health aides are the backbone of the home health agency. We make it possible for nurses [RNs] to do their nursing work. When we go to the homes, we hear all the complaints about the hospital, how the doctor did this and the nurse did that. People say to us, "But you people are different in the home," so we make [the HMO] look better. We are the ones who really see the patients and find out what is happening to them. A nurse may go out once a week, or even once a month. We may be there every day or two or three times a week.

For example, a patient of Deere's with a physical disability, worried that her husband was "stepping out on her" because they did not have sex. Deere "told the RN and the social worker and the physical therapist, and we [*sic*] talked about what to do and got her some booklets so she could read about sex."

The medicalization of aide work and the decline in housekeeping may lessen the frustration of African American aides who tend white racists (Donavan 1987). Aides describe how some patients express their bigotry freely and insultingly, for example, by asking African American women not to use their toilet. Others refuse to have women of color as an aide. Some patients fear "racial" contamination or have suspicions that arise from racism, which hurt and anger aides. Sandra Green says she "follows the rules and regulations to keep out of trouble with my clients" ever since a patient accused her of taking $5. A mixup had occurred: the patient had given the money to her church and forgotten that she had done so. The resolution was unpleasant: Green was not sent back to the home because there "would be hard feelings."

Lack of time also leads to stress and frustration for aides. Patients want more than the aides can give them: "If you give as much as the patient wants, you would be there all day. They watch the time and right before you leave they find things for you to do. I say to them, 'I'll do it the next day' or 'Write it down.' They try to give you gifts so you are obligated, but we are not supposed to take gifts."

Sandra Green said that aides need, most of all, to have lots of patience and "put up with people." The majority of people she cared for were "very lonely, and they looked for you. You are their company. They may not see another person from day to day, or week to week."

But what aides like about their jobs may conflict with federal cost-containment measures. Deena Brandt sums up the anomaly of aide work:

> Home health aides are available for personal care defined as a bath, foot care, or a shampoo. They cannot be sent out only to cook, shop, or make sure the elderly patient is safe. The government does not care if a patient starves or is unsafe. The kind of care that the elderly really need is not daily baths [the personal care that the government requires]. Medicare is trying to say that to get aide help seven days a week, the patient must be *bedridden*, not just housebound, which again ignores the needs of patients, especially the elderly.

Alice Dale sums up the cursory care that can occur when decisions based on cost containment replace a human service ethic:

> I don't think that it is fair. People are making all these cuts and they don't understand. Some patients could stand the cuts, others cannot. Sacramento and Washington just cut, and they leave it to us to figure out what *we* must cut. They should send someone from Sacramento and Washington down

here to see what goes on, to go into some of these homes, to see what people need.

They don't understand what the patient needs and wants. The patient is grateful to see someone just to say hello. Some of the patients would like to go out and walk with you so they wouldn't be mugged or knocked down.

Rosemary Sharp, a white woman, has worked in health care for nearly twenty years. She is vice-president for home health care at an HMO. She sees the new federal policies as changing the hospital's ability to care for those without family support or for those health experts believe need to be in the hospital, not their home:

> Until the DRGs, we practiced "social admissions," admitting people to the hospital because home care was inappropriate or unavailable, because those in the home were incapable of giving care. For example, an elderly patient who was living with an elderly spouse who was unable to care for him would have been admitted to [our HMO]. We would have included this as part of our general running cost. This is no longer possible under the new Medicare guidelines unless we are willing to pay the total cost of hospitalization.

Social needs are now a responsibility of social workers and discharge planners, family and friends who rely on whatever community resources are available. They must pull together social resources that may barely substitute for the lost "hotel" services provided by hospitals. The medical model of recovery continues to focus on the disease or injury, ignoring the social and emotional aspects of recovery.

Aides and RNs

Aides say that the patient's condition is more than physical or medical, that feelings, "spirit," and small complaints count too. The hierarchy of workers places aides on the bottom and discourages an exchange of information and mutual appreciation among health workers. Racism and class barriers, as well as time pressures, often result in useful information not being sought. (LPNs also complained about not being appreciated by RNs, who in turn complained about physicians and administrators.) Social worker Deena Rattner's view on the importance of the aides she supervises is this:

> They know the cast of characters in the home better than anyone else. They know when the case manager wants to be rid of the patient, and they know

when everyone in the building hates the patient or when the patient is having family problems. The home health agency ought to have multi-disciplinary conferences where RNs, aides, physicians, and social workers come together to discuss a patient. Aides need to have a sense that they can actually make an important contribution to patient well-being by giving their information to the staff. The aides could be useful in helping to plan the case because they do have information that the RN does not.

Rattner believes that RNs in home care respect aides more than RNs generally do because the nurses themselves have lots of autonomy. She says that home health RNs "do not need to turn and pick on the lower guy. They express appreciation of the aides but they see no priority in getting information from them. They see them as highly skilled, but a lack of time means that they do not talk to them."

Priscilla Green was coordinator of home health care at an HMO. Green tried to encourage closer cooperation and more respect among workers across grades, and especially to encourage RNs to appreciate aides. This was so unusual that aides and other coordinators noted it. Before Green began to coordinate the home health agency, the dress of workers showed their place in the hierarchy. The aides worked in white uniforms, while RNs and therapists worked in their "street" clothes. Green told the RNs and aides "to talk it over"; together, they decided that the aides should also wear street clothes. Aides said they felt more appreciated, respected, and professional, and less subject to harassment by neighborhood residents who thought from their uniform that they carried narcotics. Green says her agency is unique.

> We're the only agency in which everybody socializes together, the RNs and the aides. The aides from elsewhere tell stories about having to punch a clock, difficulties with RNs, and being kept tabs on all the time by their supervisors. When we have meetings, everyone has to go—the RNs, aides, social workers, and at least one doctor. Our home health agency is different than our hospital [where the separation continues].

One aide described the shocked reaction of another coordinator to aides being treated as colleagues of RNs: "[Priscilla] was at a meeting last week. A supervisor from another agency said to her, 'Where do your aides go when they come to work?' My supervisor said, 'What do you mean, where do they go?' The other supervisor said, 'Well, do they have a room or what?' My supervisor said, 'Everyone is in one big room.' The other supervisor looked surprised."

Green is an African American, as are the majority of the agency's aides, and is sensitive to the racist implications of segregating these workers from the usually white RNs. Race may be one barrier to socializing and respect across grades, but the organization of the workplace seems to matter too.

Health workers (including RNs) sometimes question the motives of hospital managers, wondering why they reorganize the labor process so as to exclude aides and licensed nurses, but increasingly rely on them in home health care and nursing homes. Some believe that the push for an all-RN staff, supposedly needed to care for very sick patients, hides the desire for an all-white staff that, in a competitive market, would attract upper-income patients. Others believe that the expansion of aide work in home health is largely to assist the (usually) white RNs to be professional. More likely, race and ethnic differences exacerbate sexist beliefs and practices. Historically, African American women were segregated in private domestic service, with limited opportunities. Subsequently, they shifted to health services and into aide jobs, in which personal care and household chores were central. Through the prism of racism, managers may recognize the domestic continuity but not the shift toward more nursing responsibilities; they may discount the distress LPNs experience as a result of job loss and pay inequity. Gender, race, and ethnicity may thus mutually reinforce devaluation of positions. In all, aides can be used to facilitate the work transfer to the home at a comparatively low cost to third-party payers.

The Home as Factory

[Medicine is a] big business and a major problem because home health agencies now need to make a profit to stay alive. There is a conflict of interest. The agency wants us to be more and more productive. They want us to see five patients, which is reasonable. . . . They will pay you twenty-five dollars for each patient you see each day over five. Other agencies pay their home-care nurses on the basis of how many visits they make per day, which seems to me to be really unprofessional.
—Carol McIntosh, home health care RN

The emphasis on high productivity produces the content of the work transfer. Since DRGs, RNs and aides make fewer and shorter visits to each patient, as mandated by federal regulations. To stay solvent, agencies have tried to increase the numbers of patients seen without using more workers, that is, through a speed-up. One agency gave RNs a $25 bonus per patient if they saw more than their assigned five patients a day. Another agency asked RNs to do the vastly expanded paperwork after working hours and to spend the entire workday on visits. This, of course, means unpaid overtime.

Other attempts by agencies to increase productivity, such as by establishing practice committees that "problem solve," seem similar to "quality of working life circles" (Madsen and Harper 1985: 13). Some have "Taylorized" nursing, using time-and-motion studies to decide how many patients their workers can be expected to serve. Every task counts. For example, an agency approved a new form after the manager concluded that it saved $120 per 1,000 charts by reducing average charting time to 4.8 minutes per patient, saving $1,314.40 per week (Weeks and Darrah 1985). Such estimates are accepted with little curiosity about whether the new charting will hamper the quality of care and whether RNs will accept this "efficiency."

Relative Intensity Measures (RIMs) are another approach for estimating productivity. RIMs measure the level of nursing needs based on tasks that must be done for patients according to their illness and dependency. Developed specifically to "cost" hospital nursing with the DRGs, RIMs measure "nursing resource use on a patient-specific basis" (Joel 1984: 44), much as has been done for blue-collar and clerical workers.[1]

Instead of RIMs resulting in RN professionalization and less use of RNs for nonnursing tasks, RNs "rose to the demands of the moment," doing nonnursing tasks if other workers were unavailable (Joel 1984: 45). RIMs did not make managers see RNs as more professional, while RNs themselves were able to sabotage or circumvent the RIMs.

In home health, productivity measures similar to RIMs have been developed to set workloads. For example, the RN workday includes time for her office work ("administrative, record keeping, making appointments, staff meetings), for in-service education, supervisory time and clinic time." Time is allotted for travel time to the home, though the agency is not reimbursed for the travel time if the patient is absent from home. Case mix sets time allotments, more for an extremely ill patient or for a new patient for whom time-consuming paperwork must be done. Only a short time is allotted for a well-baby visit to a mother and child who were in the hospital for less than twenty-four hours.

Forms similar to RIMs have been introduced into home care, and the concern with productivity has led to a close look at paperwork.

Hence, as in RIMs, discharge statements have been changed from a narrative to a check-off form, to decrease RN time on documentation. This may mean that RNs must do the work at home, after hours, and thus for free. Perhaps most telling of the uneasy relationship between productivity and professionalism is that "nursing dependency" was left out of the construction of the curtailment of home care.

Changes in the Labor Process

Changes in the labor process challenge some commonly held theories. First, nursing work has not been characterized by a one-way move toward an increasingly detailed division of labor. In recent reorganizations of the labor process, the division of labor has been reversed and top-level jobs have been broadened in scope to include former tasks of lower-grade workers. Second, the jobs of lower-level workers have been upgraded in job content, but without any compensatory increase in wages. Third, workers have been redistributed in a new arrangement among different health sites (home, nursing home, hospital, outpatient clinic) whereby different grades of workers predominate in distinct sites: RNs in hospitals and home care, LPNs in nursing homes, aides and assistants in home care and nursing homes. This site specialization is a consequence of the reversal in the division of labor. Fourth, polarization occurs: the "occupation" may be upgraded, but the "jobs" may be downgraded or remain fixed. Nursing may appear to have been upgraded because of increasing percentages of nurses with more schooling than ever before: in the RN ideal, though not in actual practice, RNs with baccalaureate degrees are "professionals," while other RNs are "technical" nurses. Fifth, home health work seems to mean a combination of *informal* (unpaid) self-care and family care, and *formal* care by RNs, aides, and others employed by home health agencies. However, RNs and aides also do "informal" care, responding to the reduction of services to patients as health care has been transformed from a human service to a for-profit industry and as the federal government has reduced spending. Hence the boundary between paid and unpaid work blurs in the job performance of aides and home health RNs as they take on tasks voluntarily.

The increased use of home health services tends to polarize nursing jobs. The responsibilities of both top-grade RNs and bottom-grade aides are increased in ways that managers and some workers view as professionalization. One cost is the decline of the middle-grade LPNs, for whom jobs in hospital diminish without any increase in other work sites. Another grade is added into the job hierarchy, informally to be sure, not in the organizational chart: the home provider combines the work of the professional nurse, albeit in an "unskilled" way, with the lowly domestic labor of the aide. The training of family providers in the *steps* that need to be taken to care for the patient presents a model to administrators of how task elements can be shifted from RNs to aides. And, of course, agencies are already shifting such tasks to aides.

Changes in the labor process seem to exacerbate existing tensions between women health workers over what is appropriate to each grade and reflects the continued devaluation of work that meets "natural needs." Even as aides and administrators describe aide work as upgraded, they are both devaluing domestic labor and implying that valuable work is "technical." In part, this may be rooted in the confinement of African American women in the United States, for generations, to private paid domestic labor, where they were oppressed in personal relations and deprived economically. But I suggest that their views also are shaped by fundamental views of gender—that women's work, especially on activities similar to those done in the home, is automatically "nontechnical," estimated to have little economic or social value.

Racism reinforces these interpretations in that many who do paid domestic labor are women of color. The job shifts of many women of color from paid private domestic labor has been into public labor, where the benefits may be many (unionization, higher wages, impersonal rules guiding work, etc.), but the work is still domestic labor with only marginal gains in appreciation.

Eliminating LPNs, aides, and other ancillary workers from hospitals has broadened the work of RNs. Hospitals administrators no longer automatically assume that labor costs will be reduced by tasks being redistributed from more skilled, higher-paid workers to less skilled, lower-paid ones. Administrators expect that lower hospital labor costs will result from turning hospital RNs back into generalists. Measures of productivity, modeled on those used for factory and clerical workers, have been adopted to assess how work ought to be assigned to RNs. The measures are used, too, as the basis for billing patients and third-party providers for nursing services, and as documents in lawsuits (Bly 1981). These measures have been interpreted by nurse researchers, educators, and managers to show an excessive amount of time wasted among lower-grade LPNs and aides, who have to be supervised by RNs. Similarly, technical staff members (e.g., ward clerks, laboratory technicians) have been described as "unproductive" because they cannot easily be kept continuously occupied (Franz 1984). (Retailers complained similarly about the "wasted" time of the salesclerk who had to wait to serve customers. Retailers urged that clerks do stocking, cleanup, and other assorted tasks to fill the "unused" time. Eventually, this led to the elimination of specialized workers in most large American stores and to transferring the "unproductive" labor to customers.) The belief that "semiprofessional" workers must be kept busy constantly, like factory workers on an assembly line, justifies the new labor process too: work that remains after ancillary staff and other nurses are laid off is redistributed by *job expansion* among the remaining workers. They face a speed-up as they take on tasks from positions eliminated by layoffs and retirement, doing more work in the same amount of time.

In capitalism, ideology justifies the continuing low pay of aides and those who do "housekeeping" work. Women, like men, accept the ideology of capitalism that sets workers against each other for a supposed limited pool of rewards and allows the invisible transfer of the work that they are no longer allowed to do to women as unpaid family caregivers. Essentially, changes in the labor process are capricious, often unverified tactics for coping with unpredictable reimbursements seen as threatening the quality of patient care and the financial well-being of the providing organization.

The last two chapers have detailed my fundamental thesis, as it occurs in paid work in the health services industry in the United States: Paid and unpaid work form a seamless web of activities that provide services. The reorganization of the labor process in the workplace sets the conditions for the work transfer, motivated by employer intentions to reduce wage costs. The reorganization by managers of the labor process eliminates, consolidates, and develops new work for paid workers. What work is no longer done by paid workers is shifted to those who buy or use services and to their relatives and friends.

10

The Home as Workshop: Amateur Nursing–Medical Caregivers

I did not realize until recently how much work spouses do and how much work adult daughters and daughters-in-law do . . . that the family simply wears out trying to care for a sick patient. The family is replacing what the hospital did, such as bedpans, turning the patient, and being on-call.

Another week in the hospital would make an enormous difference in recovery for the patient and for the family to develop skills to care for the patient.
—Social worker supervisor of home health aides, VNA

We Americans do not have the resources to use the family as a caregiver. The government is saying that we should take care of the elderly ourselves in the family and in our communities. But it's not possible because children are scattered around the country.
—Director, home health agency

I think it is one of the best things that HMO offers. Hospitals are horrible places to be. In the hospital, we control everything, and eventually, people stop recovering or doing very well.
—Home health care RN

Erving Goffman (1961: 321–386) called the hospital the physician's workshop. Today, the home is an extension of the hospital in an unprecedented fashion, a place where high-tech work initiated by physicians, RNs, and other specialists is continued or concluded. It has become the workshop for amateurs,[1] doing unpaid labor essential to the U.S. health care system by completing the work of paid providers. Unpaid work has changed from housekeeping and minor nursing to encompass the administration and monitoring of complex nursing–medical regimens as acute-care hospitals have lost their near monopoly on care (Franz 1984). The consequences are unequal for family caregivers: money buys release from constant home care of kin; and hospitalization, posthospital institutionalization, and access to home health care vary by gender, class, and racial–ethnic membership.

My descriptions of the home-care experience of patients and family caregivers rely on interviews with RNs and home health aides, nurse managers (administrators and health agency coordinators), and social service workers. Unfortunately, I was unable to interview acutely ill patients discharged to home health agencies or their caregivers. One voice is heard: a patient who spoke to me over many months of the complex feelings and experiences of dying at home, to which I have added my own observations. Many studies have been done of the formal and informal care of the chronically ill (Stone et al. 1987) and the frail elderly and their family caregivers. But little is known about the acutely ill, who are the increasing users of formal and informal home health services (see Abel and Nelson 1990; Finch and Groves 1983).

Home Care: An Experience

Returning the care of the sick to the community has complex social and emotional meanings for both patients and caregivers. Since 1980, care has been evaluated largely by government agencies in monetary terms, and the quality of care measured in hospital readmissions or mortality rates. Home care has facets other than survival, its own cycles and stages, and its own difficulties and pleasures. People from many social groups, institutions, classes, and ethnic groups may be drawn into a network of paid and unpaid support.

One professional writer died at home after receiving care for many months from a network of forty friends, colleagues, and acquaintances. This was a heroic effort. Members of the "network" did their caregiving shifts of four or eight hours each week fairly faithfully. They gave what hospitals call "hotel services" (preparing food, changing bed linen, washing dishes) and personal care (bathing, washing hair, clipping toenails, toileting, and so on). They kept records on the administration of medications and breathing exercises. They charted the patient's condition by recording such information as "ate two muffins," "drank orange juice," "in considerable pain," "refused to eat lunch." They gave additional time to errands, such as shopping, doing laundry, delivering mail, and corresponding with publishers.

The experience was full of mixed feelings for the caregivers and the patient. Caring for a dying person is an unfamiliar activity for most Americans, one that raises existential concerns about mortality and aloneness. Some caregivers say they felt ashamed and guilty about what seemed socially unacceptable feelings of resentment toward a person who was dying: for having the usual measure of personality quirks, unreasonable expectations and unpredictable tastes, and struggles about imminent death.

This patient fought hard to remain at home; resisted being moved to a nursing home, a friend's, or a daughter's home in a neighboring state; and continued to "live alone." Her caregivers found the work physically and emotionally exhausting; they reported fatigue, upset stomach, headache, and trouble sleeping. They complained about lost time that they might have spent visiting friends, caring for children, and pursuing careers. And they expressed guilt as they struggled with their feelings of helplessness and shame at resenting the loss of time to someone who was losing life itself. Caregivers also took considerable pride in their collective accomplishment: as an informal network, they saved a friend from institutionalization and unwanted dependency.

Their patient was relieved to be able to "live on my own," but not in a rosy world. She talked about a lack of privacy, about being "taken over" by caregivers, feeling invaded, without boundaries, and out of control. No doubt some of these feelings were about impending death or a mix of feelings about death with the effects of the disease and medications. But these feelings were also a reaction to the social reality of being tended. The patient lacked personal physical and psychological space as much as the sick do in hospitals, nursing homes, and hospices. She was in quasi social contact with "strangers" (the patient's term for those who were not good friends before the illness was diagnosed), who were giving the most intimate physiological and psychological care.

Caregivers treated the patient in different ways, including as if she was no longer a person with "all [her] faculties intact" (Salinger 1960: 110). Some enunciated carefully and spoke slowly in the high-pitched voice that adults reserve for conversations with dogs and small children. Unsurprisingly, the patient interpreted whispering, intended not to disturb, as hiding that most dreadful of secrets, immediate death.

Before being bedridden and totally dependent, the patient talked about the absence of "meaningful relationships" and "meaningful conversations," despite the streams of caregivers. She seemed to need to feel *cared for*, as distinct from being *tended to* (Parker 1981). Given that the relationships were neither familial nor waged, the patient seemed to want to "give back" for care by interacting supportively with caregivers.

As death neared, she stated more feelings about being alone though surrounded by caregivers and sought various ritualized connections as reassurance that people cared. Her ambivalence about the experience was expressed in an answer to a question about how things were going: "And I wrote so many good things about collectives, too many . . . though I *did* also write about the bad."

No network of caregivers can hold back death. But sending patients "back to their families" or "the community" has to be understood as having social and psychological effects, negative and positive, on caregivers and on the sick. Home health care is a complex social experience, one barely portrayed in its complexity by social scientists and seemingly ignored by policymakers. It needs a complex and well-conceived system of social support that includes more than the present stingy financing by the federal government and various insurers.

Women's Work

For over a decade, insurers have been promoting more use of home health care and home high technology as a substitute for hospitalization. The result has been twofold: the changed labor process for paid workers (described in Chapters 8 and 9), and new work for family caregivers. In the United States, before hospitals improved, wives and mothers, adult daughters, and daughters-in-law nursed ill family members. Today, women must learn high-technology health work to be able to care for family members who are more seriously ill at home than before, and many of whom are alive only because of continued reliance on high-technology medicine.

Changing reimbursement policies make more work for women and others in the family, but the sex–gender system and race–class subordination make the work transfer feasible. In the United States, with its weak welfare system, most children and nonemployed adults have access to social resources such as health care through family membership via the employed heads of households. Only the elderly, the poor, and the disabled, along with veterans, members of Congress, and the president and his cabinet, enjoy "socialized" medicine—at least partial access to care through federal insurance or in federal hospitals. This fits well with the commitment in the United States to the individualistic model of illness causation and treatment (Krieger and Bassett 1986) and matches the philosophy of the American Nurses Association (1978: 3), which supports home care because "health is a personal responsibility."

INDIVIDUALISM AS FAMILIALISM

"Individualism: self-help, self-support, self-sufficiency" appears to reject dependency on other people and groups, but "in practice, the unit of self-support is not the individual but the family" (Barrett and McIntosh 1984: 45). Those whose families lack the money and know-how rely on welfare institutions or go without (Barrett and McIntosh 1984). In contrast with the United States, in capitalist societies with strong welfare systems, such as Sweden and the Netherlands, citizens claim social resources as individuals (Bystydzienski 1989: 678; Folbre 1987). Especially in the 1990s, the United States has moved away from individual rights, reducing federal services and enlarging dependency on families while increasing state controls over individual health decisions (e.g., abortion, suicide, refusal to accept allopathic medical care).

Health care can be shifted from the formal health delivery system to the family and the women within it because of these ideologies and practices including women's continuing responsibility for unpaid domestic labor. Hospital administrators, middle-level managers, and discharge planners also view "the family" as responsible for patients.

Women's unpaid labor in the home is an ignored segment of health care delivery. Supposedly, technical health care delivery is done only by professionals. Thus the care of the sick in the home is largely invisible or is treated as routine housekeeping, not essential to the health care delivery system and not requiring nursing skills. Only a few sociologists have seen that caregiving is "work" (Carpenter 1980), that caregivers may struggle to learn the new technologies (Fox and Swazey 1974; Post 1989), and that declining welfare services make caregiving difficult (Corbin and Strauss 1988).

Within the household in capitalist societies, women are responsible for the social reproduction of the labor force, including the health care of husbands, partners, and children. Domestic labor entails women's care of other family members who are socially and economically dependent, namely, the retired and the sick, who may need ongoing or intermittent physical, emotional, and financial help (Strong-Boag 1986). The invisibility of women's unpaid labor in health care and the hidden financial costs of home care for the family show in the easy acceptance of the prospective payment system as having "accomplished its primary goal without shifting costs to other payers"—as if the family has no costs (MacLaury, in Russell 1989). Thus the underpinnings of the "accomplishment" is women's often invisible domestic work. The work transfer takes tasks from paid workers, many of whom find their jobs have been eliminated or reduced to temporary or part-time. Mothers, wives, adult daughters, and daughters-in-law of the ill are socially obligated to provide the labor that completes the labor process begun in organizations outside the household—in hospitals, clinics, and other health care facilities.

RACE AND·CLASS

Not all women experience the work transfer identically, since changes in hospital use and posthospital care vary according to the age, race, and family income of patients. Between 1983 and 1985, the admission of children to hospitals dropped more than for others, 19 percent compared to 11 percent (Moss and Moien 1987: 5), making more work for mothers. The admission of African American patients decreased over twice as much as that of whites, 27 percent compared to 11 percent. Admission rates of those with family incomes under $10,000 declined by 19 percent, compared with 11 percent for those with incomes over $35,000 (Moss and Moien 1987: 7).

Discharge to nursing homes was more common for "well-off" patients on Medicare, while discharge to home health services was more common for those on Medicaid (Neu, Harrison, and Heilbrun 1989: 61). Patients with private insurance stayed in nursing homes longer than Medicare patients, who went home sicker, whether or not they received home health services (Morrisey, Sloan, and Valvona 1988, Exhibit 3: 59). African American patients were more often discharged to home health services than to nursing homes (Neu, Harrison, and Heilbrun 1989: 57).

Perhaps because women are more likely than men to live alone, they are also more likely than men to receive home health services (56 per 1,000 women enrollees compared to 43 per 1,000 men) (Ruther and Helbing 1988: 107). Providers too assume all women can and should care for the sick men in their families without paid help.[2]

Data on caregiving to the chronically ill suggest that women cope with the work transfer differently depending on class. Women from higher income levels are less likely than others to care continuously for their elderly parents. The poor are more likely than the better-off to be in the same community as needy relatives and parents and thus to be caregivers. Women in working-class jobs find it more difficult than those in professional jobs to do tasks such as telephoning to ensure adequate caregiving (Abel 1990: 73). Women from households with high incomes can hire substitutes for themselves: private-duty RNs, nurse assistants, and attendants. In contrast, working-class women rely only on any home-care nurses and aides that their insurance may provide. Finally, the government discriminates against the poor by giving less service to indigent Medicaid patients than to elderly Medicare patients.

Patients in Their Homes

Some people would like to stay in the hospital because it is quiet, comfortable, and someone waits on them. But the majority of people sleep better at home with family or familiar things around. —Home health care RN

The patient and family work may begin before hospitalization. Patients who will be admitted to the hospital for only a few hours, for minor surgery or invasive diagnostic procedures, may come to the hospital or outpatient clinic before admission for tests that once were done in the hospital. So will patients preparing for major but nonemergency surgery. If patients come from some distance, they must find housing for themselves or commute to the hospital twice in a few days—once for tests and once for surgery. Out-of-town patients may rent beds in the wards, which have emptied because of DRGs. In the hospital, patients and family caregivers may be taught about some of the health self-care that they must later do in their homes.

Home care for families is more difficult today than earlier because of earlier hospital discharge. Hospital aides used to help patients in ways that encouraged physical recovery. For example, they helped slow-moving patients walk to toilets rather than place them on bedpans, as RNs may do to save nursing time for serious problems. Walking helps bring back body functions, and toileting prevents the use of catheters, which encourage incontinence in older patients. Today's short hospital stays and the lack of aides result in more patients going home before they can walk and more work for the home caregiver.

THE MEDICAL IDEOLOGY OF HOME CARE

For fifty or so years, the medical community insisted on, and most of the public accepted, the hospital as the best place for the sick. Hospital administrators, managers, and home health RNs now describe home care as desirable because of personal and psychological benefits and lower costs. Many health workers believe that patients recover faster when they have private personal space, psychological comfort from family, and can control their daily routine. Rachel Brown, the white director of ambulatory care at a major teaching hospital, gives the current view:

> A lot that goes on in our heads affects how we feel. That's what happens with elderly people in hospitals, who may get confused and wander, and fall out of bed and over the side rails, and those kinds of things. Not that they can't fall at home, but at home it is a familiar environment. The hospital is noisy, there are people in and out all night long, and there is a very clear psychological, physiological response to being there.

Christine Michaels, a white RN in home health, says that patients prefer to be home "because it is quieter, without the disturbing hospital routine that wakes people up to deal with their illness but not with their individual needs." Families do not have to travel back and forth to the hospital, and RNs work in a setting that is more pleasant than a hospital.

Even RNs who mention negative aspects of home care consider the home a better place than the hospital. Susan Carter, a white RN, considered home care "wonderful, though I emphasize the bad things": "At home, people eat their own food, sleep in their own bed, and are with their own families. It is so stressful for patients in the hospital that they do not even remember what we taught them. We have to review everything, food, medication, driving, sitting and so on, in their homes."

HEALING AT HOME

Some workers see no medical research that supports early discharge and home health; they see only new political pressures. The director of home care at a major medical center explains:

> I have asked doctors why they discharge patients or keep them for different amounts of time, and the physicians themselves admit that they do not know because there are no data.
>
> We make judgments that are convenient to administrative decisions. There are now stringent attempts to police even home health agencies on [the] political grounds that we are spending too much. In this political climate, health is considered just too expensive . . . we are being asked to do more and more for less.

Some nurses, critical or not, conclude that administrators and federal regulators do not care about two major outcomes of early discharge: the work transfer to patients and families, and inadequate care. I asked Pauline Atwood, a white director of discharge planning at a major medical center who has worked in health care for thirty years, about the scientific basis for short hospital stays. She replied: "In the 1920s and 1930s, in the push to develop hospital insurance, everybody wanted people to come and stay forever. And [the hospital owners and administrators] wanted hospital insurance to cover that. Now we have [DRG] caps, so we want to get them out, so we are saying, 'Yes, it is safer at home than here.'"

There may be convincing evidence for shorter hospital stays, but if so, the information has not reached the nursing managers or home-care nurses I interviewed in 1984–1985. For example, Pauline Atwood could mention only one study that supported early discharge. It compared patients with myocardial infarction treated in a coronary-care unit with those treated at home and concluded that the patients did equally well. "Hospitals," Atwood explained, "had wanted people to come in for everything because they got paid for it, and they said that one could not do things as well at home as in the hospital."

She also was skeptical of what she called the "technological fix" and saw the shift of high technology to the home as a "money-maker" for home health service agencies and home-equipment suppliers. She believed that the extensive use in 1985 of total parenteral nutrition (TPN, a non-oral feeding system) was because it was "making money," including as it did the sale or rental of infusion pumps and solutions with nutrients for infusion. As she anticipated, in late 1985 the federal government capped the use of high-technology equipment and procedures and mandated the use of modified and cheaper nutritional programs over the more expensive TPN. By 1988, medical interpretations conformed to this reimbursement policy; physicians and nurses reported that the modified treatment was superior to the more expensive version.

SAFETY

RNs believe that in some ways the home environment is safer than the hospital. In the home, there is less chance for patients to get bacterial infections or react to toxic chemicals, and night sleep is not interrupted as often. But discharging patients "quicker and sicker," as health workers call it, makes for home-induced illnesses. Patients may go home with draining wounds that require RNs to make twice-a-day visits to do dressing changes. Such wounds are easily infected. While these infections would be treated quickly in the hospital, the spacing of home visits delays treatments. The result is that RNs make home visits to change dressing and then may make additional ones to treat infections. The danger of infection increases as family members or home health aides do "wound care" in place of RNs.

Technologies in the Home

High technology in hospitals was often cited as the major cause of the rise in health care costs.[3] Now the expectation is that using high technology in the home saves money for insurers and hospitals and permits hospitals and nursing homes to send very sick people home to family caregivers. Before 1981, many corporate insurers fought against the extension of coverage to illnesses not requiring hospitalization. They now believe that home care may lower costs, but some of them also worry that a new home-care benefit will lead "some people who do not need it to take advantage of it anyway, thus adding to costs" (Roe and Schneider 1985: 52). Their images seem drawn more from the consumption of dinners, Broadway plays, and meetings in luxury resorts on executive expense accounts than the consumption of intravenous antibiotics by those with bone infections, apnea monitors by newborns, or parenteral nutrition by those recovering from colostomies.

Social scientists and social policymakers often seem to consider technology to be an autonomous system, generating inevitable social change, its own increased use, new inventions, and so on, as if technology were independent of social decisions (Litwak 1985: 14–15; Ruderman 1986). I see no such inevitable outcomes. Technology is socially constructed[4]; its origins, promotion, and use are all embedded in social relations—including the relations of production, sex–gender relations, and racism—and conflicts over social entitlements.[5]

TECHNOLOGY AND "EMPOWERMENT"

The use of high technology by family caregivers is not automatically "empowering"; they gain no more social power or technical knowledge by using high-tech health equipment than by adjusting electronic thermostats. Women's use of high-tech home equipment in the work transfer gives them no control over what Cockburn (1985) has called "the machinery of domination" in gender relations; women gain no influence on health policy, but only assist kin to remain outside institutions. Control over health decisions remains with men and is located largely among those in the corporate class, government bureaucracies, and hospital managers. Furthermore, medical–nursing technologies have usually been designed by men, often by engineers with mechanistic views of social life, fears of women and sexuality (Hacker 1981); and it is men, not women, who learn the intricacies of repairing and servicing machines in the home.

To compete in the capitalist marketplace and attract patients, hospitals have adopted expensive technologies (Budrys 1986; Greer 1986).[6] Medical technologies are mediating or enabling features in home health care, allowing hospitals to practice "cost containment" by transferring work to the home. There, patients range from those who need simple monitoring for sleep disorders (e.g., for apnea or the intermittent cessation of breathing in an otherwise healthy newborn or middle-aged adult) to a totally dependent quadraplegic whose life depends on ventilator-supplied oxygen.

TECHNOLOGY FROM HOSPITAL TO HOME

I shouldn't be as cynical as to say that it was all done to get more money. People thought that sophisticated technology would result in better care.
—Pauline Atwood, director of discharge planning

The use of high technology in the hospital predated home use by decades. Most equipment was designed to improve hospital services or facilitate the exploration of space, rather than allow home care. Hospital technologies have been modified for home use much as commercial stoves, refrigerators, and vacuum cleaners were modified for the home. Typically, the redesign is minor, such as miniaturization or changes in monitoring features that substitute an alarm system for the watchful hospital worker. According to a marketing manager from one of the major U.S. suppliers of home respiratory technologies, home equipment differs from hospital equipment in "having fewer bells and whistles." Only on occasion have technologies been redesigned for home use (e.g., the home morphine drip).

The high-tech equipment and procedures listed in Table 10.1 were those most often used in home health services in the 1980s (Haddad 1987), allowing very sick patients to recover or to prolong life and ease the pain of dying. The major high technologies in home care now include the intravenous administration of chemotherapy, antibiotics, and essential fluids; monitoring of newborns and adults who cease breathing (apnea) while they sleep; phototherapy for newborns with liver problems; nutrition through veins or the nose; and oxygen supplementation for those unable to breath unassisted (Barfoot and Ross 1988; Bontempo and Eggland 1988).[7]

The Broviac and Hickman catheters, and the Heparin lock, are essential components for giving nutrition in a way that bypasses both eating and repeated intravenous treatments. The infusion pump regulates the administration of pain-control drugs and chemotherapy solutions, and because it is mechanical rather than gravity-flow, allows patients to move around, travel to work, and live "normally" rather than be confined to a bed or chair.

The dates when these procedures were first used in the hospital and in the home are listed in Table 10.1. These dates support my view that it was not the availability of technology or its lack, but social policy that prevented and then allowed the expanded use of these in home health services. The dates listed in the table are based on reports in the medical literature showing when the technology or procedure was first used in the hospital and then in the home.

While it may be "cost saving" to insurers, home care has been profitable to U.S. industry. Corporations that sell technologies, supplies, and health services for home care have grown since the adoption of DRGs. In 1985, Baxter Travenal anticipated a tripling in its home health product sales. Six major home-care corporations (Baxter Travenal, Abbott Labs, American ContinueCare, Healthdyne, Omnicare, and Home Health Care of America) competed for a share of the home infusion market, expected to increase by 191 percent in three years (Edmonson 1985: 31–32). According to investment firms (the government keeps no records), home health expenditures on high technology increased from $3,067.7 billion in 1983 to $5,434.7 billion in 1987 (Roe and Schneider 1985: 52). Business analysts expect the market to grow from $3.9 billion in 1983 to $24.3 billion by 1995 (Edmonson 1985: 29). Even corporations that were active in business circles to curb health costs, such as the Washington Business Group on Health, reported that business investments were "penetrat[ing] home markets." Well they might: between 1983 and 1987, home health care spending on respiratory therapy grew by over 50 percent (from $370 million to $572 million), spending on

TABLE 10.1
Technology and Procedure Use-Dated

Procedure/equipment	Hospital use	Home use
Hemodialysis	1945[8]	1963–1964[2]
IV antibiotic therapy[a]	1964 + [17]	1974[14]
Cancer chemotherapy (portable infusion pump)	1963[19]	1979[12]
Apnea monitor[b]	1969[4]	1973–1974[9]
Phototherapy	1966[10]	1979[16]
Oxygen therapy	1956[11]	1965[11]
Ventilator	1952[13]	1957[1]
Broviac catheter	1972[3]	1972[3]
Heparin lock	1972[18]	1974[14]
Hickman catheter	1979[7]	1979[7]
Total parenteral nutrition	1967[5,6]	1970[15]

Note: Dates are of the publication in the medical literature that first reports the use of the procedure and/or equipment in hospital and home. Sometimes an earlier date is specified in the report itself. The documentation for this table was compiled by Sharon Smith and Jean Campopiano.

[a]Carbenicillin, used by Rucker and Harrison[14] for outpatient IV antibiotic therapy, was developed in 1964, but no clear date is available for when the drug was first used in hospital clinical trials.

[b]Apnea refers to the intermittent cessation of breathing.

Sources:

1. Affeldt, John E., Albert Bower, Clarence Dial, and Nobby Arata. 1957. "Prognosis for Respiratory Recovery in Severe Poliomyelitis." *Archives of Physical Medicine and Rehabilitation* (May) 38:290–295.
2. Blagg, C. R., R. O. Hickman, J. W. Eschbach, and B. H. Scribner. 1970. "Home Hemodialysis: Six Years' Experiences." *New England Journal of Medicine* 283(21):1126–1131.
3. Broviac, J. R., James J. Cole, and Belding H. Scribner. 1973. "A Silicone Rubber Atrial Catheter for Prolonged Parenteral Alimentation." *Surgery, Gynecology and Obstetrics* 136(4):602–606.
4. Daily, William, Marshall Klaus, and B. P. Meyer. 1969. "Apnea in Premature Infants: Monitoring, Incidence, Heart Rate Changes and an Effect of Environmental Temperature." *Pediatrics* 43(4):510–518.
5. Dudrick, S. J., D. W. Wilmore, H. M. Vars, and J. E. Roads. 1968. "Long Term Total Parenteral Nutrition with Growth Development and Positive Nitrogen Balance." *Surgery* 64(July):134.
6. Flack, Herbert L., John A. Gans, Stanley Serlick, and Stanley J. Dudrick. 1971. "The Current Status of Parenteral Hyperalimentation." *American Journal of Hospital Pharmacy* 28(5):326–335.

7. Hickman, Robert O., C. Dean Bruckner, Reginald Clift, Jean E. Sanders, Patricia Stewart, and E. Donnall Thomas. 1979. "A Modified Right Atrial Catheter for Access to the Venous System in Marrow Transplant Recipients." *Surgery, Gynecology, and Obstetrics* 148(6):871–875.

8. Jones, Katherine R. 1982. "Hemodialysis and Kidney Transplant Surgery." Pp. 175–183 in *Strategies for Medical Technology Assessment*. Washington, D.C.: Office of Technology Assessment.

9. Kelly, Dorothy H., Daniel Shannon and Kathleen O'Connell. 1978. "Care of Infants with Near-Miss Sudden Infant Death Syndrome." *Pediatrics* 61(4):511–514.

10. Lucey, Jerold, Mario Ferreiro, and Jean Hewitt. 1968. "Prevention of Hyperbilirubinemia of Prematurity by Phototherapy." *Pediatrics* 41(6):1047–1054.

11. Petty, Thomas L., and Louise M. Nett. 1983. "The History of Long-Term Oxygen Therapy." *Respiratory Care* 28(7):859–865.

12. Plasse, Terry, Takao Ohnuma, Howard Bruckner, Karen Chamberlain, Terry Mass, and James Holland. 1982. "Portable Infusion Pumps in Ambulatory Cancer Chemotherapy." *Cancer* 501:27–31.

13. Price, J. L. 1962. "The Evolution of Breathing Machines." *Medical History* 6(1):67–72.

14. Rucker, Ralph W., and Gunyon M. Harrison. 1974. "Outpatient Intravenous Medications in the Management of Cystic Fibrosis." *Pediatrics* 54(3):358–360.

15. Scribner, Belding H., James Cole, T. Graham Christopher, Joseph E. Vizzo, Robert Atkins, and Christopher R. Blagg. 1970. "Long-Term Total Parenteral Nutrition." *Journal of the American Medical Association* 212(3):457–463.

16. Slater, Lawrence, and M. Frederick Brewer. 1984. "Home Versus Hospital Phototherapy for Term Infants with Hyperbilirubinemia: A Comparative Study." *Pediatrics* 73(4):515–519.

17. Sneader, Walter. 1985. *Drug Discovery: The Evolution of Modern Medicines*. New York: John Wiley.

18. Stern, Robert C., Susan Pittman, Carl F. Doershuk and LeRoy W. Matthews. 1972. "Use of a 'Heparin Lock' in the Intermittent Administration of Intravenous Drugs: A Technical Advance in Intravenous Therapy." *Clinical Pediatrics* 11(9):521–523.

19. Watkins, Elton, Jr. 1963. "Chronometric Infusor—An Apparatus for Protracted Ambulatory Infusion Therapy." *New England Journal of Medicine* 269(16):850–851.

venal and nasal nutrition tripled (from $180 to $554 million), and home dialysis increased by 70 percent (from $246 million to $432 million). The Washington group cautioned that cost containment would determine the enthusiasm with which this growth was welcomed (Roe and Schneider 1985: 52).

USING THE TECHNOLOGY

"Technology" includes knowledge, procedures, and materials. Knowledge is broader than just how to use something; it includes information about the reasons for procedures and what patient symptoms require help from a professional. Procedures refer to how to use the materials (equipment and supplies) and rely on what are called *protocols*, which give each step and their timing in, for example, the administration of an

IV. The materials include such items as closures, solutions, syringes, alcohol, and dressings.

Medical technologies also embody social, political, and economic practices and ideologies. By this I mean that the availability of technologies for home use emerged from decisions about reimbursements, the right to health care, whether the sale of technology would increase corporate profits, and so on. As the home-care market expanded, suppliers competed with one another for buyers (i.e., home health agencies), sometimes bidding so low that the suppliers feared that the quality of patient care would be low too.

Medical technology may make it easier to do home care, but much early home care was done without equipment designed for the home. For example, the portability of machines for treating jaundiced premature babies has been reduced to the size of a large suitcase. Yet the first home dialysis machinery, widely used in home care, was large and unwieldy. Portable dialysis (what is called ambulatory peritoneal dialysis) allows patients to move around during treatments, but they are still restricted to their homes during the four to five times daily draining of their kidneys by the need for sterile conditions.

Home care is made easier for paid workers and family caregivers by detailed steps for caring, what are called standardized protocols, but the absence of protocols does not deter home care. For example, parenteral nutrition has been done in the home since the late 1970s, even though a standardized protocol for use in the home was not published until 1985. Prepackaged materials designed for hospital use have been followed by similar prepackaged sterile supplies for the home. Thus adult diapers, colostomy bags, packaged and sterile needles and bandages, premeasured antibiotics, packets of pain-control drugs for insertion into infusion pumps, premeasured drugs for IV chemotherapy, and IV pain medications all make home care easier. Before these goods were available, the RN and the family improvised, for example, measuring medications or using the family oven as a makeshift autoclave to sterilize needles and bandages.

GOING HOME SICKER AND TECHNOLOGY

We joke. We say, "Patients will go from intensive care to the home," or, "We will soon be operating on the patient's kitchen table." —Director, home health services

Home care today is more than a variation on the usual domestic chores of women: transporting, giving emotional and social support, home-making, and doing personal care. "Care" has come to encompass a new range of nursing–medical tasks. Family caregivers now monitor patients for a wide array of problems, everything from reactions to medication to major crises that require emergency readmission to hospital.

Family members, mostly women, use high-technology equipment to deliver treatments for acute as well as chronic conditions. To give such care, women must learn to use the technology designed by bio-medical engineers and physicians for use by registered and licensed nurses and therapists. According to one home health agency director (with an unflattering view of RNs), what patients and family caregivers must learn can be very technical but is easily taught because "even simple people can learn to do things that [hospital] nurses do." The work that family caregivers learn may be fairly simple, such as supervising breathing exercises, or may be complex, such as keeping equipment from being a conduit for dangerous bacteria into the heart. Caregivers supervise exercises and give mechanical relief to patients with breathing disorders, feed by tubes or IVs those unable to take food orally or digest normally, give intramuscular injections, and monitor patients who are getting antibiotic and chemotherapy treatments. Caregivers may rely on written instructions to check patient symptoms and decide if the symptoms call for readmission to the hospital.

RISKS IN USING HIGH TECHNOLOGY

The use of high technology in the home is not problem free. Susan Carter, a white BSN in home health, worried about nurse and patient safety. She believed that some RNs were uncertain about their proficiency in using high technology and their ability to teach it to others. As an activist in the American Nurses Association, Carter had received complaints from RNs about what they believed to be dangers to home patients. For example, some home patients depended on high technology, such as a constant mechanical supply of oxygen, for their lives. Their ventilators have back-up systems that kick in when there are power failures, but this may not lessen the anxiety of the RN, the family caregiver, or the patient, because the extensive back-up of the hospital is missing. Susan Carter described a young man who was sent home though he vomited every time his tracheal equipment was changed; he could have choked to death. While she continued her regular care for about forty other patients, she also "spent hours talking with the doctor, the family and so on, to try and get them to train her and the family properly." Finally, she refused to change the tube, saying that she did not know how to do it and so could not teach family members to do so. The physician was irate. Physicians do not make house calls, so the patient had to be readmitted to the hospital.

The use of the Broviac catheter also carries risk. RNs sometimes say that they themselves are nervous about using it even in the hospital, and are more nervous about it in the home. Inserted into an artery running into the heart, the catheter allows the RN to draw blood and give medications. The patient or caregiver must learn to use only sterile materials in the care of the catheter so as to prevent embolism and infection. Carter reported that the first patient in her agency to go home with a catheter was taught its care in the hospital by the physician and that the patient then taught the home health nurse. Whether this story is true or not, it reflects fears by RNs that they lack necessary skills. In Carter's agency in 1985, there was no inservice training for catheter care, and the RNs depended on physicians for their instruction.

Even IV antibiotic therapy, a relatively easy procedure, is not without complications. Among 310 patients in six health care services, despite a high "success" rate (cure without recurrence or death and savings to reimbursers of 69–79 percent over hospital care), patients experienced hospital readmission, chills, diarrhea, drug reactions, and problems with equipment and caregivers. To counter complications, the evaluators proposed a lengthy "instrument" for "quality assurance" and the control of potential problems in drug use, home management, and psychosocial and patient costs, but they questioned whether patients do better in the home than in the hospital (Dolbee and Creason 1988).

One RN described a patient with a leg amputation who was sent home six days after his operation. The stitches were still in the wound:

> He was discharged on a Friday, though we had all expected him to stay in hospital until Monday. He was sent home with ineffective pain medication, no commode, and no walker. He fell at home, the stump developed an infection, and I sent him back to the hospital for one week. The same intern who had sent him home without adequate technical support ripped out his stitches and sent him home the following Friday. I went out on Tuesday, and the patient again had an infection.

In Susan Carter's view, physicians and interns themselves do not have an adequate understanding of home care. Interns may discharge patients without recognizing that home care requires distinct treatments and concerns:

> I saw an eighty-nine-year-old woman with a Foley catheter [to drain the bladder] inserted because she was having trouble holding her urine. She was sent home with a little leg bag that had to be emptied every two hours. Nobody in the hospital told her to change to a big bag for the night, so she was getting up every two hours. A new doctor, not an intern, inserted the Foley, but he did not think about how totally limited this would make her homebound life, nor did he do education.

Other technologies that have been moved from hospitals to the home include convertors that produce oxygen from room air for use in respirators and ventilators. This reduces the risk of explosion and eliminates the need for regular home deliveries of oxygen. Apnea monitors are used in the home for both adults and newborns. The Hickman catheter and lines and the Heparin lock allow repeated access by RNs for medication and blood samples. The infusion pump regulates the dosages of antibiotics and pain-control medications. Even simple equipment, such as "hospital" beds, commodes, and "low-tech" items, make home care easier on patients and caretakers.[8]

LEARNING ABOUT THE NEW TECHNOLOGIES

Instructions are given by RNs to amateurs who are expected to learn procedures quickly and to care for family members with only intermittent supervision. RNs write out instructions for complex tasks and try to detail the symptoms that require emergency help. Home health RN Raye Knight describes the specifics: "The RNs teach the patient how to do their own IVs. They show them how to clean the Heparin-plug [that prevents blood clots] . . . and prevent clots from forming . . . to learn all of the procedures, to use pumps, how to use all of the supplies, and to keep track of what they need."

Caregivers may learn how to turn an invalid to prevent bedsores or how to use a Foley catheter to empty the patient's bladder, how to change dressings on an open wound or clean a line running into an artery. Family members learn from oncology, respiratory, and IV specialist RNs how to use and clean equipment, such as the infuser pump, intermittent positive pressure breathing equipment, and nasogastric tubes. Even family members who cannot speak English learn to care for sick relatives. One Vietnamese family, in which only the husband spoke English, learned to care for his dying wife. It took ten visits for the husband to learn the procedures for irrigating a Hickman catheter and for other family members to learn to give intravenous chemotherapy, pain-control medication, and monitor the wife for symptoms that might require emergency help.

Pauline Atwood describes the difficult work that family members are willing to do:

> About six months ago, an infant was sent home from our intensive neonatal care unit after being in the hospital about six months with "severe respiratory distress syndrome." The child needed oxygen and very careful administration of multiple medications in syringes and such, and special feeding. The child had a tracheotomy for breathing.
>
> Thirty years ago, nobody would have thought of sending such children home. Parents now take these children home and go through many sleepless nights until they work out a system of knowing when the child is in distress.

Family caregivers may also give treatments that are dangerous to the caregivers:

> Caregivers seem to be willing to take on such things as dealing with a catheter inserted into the hypatic artery [into the liver] for administering chemotherapy. A family was willing to take this on because the woman had only a few weeks of life left. The chemotherapy was more a comfort than still active treatment; it was to diminish symptoms. It was very risky and hazardous to them, but they were still willing.

The Irony Of Amateur Caregiving

The highest level of care being done is in the home. The people who are asked to do this are unskilled family members or minimum-wage workers.
—Wendy Jenkins, coordinator of major medical center, home health agency

Health care that is sold is embedded in elaborate state and federal regulations of training and licensing and in a hierarchy of responsibilities legally designated in "practice acts." These acts are state laws that specify a chain of command and detail the responsibilities of various health workers. For example, an act may state that RNs have the right to do IVs, but LPNs do not have the same right. RNs, and sometimes LPNs and even aides, learn to use complex medical technologies in inservice training workshops, supplemented by periodic retraining. Under cost containment, customary expectations about training and practice acts have been abandoned. In home care, the most skilled workers, RNs with the BSN degree, teach persons unskilled in health care—patients and family caregivers—to do technical nursing work. If family members cannot be trained and a patient is poor (receiving Supplementary Security Income, or SSI), a minimum-waged "chore worker" may be hired and trained by an RN to do the work. Thus federal regulations basically assume that nursing competence, supposedly learned only in formal training, can be reproduced easily. Regulations presume that in-hospital teaching of patients by RNs, during a period of likely emotional upset, and brief training of patients and family members in a few RN visits, result in sufficient skills.

Potential caregivers, however, may refuse to learn nursing procedures because of fears, resentments about being asked to care, and resentments against patients. One nurse described an elderly man whose wife "expressed her anger at years of a sour marriage by passively just not learning what needed to be done." Patients cope also with the empathetic limits of their spouses, even for trivial caregiving: a husband fussed about a week of meal making and clean-up because "my wife brought on her [bunion] surgery herself by wearing high heels." Some caregivers seem unable to learn the rigorous routine for sterilizing lines used for non-oral feeding or carry out the routines irregularly. Friends may need to be recruited to care for a sick person whose spouse is unwilling or unable to do so, or for someone who lacks family. The gay communities in San Francisco, Los Angeles, Portland (Oregon), and Seattle, among many other communities, have organized networks of helpers to care for men with AIDS. One RN recruited a neighbor to a "virtual lifetime commitment" of preparing insulin syringes for an elderly and blind diabetic woman who became ineligible for home care because she became "stable." The RN herself promised to be available for (free) emergency help.

Family members may be willing to do the work but may lack resources. Wendy Jenkins, a white coordinator of home-care services with thirty years in health work, explains:

> We see stress in the family which shows in the increase in the number of cases that require social services, the social workers attempting to bolster the family. Being a twenty-four-hour caretaker to a newly discharged

stroke patient who needs care, day and night, with no respite, is stressful. The caretakers cannot give the care; they disappear or they become stressed because of the financial situation, especially those people slightly over Medicaid's level.

Christine Michaels, a white RN in an HMO home-care department, explained that patients may feel overwhelmed if they are sent home after a stroke, with complicated dressing changes or incontinence. She says:

> Care is also frightening to the families, to have a terminal person at home or a person with a breathing problem or a bleeding problem. It's also lots of work. There are lots of little old ladies taking care of their husbands with strokes who do not have the money to have somebody come in to watch the patient, often with multiple and chronic problems, at night. They just suffer, take care of the patient, and don't sleep well. Home health aides do help, Medicare provides some, and non-Medicare plan patients [in this HMO] pay $3.75 per visit.

Some caregivers lack the time and energy to do adequate care. Some make long trips from their homes, after a day on the job or sandwiched between other pressing family tasks, to give care to a relative. Some caregivers are men who are unfamiliar with housekeeping and the basics of nursing and struggle to learn nursing routines along with how to shop and cook. Poverty makes some home care unsafe and unhealthy because of inadequate heating or bathing facilities in the home.

Some potential caregivers have their own health problems. A manager of a supplier of high-technology materials, which services patients on ventilators and respirators, described an eighty-year-old retired physician. Under ordinary circumstances, he would have been sent home months ago. But his wife's frail health prevented her from caring for him at home, so he remained in the hospital, and probably will until he dies, with his bills written off by the hospital as bad debts. Because of the low reimbursement given to nursing homes, none will accept this patient, and federal reimbursement policies prevent home health agencies from giving him the round-the-clock chore worker who would "substitute" for his wife.[9]

To meet their care needs, home health patients depend on a variety of community resources including counseling by RNs and organizations such as Catholic Services, the American Cancer Society, and the hospital's social service department. Yet adequate community services that provide meals, transportation, companionship, and other help are increasingly scarce as the agencies cope with budget cuts.

Patients and their informal caregivers face other problems. Bernice Slater, a white home health RN, described her attempts to help an elderly woman with a chronic condition, diabetes, cope with insulin injections and tests for blood glucose levels. The patient had limited vision, a common problem with diabetes. Because she had been diabetic for many years and "knew all about" the disease, Medicare would not pay for home visits except briefly after her diabetes had become unstable. The patient's physician wanted her blood glucose levels checked three times a day. The woman was able to prick her finger and put the blood on a test strip but was unable to read the results on the strip because of her limited vision. Slater says,

> I found a new machine [for monitoring the diabetes] called a glucose scanner that costs $250, but I got it used for $100. I would go back to the office screaming, "This is ridiculous, this woman is almost blind." I said that if something happened that she could always call on me, I would come over and fill her syringes. I left her my card and tried to reassure her.

RNs also worried about the ability of caregivers to learn to interpret symptoms, such as when bleeding from a wound is "too much" or when pain signals a crisis. Nurses discussed several cases that were receiving media attention during the months I was interviewing. For example, because a hospital would not admit a patient on the basis of his wife's request, he died twenty-four hours after his discharge from "in-and-out" surgery.

The lack of strong family support may mean the failure of home care. Wendy Carr, an RN who left home health because she was unable to accept Medicare and Medicaid limits on home health care, says, "I would teach a caretaker and come back to find a new caretaker and have to reteach. I might be forced to close the case [withdraw services] because Medicaid will not pay to have you teach several different caretakers every few weeks. Then the patient would get sicker and be readmitted to the hospital and we would start all over again."

Home health care has the *potential* to give patients care that makes them happier, if not "healthier," than hospital care. But this requires adequate levels of services. Otherwise, home health care may be a disappointment to both health workers and their patients and may be seen as a new "scam," a way of cutting federal aid and corporate costs at the expense of patients, their families, and home health workers.

Patients cannot get significantly more home care because they live alone or live-in family members cannot give them adequate care. Elderly patients may lie in bed surrounded by their own excrement until the RN arrives. Patients may go without food. Patients may be sent home without necessary equipment such as crutches, wheelchairs, or commodes. Wendy Jenkins describes her frustration at the lack of community resources for supporting home care: "I call Meals on Wheels because I discover a patient has not eaten for several days, and there is nobody to provide food. They can't come out because of a waiting list for four or five days, and I have to figure out what to do because obviously the patient cannot survive."

Patients are discharged to home health care in single-room-occupancy hotels without meal services being arranged. A home health RN cared for several men who could barely get to a nearby restaurant but forced themselves to do so to get food. But there is a "Catch 22" here. Trips for food make them technically not housebound and hence ineligible for home health services. RNs hide the problems these men face in home health care and seek remedies informally, without charting problems. Otherwise, they would endanger reimbursements to their agencies, and care to patients.

Reduction In Home Care

The DRG system, as expected, reduced hospital use. Occupancy rates declined from 75 percent in 1982 to 65 percent in 1987, while the number of beds used dropped from 1 million to .96 million (Russell 1989: 34). Home agencies therefore expected to care for many more patients, but the Health Care Financing Administration (HCFA) began to apply regulations aimed at preventing a compensating increase in home-care costs. Capitation (a flat fee) for Medicaid patients and stringent reimbursement policies threatened agency financial well-being. Sicker patients went home, and patient numbers still soared; staffing levels stayed constant.

Some RNs believe that the combination of discharging patients before their bodies have returned to normal and insufficient home services set up a cycle of hospital release and readmission. By 1985, federal and state agencies cut support services. For example, Medicare cut the length of aide visits from three or four hours to an hour and a half, making it difficult if not impossible for aides to do basic housekeeping tasks. According to one director of home care, Priscilla Green, her hospital reorganized the labor process, upgrading the responsibilities of all home health staff, including aides. RNs were expected to do case management, while aides were expected to do some RN tasks. Patients were now being sent home too sick for licensed nurses to make decisions about whether symptoms, as described on the telephone by a family caregiver, would call for hospital readmission. In response, the agency upgraded its telephone Nurse-Help service by replacing LPNs with RNs.

Home health departments also found themselves understaffed because of the larger workload that resulted from DRGs. RNs coped by making fewer visits to each patient. Coordinator Green spoke of the reductions in much the same way as employed mothers accept seeing their children less than they would like: "The nurses make up for the fewer visits by increasing the quality of the care given."

Grace Lowry, a director of a home health agency, saw the effect of understaffing differently: "We try to rush around and squeeze as much as possible into a visit, but it's very hard to do all the work that needs to be done."

New reimbursement policies in home health mean patients get reduced services despite their being very sick. Deena Rattner, a trained social worker who supervises home health aides, explained why her agency found itself at a disadvantage compared to newer, nonunion agencies with lower labor costs. In a 1985 experiment, Medicare used a flat reimbursement system on a capitation basis for patients who her agency served for fewer than six months. They continued a fee per visit for those served for a longer time. Many nonunionized agencies paid their staff on a per-visit basis and hence lowered their per capita costs. In addition, Medicare paid $938 per patient to Rattner's agency, though the agency's average cost was $50 more. To cope, the agency expanded aide work to include tasks once done only by RNs. For example, aides now change dressings.

Medicare intended to decrease fees by 8 percent in 1986. To cope with the expected loss, Rattner's agency was considering eliminating occupational and physical therapists, and social workers, with RNs doing all the work. Ironically, the agency had just added more social workers, anticipating that sicker patients would need complicated social support networks. In part, some RNs believe that they will now win a "turf battle." Those with a public health perspective believe that social workers and other ancillary health professionals usurped the work of RNs. Yet other home health RNs, viewing nursing as more technique and theory of recovery, complain of being overwhelmed by social service tasks (e.g., calling community agencies to find meal services).

Patient Concerns

Self-help first emerged in the 1960s. Feminist health clinics and the home-birthing movement run by nonphysicians were among the early grassroot actions. Consumer movements in the 1960s and 1970s wanted patients to have the right to home care as an alternative to hospitalization. Their demands were sidestepped or rejected outright. Patients found that reimbursement was hard to get for home-based treatment, and nursing care was denied. They could not get insurance coverage for nursing chronically or acutely ill children at home. Dying patients who preferred to be at home, and whose family or friends wanted to tend them, had to pay for most care themselves. It was unusual for patients with infections or limited health problems, who were otherwise able bodied, to be treated at home and have their bills paid by a third party. The public wanted less control by experts and more self-participation in decisions about care. Demands were not for home health care with minimal support services, the system that has emerged in the 1990s. Certainly advocates did not expect health professionals to retain control and third-party payers to have growing power over who gets care, where, and from whom. When federal legislation finally mandated outpatient treatments and made home care more economically advantageous than hospitalization for insurers, it was as a response to corporate demands for controlling health insurance costs and federal tax expenditures. Reduced decision making about care by health professionals, through flat fees, capped number of visits, and the like, was only one outcome of cost containment, and not a particularly desirable one to patients because it shifted access to care even more from patients to health professionals. That is, a physician or administrator might try to get more care for particular patients, but patients had no more control over decisions than before DRGs. Federal legislation also made third-party payers a more important gatekeeper on care by paying flat fees based on "average use," rather than on the particular needs of individual patients.

Home care was packaged by legislators, hospital administrators, and discharge planners as a benefit to patients: as assuring privacy, home comforts, and community and family support. Presumably it is highly moral because it shifts responsibility from institutions to the family, and it is sound psychologically because it lessens patient dependency and decreases the disorientation that the frail elderly may experience in hospitals. Much of what the protesting public had demanded in the 1970s was presented as available in home care, everything except a system of home care that meets the needs of patients and their caregivers.

If the new emphasis on home care undercuts the power of physicians and threatens the prestige of hospitals, it certainly reinforces the traditional view of, and oppressive demands on women in the family. With shorter hospital stays and more use of outpatient clinics, the work transfer is a crucial mechanism by which health care is delivered to increasing numbers of the elderly and the poor, and the younger well-to-do users of the U.S. health system.

The ideology of familialism supports cost containment, but, unfortunately, families in the United States are widely dispersed geographically, fractured by divorce into small units, and rebuilt by remarriage, second divorces, or informal partnerships into endless new patterns of familial ties. More women with family responsibilities are employed outside the home, supporting themselves and their children or working to keep up with the increased costs of housing and declining wages.

What RNs do must not be overlooked: they enter into the "informal" network when their work extends beyond paid working hours and when their "after hours" efforts may be what makes surviving home care possible for the most needy patients.

This chapter has discussed the content of women's work in home health care, the result of the reorganized labor process in hospitals. Hospitals have been increasingly subject to principles of capitalist rationality as the health industry has shifted from a nonprofit to a for-profit system. Women's home work is the end part of caring labor that begins in the paid workplace. In the home, women are the workers necessary for the completion of tasks begun in hospitals and other health facilities.

11
Conclusions

I have tried to understand more fully the connections between changes in the domestic work of women as family members and changes in the daily work of women as service employees in two industries, retailing and health care. I call the connecting process the *work transfer*, by which employers selectively and even capriciously reorganize the labor process. They eliminate paid workers, but some work still needs doing. They reduce the number of paid workers, but some work still needs doing. They retain paid workers, but assign them new work, taking away some of their old work, but the work still needs doing. The doers are largely women. They assume (as others assume) that they must complete the work as an integral part of their domestic responsibilities—not as an extra, not as new work.[1] I have tried to make explicit the power of major corporations and the state in a liberal capitalist society to reshape the workplace and family life and to do so by decommodifying wage labor and appropriating the nonwage labor of women family members to take its place. Women experience the consequences of the work transfer twice, first as wives, mothers, and adult daughters and daughters-in-law; and second as paid service workers.

Appropriation occurs deliberately when firms reorganize the labor process and deliberately transfer work to customers and clients. It occurs inadvertently when organizations, seeking to adjust to economic crises, change the labor process among service workers and reduce services to customers and clients. Men's nonwage labor also may be appropriated, but much less often than that of women, who are responsible for most of the work of social reproduction. The content of unpaid work is thus a result of changes in paid work. Unpaid workers must readjust their lives to accommodate the new work; paid workers must adjust their work lives to accommodate a new labor process and perhaps unemployment, a speed-up, or part-time work.

I hope that my analysis shows that the boundary between *work* in the so-called private sphere and the so-called public sphere is nonexistent or, at most, highly permeable and that the relationship between unpaid and paid work is one of interdependence and reciprocal influences.

I have argued that unpaid labor has been appropriated by capital and the state and has been used to complete labor processes begun by paid workers. I bring in a neglected dimension, the direct contributions that women's unpaid labor makes to the ever-changing domination of life by capitalist institutions in the United States, to a sex–gender system that oppresses, and to racism (including ethnicity) that harms people cruelly. Women's unpaid labor completes labor processes that are fundamental to capitalist systems of distribution of goods. Retailing is one example. Also, I argue that women's unpaid labor completes a labor process in a service industry en route to "corporatization." My example here is health services, which have been substantially transformed from nonprofit "human" services into a for-profit industry.

The success of a labor process, the work transfer, relies on and reinforces the current system of class, sex–gender, and race and ethnic inequalities. Within the bounds of privilege and inequality, women's unpaid labor is necessary for the completion of the work of paid employees, usually other women. Privileged relations allow some women to forgo doing much unpaid labor, and vast social inequalities force other women to do more than the average share of unpaid work in retailing and health services.

Work life, personal life, and family life are interwoven. First, in employment, with variations by class and race, most women are at a disadvantage compared to most men. A sizable percentage of women work in female-typed occupations, such as retail sales and nursing, where earnings average less than in male-dominated jobs. Women earn less than men in all jobs (Reskin and Hartmann 1985). Women of color face additional problems: segregation in female-typed occupations, both in older ones such as nursing and in newly emerging ones such as computer programming (Glenn and Tolbert 1987), and they usually earn less than white women in nonsegregated jobs (Gwartney-Gibbs and Taylor 1986), regardless of skills and experience (England 1984). Second, while husbands may share some of the work of social reproduction with their wives, women remain mainly responsible for childcare, housework, and social relations with kin and neighbors, schools, and health care institutions (Hochschild 1989). Women's responsibility for unpaid work influences their experiences as paid workers by limiting their hours for rest and recreation, as well as for job training and other after-hours job activities. The more money that women earn compared to their partners, the less they conform to traditional expectations about unpaid work (among other activities) in the home. The more economically independent women are, the easier they find it to challenge oppressive social relations by personal or collective actions, in the household (Dill 1986; Zavella 1987), the workplace (Janiewski 1985; Sacks 1988) and politics (Ehrenreich 1985). Nonetheless, unpaid domestic labor remains as much a female-typed job as clerical work, nursing, and public school teaching.

Self-Service: Ambiguous Autonomy

Is self-service good or bad? As a form of work, it is neither. In a society in which economic exploitation of the labor of some for the good of others is not the rule, self-service might be a way by which the community (or individuals) shares limited resources or shifts labor from a less to a more valued activity. Indeed, even in a society in which labor is exploited, self-service has value for families and friends doing the work and those needing it done; it may knit ties among family members, accelerate recovery from illness, and give people a way of meeting emotional and material needs. Nevertheless, self-service may restrict and harm women doing paid work and unpaid domestic labor. Unpaid domestic labor expands without a sufficient infrastructure of support or contracts and disappears without employed women having alternative jobs.

Skepticism about self-service as a principle for organizing women's work in a capitalist society is not a plea for a return to low-wage women's labor in stores, hospitals, offices, and social service agencies. That would hardly be a satisfactory solution for women workers. But there may be alternative ways of serving families, of meeting needs for assistance in which the exploitation of unpaid and paid labor is eliminated.

Regardless of its benefits, self-service depends on a more or less invisible use of woman's labor, a use for which women are not rewarded; and it may have dire consequences for those whose labor is replaced by self-service. The work transfer itself must be recognized as a way by which capitalism and the state attempt to lessen their responsibility for social reproduction, and then label this a social good. The alternative to self-service is not a return to the presupermarket neighborhood store or extensive hospitalization for any and all medical procedures. Nor is it to return to the time when low-wage workers had their labor exploited by a corporation.

By and large, Americans apparently have eagerly, or with only minimum resistance, accepted self-service in retail stores. And they have accepted the shift to early hospital discharge and increased outpatient services that transforms the home into a minihospital. Various ideologies may make self-service acceptable, ideologies about the right of capital to set employment levels and control the distribution of health services. For example, the widely held belief in the virtually absolute right of corporations to decide on the labor process makes job loss and job degrading acceptable to most Americans, justified by corporate demands for efficiency and corporate definitions of acceptable profit levels. Only a comparatively few retail unions and some community groups have worked, jointly or separately, against these absolutist rights and have tried to circumscribe corporate power. At the level of the customer, such beliefs as a value on self-reliance and self-control, fears of the impersonality of the large organization, and a view of personal service as debasing the server may make self-service seem desirable.

Capital and Women's Work

I have considered for-profit enterprises and those becoming for-profit—in the manufacturing, distribution, and service sectors—that dominate retailing and health care. These groups inordinately dominate the practices by which criteria are selected and used for spending on social programs. Early in the twentieth century, the use of unpaid and paid labor in tandem in retailing emerged largely in vertically integrated systems of production and distribution. In health services, after significant corporatization of the health services industry, the use of unpaid labor to *replace* paid labor emerged importantly in the late 1970s and increased in the mid-1980s.

In both instances, the replacement reversed the expected and typical process of the commodification of labor in capitalism. That is, over four

centuries labor power moved from being nonwaged, done for obligation, barter, or as part of familial duty, to being waged.

In retailing, the adoption of the work transfer was a private decision, fought over largely by retailers, hardly a response to buyer demands for freedom from salesclerks; it was accomplished with only
minor resistance from unions. Corporate firms in the *Fortune* 500, the
backbone of the most influential firms, were the driving force for cost
containment in health services. They were interested both as investors
in health services and equipment and as purchasers of considerable por-
tions of health insurance. They also pursued a fairly narrow conception
of social entitlements and resisted tax expenditures on the poor and the
elderly.

What does *domination* mean? Partly, I refer to the mechanism by
which firms invest or fail to invest in physical plants, training, research
and development, and distribution. These areas set the stage for control
of the labor process. "Control" includes legal entitlements, which are
taken for granted in much social analyses: the corporate right to "own
jobs"; the near-total control, as union power declined, over the gender,
race, and ethnic composition of the workforce. "Control" includes the
inalienable rights of employers to hire and fire workers, increasingly
strengthened by "bread and butter" unionism and weakened by gutted
affirmative action programs. Employers are able to set the size of their
workforce and change its skill levels, gender composition, wages and
benefits, pensions, and so on. Their control extends to the exercise of
political power and influence by lobbying, political action contributions, participation in the selection of candidates, and a new weapon:
lawsuits against citizen-action groups.

The power of capitalism is exercised through *cultural hegemony* too.
It occurs through the naturalization of complex social meanings. Capitalist organizations and goals, struggles, crises, and victories, and most
important, their effects on the everyday lives of people, are portrayed as
inevitable, as natural. Shared ideas, understandings, interpretations, and
perspectives are embodied in political discussions and beliefs about the
social, physical, and biological worlds, in the criteria for distinguishing
knowledge (assumed to be unbiased) from *ideology* (assumed to be infused with political and social passion and hence in error). Beliefs are
presented about mass culture and high art, the political world and personal life, and the social relations of gender, race, and ethnicity. And
social meanings confirm the domination of social life in the United

States by setting the needs of capitalist firms as the fundamental criteria for evaluating just about all manner of social life. In most liberal capitalist democracies, cultural hegemony includes a purported commitment to tolerance for dissenting opinions (within circumscribed limits), and sometimes for political parties' sharply contrasting social goals. By comparison, the United States, has a single political party with two branches, since the Democrats and Republicans differ primarily on strategies, not in commitment to the goals of capitalism. Cultural hegemony is not monolithic in the United States. But, only minimal physical coercion is needed or used, since the wide acceptance of shared social meanings maintains social order on behalf of one sector of the society: corporate capitalism.

A chain of relationships links corporate interests to retail workers, nursing workers, unpaid family workers, and buyers and patients. Strategies used by corporate leaders, whether in the retail trade or health services industries, by vendors of health-related goods and health insurance, and by retail employers all aim to increase capital accumulation. As the issue of the legitimacy of the state has faded, social expenditures have been attacked mercilessly and the American welfare state, however much a pale image compared to the Western European states, is being dismantled. Health services, among other services, have become an attractive area for capital investment, and investors have sought "rational" organization.

Ideologies of "professionalism," "self-care," "personal responsibility," and an idealization of the homemaker in charge of consumption justify shifts from one paid worker to another, and from paid to unpaid workers. The reorganization of the labor process and the ideological justifications for reorganization used by capitalists, nursing leaders, and managers suggest that some sociological theorizing needs modification.

Trends in women's paid employment under capitalism pressure women to do paid work, weakening distinctions between the public and private spheres of work. Woman's world is now firmly in both realms, and the separation of paid from unpaid work is outdated imagery. The changes in the content of domestic work and in paid employment means that most women during the course of their lives will experience fully the contradictions of life in capitalist society. The belief in the home as a haven is mythic. Women must now maintain their traditional responsibilities for the household (there is little evidence of any significant shift in the gender division of labor in the home), but the double day is normalized because women increasingly are expected to do paid labor outside the household, regardless of family responsibilities. Also, women are the backbone of the volunteer force in the United States, the source of much of the labor that runs cultural institutions such as museums and symphonies, substitutes for paid aides in the schools, and provides personal contact and nurturing in hospitals. To these widely recognized categories of work in capitalist societies must be added the unpaid labor of women in consumption.

Guided by the drive to accumulate, capitalists strive to decrease the wage bill (earnings and benefits) except in times of rapid expansion when they see rising labor costs as a minor cost of doing business and high wages as fueling consumption. The decommodification of labor that shifts once-paid-for work to women as family members is an anomaly in the historical emergence of capitalism because it is a departure from the commodification of labor power, goods, and services. Generally, therefore, decommodification is invisible. It appears to us as an accommodation to crises in the service sector, where considerable work exists that resembles tasks women do as part of their socially assigned domestic responsibilities. Wives and mothers meet the myriad needs of other family members by mediating between the marketplace and the household. Of course, the resemblance is to once-paid-for labor in the marketplace. That is, women mediate because family members do not directly consume clothing, household furnishings, and most forms of entertainment in the marketplace. Most consumption for households is mediated by the actions of their members, most often by wives and mothers. For example, in mediating between the retail trade industry and the household, women buy raw food and prepare it for consumption, even if only by ensuring that all the components for eating are present. In mediating between the health care system and the household, women transport children to medical offices, buy pharmaceuticals, care for children and partners in the household, and later assume responsibilities for aging parents. The decommodification of labor and the subsequent reorganization of the labor process regulate only how much work women do, not whether or not they labor in order to consume services bought in the marketplace.

Periods of crises lead capitalists to use a short-term strategy of decommodifying labor: crises include labor shortages accompanying rapid growth in consumption. There is no growth in what employers view as an acceptable labor force. For example, expanding consumption in the

South led to the first successful chain of self-service grocery stores in the United States; self-service permitted store owners to avoid hiring black women and men as salesclerks serving white customers. Labor shortages resulted also from expanding opportunities for workers outside the retail trade industry. Decommodification during World Wars I and II solved the problem of the shrinking labor pool, which led workers to press for higher wages. In health services, a different crisis sparked the decommodification of labor: the movement of capital into a sector that had been protected from "capitalist rationality" by being a human service subsidized by the state rather than an "industry" bent on profits.

Health care has long been profitable to physicians as practitioners and as hospital and nursing-home owners, and more recently to pharmaceutical manufacturers. Until the mid-1960s, the health services industry was not an attractive investment however. It became so as the federal government began to underwrite the cost of health care for the elderly and the very poor. Ironically, government subsidies for health care attracted major corporate investors, transforming the industry from a public human service to a private, for-profit industry that sells health care as other industries sell guns, autos, VCRs, and housing. Today, few human services escape the impact of private capital, probably only those provided through local taxes, such as most public schools, and then only because their uncertain funding by school districts makes them unattractive to large-scale investors.

Public Versus Private Spheres

I reject the conventional social science view that women's domestic work is directly for the family and only indirectly for capital as an artifact of sexism and a blindness to how women's domestic labor has been forced into the labor process outside the home. Women must work in order to buy goods and services. The concept of social reproduction captures only the indirect contribution that women (as wives and mothers) make in their daily routines to the maintenance of capitalism.

I reject also the view that the family and hence women's domestic work is "in" and "for" the private sphere and that only paid work is in the public sphere. Daily life has been organized by the decisions of corporations and state and federal agencies so that women's unpaid work outside the household becomes a critical aspect of the contemporary cycle of production and distribution in capitalism, the final step in purchasing and using goods and services. There is no need to argue that women's work connects to capitalism through social reproduction only "in the last analysis." There is no need to argue that women's domestic labor is only embodied as dead labor within the living labor of workers today and in the future labor of the generation women raise. Instead, we can look directly at the present material conditions of women as buyers and see that women's work is essential to retailing and health services.

The ideologies of convenience, personal control, free choice, and cost savings to consumers may make self-service palatable to women. These ideologies fit well with those that legitimate women being in charge of a presumed private household, that applaud women heads of households for their willingness to include new tasks as part of their domestic responsibilities. These ideologies are important because capital and the state, under cover of intermittent worldwide crises, use the work transfer as a short-term strategy to cut labor costs and social entitlements. The work transfer is put forth as beneficial to family members, the community, and the unpaid workers themselves. Many shifts have occurred: budget cuts have meant that responsibilities have shifted from teachers to parents in public schools; cuts in funding of legal services for the poor have led to training sessions in do-it-yourself law for battered women and poor tenants facing eviction. These shifts rely on women as family members doing more unpaid work and mask how cuts in the welfare state rely on women's unpaid work.

What this means for women must be recognized. Work transfers are mainly to wives, mothers, and other women with family responsibilities. Of course, everyone in the United States experiences the work transfer to some extent. The increased use of the work transfer in the public sector suggests that analysis (and political organizing) ought to take into account this exploitation of women's labor.

A convergence is occurring in conditions of employment in retailing and health care for women, especially affecting women of color and others in low-grade jobs: low-wage, part-time, and temporary work with no or minimal benefits. The feminization of retailing accompanied a change in the structures of the workforce: from clerk to less-skilled cashier. Women workers in retailing retain the qualities of a reserve army of labor, where a majority work part-time and seasonally, do not earn a reasonable living, and rotate in and out of the workforce as a response to employers' needs, which are themselves shaped by business cycles.

In nursing, women workers are experiencing vast changes in the labor process. The number of lower-grade workers is growing at a faster rate than others, and middle-grade workers are facing job loss while upper-grade workers face job expansion and a speed-up. Health workers are increasingly part-time and temporary: in 1985, about 20 percent of hospital RNs, and nearly half of all health workers in home health, were employed part-time or as temporary workers not entitled to job security or fringe benefits (Szasz 1990: 200). Two-tier wage and benefit systems are being adopted, and productivity measures are used widely to evaluate the work of professional workers, who are also being threatened by competition from "physician extenders." The nursing shortage, tax expenditures, hospital costs, and insurance payouts would, of course, be much greater for the same level of care if work had not been shifted to women in the household.

Home health care is not automatically cheaper than hospitalization, as industry and government had expected and predicted. Partly this is so because home health equipment and service vendors maximized their profits by charging prices for goods and services that eventually outraged federal administrators (i.e., renting commodes for home health care as if these were made of gold). But it is also because the discharge of very sick patients to their homes has been done in tandem with expensive paid health services and equipment, and perhaps more hospital readmissions.

Theoretical Implications

IDEOLOGIES ABOUT COSTS

Retailers presented self-service as a way to accomplish great financial savings for customers, though the savings were mainly in employers' labor costs at the price of increased unpaid labor by housewives. Self-service was presented as in the best interests of the customer: a way to gain personal control, freedom from interference, privacy from salesclerks, the ability to gather the information needed for decisions on self-service buying (actually, self-service *selling*). Similar interpretations were later invoked to justify more work for patients and caregivers.

These are minor points compared to the major one that Americans cannot afford the current costs of health care. Public debates about health care accuse nonprofit hospitals of having been greedy. That may have been so, but their greediness was not in the interests of high profits but for more technology, better buildings, experiments in care, and, no doubt, higher physicians' earnings. In contrast, for-profit health corporations have been greedy for profit. Profit emerged as an issue only as private investors sought to use federal funding of health services to invade the not-for-profit public sector. These investors succeeded in moving health care from the public nonprofit sector to the private, for-profit sector. Along the way, they made health care "too expensive."

I cannot overemphasize that while changes in the labor process in health services may be framed as cost savings to "society," the changes are prompted by *corporate* attempts to accomplish two goals: (1) to further capital accumulation and increase profits, and (2) to shift the responsibility for social reproduction to workers and their families. What is ignored in corporate attempts to contain rising health service costs is that the ultimate financial beneficiaries of spending are some of the leading U.S. corporations and their investors. Neither the well-insured sick nor the indigent get richer with rises in health care costs. The rising cost of health services provide modest benefits to most health service workers, physicians, distributors of supplies, ancillary staff, construction workers, small manufacturers of technology, and so on. The major producers of pharmaceuticals, and the major conglomerates that manufacture high-tech diagnostic and treatment equipment and supplies, reap the largest single share of U.S. spending on health care. Yet these high levels of spending on health services have not led to better health for Americans.

Expensive technologies are profitable to corporations. It will be interesting to see just how much "cost containment" will be tolerated by American corporations before a shrinking domestic market for health goods threatens profits. Indeed, consumers, faced with increased payments, may become just as acute shoppers for health services as for automobiles, with equally unsatisfactory results for mainstream American health service industries.

IDEOLOGIES ABOUT THE LABOR PROCESS

Hospital administrators and managers in corporate-owned facilities face investor demands to curtail costs and increase profits. Public hospitals have been forced to curtail costs to survive DRGs and an accelerated corporate takeover of health services. A ready-made ideology of RN professionalization is used by managers to justify both changes in the labor process and the expansion of RN work. The insistence of nursing leaders on creating distinctions between "professional" and "technical" nurses makes it easy for managers to justify increases in RN responsibilities and decreases in ancillary staff. Hence the elimination of respiratory therapists and aides can be justified by the need for RNs to do "total care" if physicians and administrators are to give nurses the professional recognition they seek. "Autonomous function" without ancillary staff is expected of RNs faced with a lack of ward clerks, therapists, aides, and so forth. Physicians, however, are not expected to understand reductions in their support staff (e.g., RNs, receptionists, and secretarial help as a reflection of their autonomy). Radiologists, for example, are not expected to do their own typing or take X-rays to demonstrate "autonomy." Instead, hospital administrators report that physicians, displeased with staff reductions, need to be convinced of the long-run benefits of cost containment.

Ideologies about consumer self-help have been coopted and transformed into "self-care" to justify more outpatient and home care. Self-care at home and outpatient treatment may seem to be responses to two decades of criticism, ranging from protests against the medicalization of everything to a rejection of medical care and concern about emotional effects of lengthy hospitalization on the elderly. The counterculture and the women's movement attacked the efficacy of medical judgments, the greediness and sexism of physicians, and narrow concepts of health. The call by the public, however, was for the patient's right to know, to make decisions about care, and to have home care with adequate support. The current response to self-care is tangential to most of these criticisms and is more akin to the notorious "deinstitutionalization" of the 1960s, when patients were dumped into the community.

The Labor Process

The loose boundary between public and private spheres, the decommodification of labor, the reversal of the detailed division of labor, and site specialization are interwoven. The decommodification of labor power and the work shift to women as family members show how permeable are the boundaries between the public and the private, and between paid and unpaid labor. The reorganization of work in the retail store permits a reshaping of its workforce, shifting from clerks with a wide array of skills to less-skilled cashiers to further deskilled cashiers by the use of electronic scanners. The reorganization of work in the hospital depends on the redistribution of work between the paid staffs in hospital and home care and between paid staff and unpaid domestic workers.

THE DECOMMODIFICATION OF LABOR

Marxist theory treats capitalism as exhibiting a one-way trend: toward increased commodification. My analysis suggests that the process can be reversed when it is useful to capitalists, administrators, and managers to do so. The long-term trend of capital will continue to be to commodify labor power as well as goods and services. In an expanding economy, higher wages and high employment rates in the service sector are not just "tolerated" by employers, but contribute to capital accumulation. In a period of contraction and declining profits, however, the decommodification of labor power can be a tempting and useful cost-cutting strategy for capital, with consequences for both the paid and unpaid work of women. Insofar as service work is not a lucrative source of capital accumulation, unpaid work will likely continue to be a substitute for once-commodified labor. This has been true in retailing, where since 1912 retailers have inserted the customer into the labor process to solve a spate of crises: rising labor costs, declining sales, and the economic collapse of the Great Depression. The health care analogs of self-service are early patient discharge, outpatient treatment, and care by family members. In health care, corporations have been pressing for "cost containment" since shortly after Medicare was established in 1965. Corporate investments and corporate interests in cost containment have been at cross-purposes, with the former interested in higher profits and the latter in reduced federal spending on social programs. A compromise has been attempted: decreased use of hospitals (nonprofits and for-profits bearing equal shares of cost reductions), but initially without a decline in health expenditures. One tactic has been cost shifting, that is, asking workers to pay a larger proportion of fees or insurance premiums. The other has been work shifting, with the care of the sick going back to the vaguely labeled "community."

Finally, paid workers may voluntarily do work they are no longer "supposed to do"—tasks eliminated from their job descriptions—to curtail operating costs by reducing or keeping constant the size of the workforce. Therefore the activities of paid workers also blur the boundaries between the spheres of paid and unpaid labor.

THE DETAILED DIVISION OF LABOR

Theorists of the labor process posit the detailed division of labor, subsequent deskilling, and the degradation of work to be a one-way process and a well-tested strategy used by capitalists to lower the wage bill and divide workers to discourage solidarity actions. For most jobs, these theorists are probably correct. In human services, however, the reversal of the detailed division of labor can be used to cut corporate costs.

In hospitals, the labor process changes by the elimination or reduction of staff and the reassignment to RNs of tasks allocated earlier to ancillary staff or other nursing workers. Some RN tasks are reduced or eliminated because of rising patient acuity. But if work needs doing, the RN may be the only worker present to do it. Other work once done in hospitals may change. Nursing of the acutely ill and their return to normal body functioning now takes place routinely in nursing homes or home care, though it once was done in hospitals. The work of caring for the sick does not disappear. Changes in the labor process create new work for home-care nurses and aides, nurse assistants, and patients' families, friends, and neighbors.

Managers attempt an economical use of labor through site specialization. A core of nursing work is done at all sites (hospitals, nursing homes, outpatient clinics, patients' homes) so that some work is done by highly trained and well-paid nurses in one site (hospitals), but less-trained and less-well-paid nursing workers perform in other sites (nursing home, patients' homes). Less-skilled nursing work is reassigned across the spectrum of the hierarchy; for example, RNs and health aides both do bed baths, feeding, bedpans, and linen changes. Some work may be done by RNs only in hospitals, but not in home care. Even that distinction fades as complicated and dangerous procedures such as intravenous chemotherapy are done by RNs with the BSN degree, and respirators are used by family members in home care.

JOBS VERSUS OCCUPATIONS

Polarization occurs within health services. The levels of schooling, skills, earnings, and status of nursing personnel has risen, although some jobs have been downgraded. Hence, while there are more RNs with doctorates and masters', and bachelors' degrees than ever before, there is also a higher proportion of RNs with the two-year associate degree in nursing. Nursing personnel include a much larger proportion of the lowest-grade worker, the aide, than ever before. RNs face a new lower-grade hospital worker, the "registered care technologist," trained with the support of the American Medical Association to alleviate the RN shortage. Even within job levels, there are variations: the battle to define "professional" and "technical" nurses may appear to have been won by RN educators insofar as most states accept the view that entry-level RNs should have BSN degrees. In practice, however, the RN shortage is too acute for hospitals to act on this principle. Deskilling, downgrading, and polarization do not occur between or within jobs in any simple way; occupation and job levels within each segment have to be examined case by case.

Site specialization may make solidarity across class and racial–ethnic lines and the use of nursing associations as political tools of change increasingly difficult. Mergers between hospitals and between visiting nurse agencies and hospitals have been carefully crafted by lawyers to eliminate unions. For example, unionized visiting nurse agencies merge into nonunionized hospitals, while nonunionized visiting nurses are not allowed to join existing unions in the hospitals into which their associations merge. "Troublemaker" BSN nurses report being encouraged to leave their hospital positions, where they have more chance to organize workers, for home care, where they will work in relative isolation from others. The physical dispersal of visiting nurses may make collective action more difficult in home care than in hospitals. And distinctions in class and race do the same. American corporate decisions about health services affect many more people than the patients. Most health workers are women, and many are women of color, likely to be in poorly paid jobs. In home care, women "care" for free. Changes in health services are an issue for working-class women employed within and outside the health services industry.

"Woman" as a Concept: Female Solidarity

The division of labor among women in the workplace underlines the limits on using "woman" as an analytical concept. "Woman" may be useful as a political concept for arguing in the academy for women's studies and for scholarly studies of females. But my analyses of women's experiences with work demonstrate far-reaching class and racial–ethnic variations. Diverse interests between women of different classes and races, between patients and workers, and between the paid and unpaid workers make it impossible to do an analysis of a single gender-based experience.

Nursing personnel are fractionalized by many issues, whatever common experiences they share as women: there are differences between RN nursing leaders compared to staff nurses, BSNs compared to other

RNs, RNs compared to LPNs and aides, and LPNs compared to aides. Cross-cutting, intensifying, and interacting with these occupational-based differences are those of class, race, and ethnicity. Nursing workers exemplify how capital and the ideologies that legitimate racial, ethnic, and class subordination set women against other women. Sociologists and ideologues of capitalism have used "meritocratic" principles to justify occupational differentiation, social inequality, oppression, and exploitation. When women workers face the capitalist workplace and managerial actions that result in job elimination, downgrading, burnout, occupational hazard, job expansion without extra pay, a two-tier wage system, and technological displacement, they react as women who are "workers," and workers in particular grades from particular social classes and racial–ethnic backgrounds. The recognition of diversity means understanding women's relationships to one another, as well as to men, and within and across the boundaries of multiple domains.

The postindustrial economy has not curtailed service work for the public. Instead, it has depended on the free labor of women as members of households. This transformation drew on the ideologies of gender responsibility and individualism and supported anarchy in the marketplace. That is, any service work could be transferred to customers with the disingenuous offer of freedom. Most of the changes supported the concept of the isolated customer, rather than a community of buyers seeking a social good. Within the framework of capitalist production, this "consumer" experience paralleled that of wage workers. Just as workers had no inherent right to a job, buyers had no inherent right to goods or services that met real social as distinct from invented individual needs.

Appendix,
Notes,
References,
and Index

Appendix

A. Methods

In the tradition of qualitative and historical comparative research, I present a theoretical analysis that merges prior understanding with unanticipated observations. Those unexpected observations are a major reason for doing qualitative research. To learn about the organization and reorganization of work, I used semistructured and open-ended conversations ("interviews") with women and men who work in the health services industry. Using interviews as well as historical documents, census materials, and some content analysis of trade publications, I lay out a sociological understanding of historical changes in women's paid and unpaid labor.

Data about current changes in the labor process draw mainly from open-ended interviews conducted in California with fifty-three persons I located through referrals, and from a dozen other interviews done over several years in New York, Oregon, and Massachusetts. I worked in two ways, from the top grade down and the mid–bottom grades up, to maximize mix and minimize interviewing persons within the same (perhaps) homogeneous network. I sought interviews "from the top down," starting my 1985 research with an interview with a hospital administrator who had been president of a district hospital for over twenty years, and who referred me to other hospital administrators. He and other administrators referred me to their assistant administrators and to nursing managers. From my various university affiliations (Harvard University, University of Calfornia, Berkeley and San Franciso, and Portland State University), I received referrals to deans of nursing schools, elected officers in nurses' associations, RN and other nursing educators. I interviewed coordinators of visiting nurses associations, with and without referrals, and branch managers of high-technology hospital and home-care suppliers. Working "from the bottom up," I asked acquaintances and friends in each geographical region to refer me to staff nurses (RNs, LPNs) in acute-care hospitals and home health care agencies, when possible, in the same workplaces where I had interviewed administrators and upper-level managers. I always asked those whom I interviewed for referrals to persons who "might have a different view than you do."

A major limit on referrals was some lack of representativeness by class, race and ethnicity. As a white woman, I began by getting referrals from mostly whites, and I found it difficult to get many referrals to people of color. Most nursing managers were white, and referred me to white workers, who referred me to other whites. In California in 1980, among employed women, African Americans were less than 7 percent of RNs, 31 percent of licensed nurses and 33 percent of aides. Hispanics were about 4 percent of RNs, 8 percent of licensed nurses, and 11 percent of aides. Asian women were 11 percent of employed RNs, 10 percent of licensed nurses and 11 percent of aides (see, U.S. Department of Commerce, *1980 Census of Population and Housing, Census Tracts*, San Francisco–Oakland, CA. SMSA PHC 80-2-231: August 1983). I do not know the percentage of home-care RNs who were women of color. In one HMO home health care agency, African American women were reportedly about one-half of RNs, while most aides were African American and most whites were RNs. I was not referred to women of color often, including by an African American woman who coordinated a major agency, and an activist African American LPN, both of whom I interviewed. I did get some information about racism in the workplace by asking direct questions.

Also, I had trouble getting interviews with many aides. I used referrals from both agency coordinators and from LPNs, but was "stood up" by aides more than by workers in other grades. Of course, administrators gave interviews during their working hours, while staff nurses and other workers could give me time only after working hours, except for the interviews arranged by home-care administrators with aides.

I interviewed health service workers in a highly urbanized West Coast SMSA in 1985 and did interviews in 1983 and 1984 with nursing educators and RNs in two western states and two eastern ones. In 1988, I interviewed several branch managers of major American home-care high-tech suppliers in the Pacific Northwest about their companies and about how high-tech equipment was introduced to new patients and serviced. On the East Coast, I interviewed nursing educators and a nursing manager in an experimental-care unit where family members are twenty-four-hour-a-day caretakers.

I asked women and men about their jobs as unit and department managers, staff registered nurses (RNs) and licensed nurses (LPNs), certified nurses' assistants (CNAs) and home health aides (HHAs). In open-ended interviews ranging from a single session of one to two hours to two or three sessions of three or more hours, I asked about the nursing work done by patients' families, friends, and neighbors, as seen by visiting nurses and home health aides, discharge planners, and visiting nurse managers. I asked hospital administrators (presidents, chief executive officers) and upper-grade hospital managers (vice-presidents, assistant administrators), nursing educators, unit managers, and all nursing workers to tell me about what they believed to be the most critical current problems in health care facing people doing their job, the impact of these problems on their work, and on patient care. If women and men did not discuss it voluntarily, I asked about patient care by the family, and the use of high-tech in the home. Women and men responded by discussing a wide range of concerns including cost containment, collective bargaining, nurse leaders, professionalization, quality patient care, job stress and conflicts, and tensions among nurses, between management and hospital workers, and between physicians and nurses. The interviewed come from acute-care facilities (hospitals), skilled nursing facilities (nursing homes), ambulatory facilities (outpatient clinics), and patient homes (visiting nurse departments and associations). Interviews were conducted in the workplace (in private rooms), in restaurants, and in the respondents' homes.

I ceased interviews at the point of "saturation", that is, when materials seemed repetitious, when I was no longer getting new viewpoints about work (Glaser and Strauss 1971). I "violated" some traditional canons by asking provocative questions (e.g., how come beliefs about hospital use versus home care seem to change depending on financial considerations?). Also, I told some managers and nurses about strategies being used at other care facilities. For example, I asked administrators what they thought of self-care units, or asked nursing workers what they thought of so-called radical caucuses of RNs at various hospitals. I did so because I did not think that a "neutral" question would get to the nub of my concern.

I conducted interviews in two different ways: after conducting about ten open-ended interviews I wrote a systematic and routine guide. I tried this in three interviews, which seemed tedious to me, off-putting to the interviewees, and from which I learned little. I returned to my original loose, open-ended style in which I followed interviewees through the discussions that they seemed to want to have, and asked them to expand on their comments, and inserted questions, when necessary, to clarify their views (see Glaser and Strauss 1971).

I gathered data only from paid workers. Lack of time, funding, and access to patients made it impossible for me to talk to the recipients of care and their caregivers. Of course, I had no access to statements by the retail clerks and customers for whom work began to change so markedly nearly eighty years ago.

B. Organizational Chart for Hospital Home Health Agency (HHA) Caregivers and Their Supervisors

President/CEO/Hospital Administrator
Director/Vice-President, HHA
Assistant Director/Assistant Vice-President, HHA
Coordinator, HHA
Assistant Coordinator, HHA

Supervisory RNs   Medical Social Worker   Home Health Aide
(case manager)   Coordinator
(social worker)

Therapists   Home Health RNs
(speech, physical,
occupational)

Home Health Aides
[Outside organization: home-care attendants]
Family caregivers: wives, mothers, adult daughters, husbands [fathers, adult sons]

This chart represents a typical line of command from which a given organization may depart. Visiting nurses associations (VNAs) have a similar organization, though without the hospital administrator.

C. Respondents

(N = 59)

Aides	5
LPNs	4
LPN/aide educators	2
LPN union	1
RNs	
Administrators, directors of services, agencies	11
Staff coordinators	6
Staff	12
Union agents, executives	3
Educators	2
Hospital administrators, agency directors, union executives	8
Others not listed above: social worker, supplier, nursing-home worker, other ancillary health worker	5

Most workers were employed at regional hospitals, major medical centers, training centers, health maintenance organizations, and independent nursing service agencies in California. A small number were from Oregon, New York, and Massachusetts.

D. Terms Used

For handy reference, I list the central terms I use in my analysis of paid and unpaid service work:

The *work transfer* refers to the decommodification of labor that decreases the number of paid workers or eliminates some of their work responsibilities, shifting work from them to unpaid domestic workers in a reversal of the long-term trend of capitalism.

Job consolidation and *site specialization* are central to my analysis of health care. *Job consolidation* refers to the reversal of the detailed division of labor: once-specialized work is reassigned to paid workers, resulting in more complex content, but older-style generalist jobs.

Site specialization refers to distinctive workplaces, within which different kinds of workers predominate, but a good deal of the work itself is identical from one workplace to another. This contrasts with a detailed division of labor within a single workplace. The *work transfer*, supplemented by job expansion, results in a new division of labor among nursing workers and a new labor process that separates nursing workers further from each other in rank, privileges, and rewards, and by workplace location that makes women's collective action across class even more difficult than usual.

Job degrading refers to the narrowing of tasks, routinization, the separation of planning from execution, and the loss of craft skills. But it also includes the literal demotion of jobs with loss of earnings. It results in the consolidation of the work of lower-grade workers into the jobs of upper-grade workers, in a departure from the usual views of work given by labor-process theory.

Job polarization refers to the enlargement of differences between top and bottom grades in an occupation and the disappearance or decline of jobs in the middle.

Notes

Chapter 1

1. The shopping cart was probably invented in 1937 by Sylvan Goldman, a grocer in Oklahoma City, to replace the market basket that shoppers carried over the arm (Folkart 1984). Thanks to Joseph F. Jones for bringing this to my attention.

2. These vignettes are composites based on historical sources, my interviews with workers in home health, and personal observations of patient experiences in home health care.

3. Paperwork, too, has been reorganized by firms to shift work to the householder. Corporate bookkeeping makes a sizable amount of corporate work: millions of clients pay bills, deposit funds, request various changes in their accounts, start and stop services, and so on. Each activity requires a record. Few records are initially computerized; instead, they depend on some kind of intermediate paperwork. Organizations try to get the customer–client to do some of this work. Bills may include various requests of the payers: to record account numbers on checks and mailing envelopes, to note telephone numbers and other identifying information on enclosures, to record amounts paid on bills, and otherwise to complete steps that lighten organizational paperwork. Dental and medical insurance holders may find that their dentist or physician requires them to do the paperwork necessary for insurance collection.

4. It has been hard for sociologists to see that the work that women do as family members is organized directly by capitalism and the state. In 1978–1979, I interviewed people in Munich, West Berlin, Zagreb, London, and Oslo. I talked with women and some men in research institutes about what their governments were doing, or not doing, to support the employment of women with family responsibilities. In the conduct of their daily lives, mothers and wives adapted their paid work to the organization of social institutions outside the household, as well as adapting their family lives to the demands of the paid workplace. For example, mothers of young schoolchildren in West Berlin could not easily take paid jobs because the hours of school were not synchronized with the usual workday. Schools lacked lunchrooms, so children had to go home to eat and mothers had to be home to give them the midday meal. Yet, in Germany childcare had been commodified and school hours had been arranged to fit women's employment under the grim conditions of both world wars. Then, private employers and the state had hired childcare workers to enable mothers of young children to do war work. In American schools, parents expe-

rience the work transfer under the so-called fiscal crisis of the state. For example, they may be called on to supervise lunchrooms and playgrounds and to organize and staff programs in elementary schools. They substitute for teachers fired because of budget cuts.

5. Married African American women, poor immigrant women, and other working-class women worked for wages more often than other women in the United States, or they did "homework" (e.g., piecework, taking in boarders and lodgers), or they worked "off the books." My discussion of the unpaid household division of labor addresses white women only because there are scant data on the unpaid domestic labor of women of other groups (see Pleck 1982).

Chapter 2

1. As Meiksins (1981) notes in discussing productive and unproductive labor, the crucial issue for an analysis is exploitation. The same warning should apply to analyses of work and domestic labor.

2. In 1983, I interviewed at, and toured, the New York University Medical Center Cooperative Care Unit.

3. See Gershuny (1978), who argues on the basis of Britain from about 1953 to 1974 that self-service, rather than service to the consumer, characterizes postindustrial society.

Chapter 3

1. Marx's use of exchange and use value does not, of course, divide the world into the two realms of family and workplace, but critiques how capitalism appropriates value. Ultimately, in this usage, he rejects dualism as part of the mystification of commodity production and the estimate of market relationships as the penultimate standard. In some feminist analyses, the terms seem to be used in a way that lends itself to seeing women as devalued largely because their work does not enter into relations based on exchange value. See Benston (1977).

2. For an excellent examination of the dialectics between domestic labor and corporate development of technology for profit, showing how capitalism shapes women's work, see Strasser (1982).

3. Patient cooperation is important for diagnosis and treatment. The question is whether *work* is the appropriate term to describe this. Illich (1981: 100) broadens the concept of unpaid work to include emotional states (e.g., "the stress of forced consumption, the tedious and regimented surrender to therapists, compliance with bureaucrats").

4. The rental of expensive equipment by the consumer is a somewhat borderline case in relating unpaid work to the maintenance of capitalism. For

example, people rent washing machines and dryers in laundromats, grommet-applying machines in hardware stores, and the use of photocopying machines in libraries and stores. Consumers rent equipment such as carpet shampoo machines, steam cleaners for house exteriors, and kits for installing door locks from locksmith shops in an attempt to lower their own costs. Consumers also buy goods to which they must add their labor, such as unassembled toys, unfinished furniture, fabrics and yarns, and, of course, raw foods. The completion of work using these materials is not part of the organizational goal of those selling or renting do-it-yourself equipment. What matters to the seller is only that consumers rent equipment or buy goods, not whether they complete tasks associated with either.

Chapter 4

1. The clerk-service store provided such information, though no doubt the worker was encouraged to put the store's interests before the buyer's. But the seller had to consider the interests of buyers to keep their trade. Clerk-service did not ensure, therefore, a shoppers' paradise. The poor, the vulnerable, and the otherwise despised suffered in relations with the clerk. Today, selling practices in the self-service store may make it difficult for people with certain disabilities, parents accompanied by small children, and those unable to read English.

2. The following definitions may help in understanding the social history of retailing. In 1920, retail stores had several ownership types and sold varying products. The *small independent* (often "Mom and Pop") store operated with a minimum of investment and the unpaid labor of family members, selling groceries but no meat, or specializing in a single product such as meat, bakery goods or clothing. Larger *independent* stores also were locally owned, had much larger inventories and investments than "Mom and Pop" stores, and some paid workers, though usually only a few. Among independent food retailers, some sold only groceries while others also sold meat. The *chains* included specialty shops, selling such goods as electric appliances, food, clothing, and shoes. Chains had more stores, centrally owned and managed. The *supermarkets* were originally independents who sold a wider variety of merchandise than either grocery or department stores. These used self-service from the outset, though some also used clerk-service as an adjunct. There are different kinds of chains (local, regional, national and international), and there are associations of independents (cooperatives, associated and allied independents) modeled on chains (Haas 1979; Markin 1963).

3. Forty years after retail food sales began to be dominated by the supermarkets, one-third of retail food stores were still run by their owners and without any paid workers (Carey and Otto 1977).

4. The Patman-Robinson Act of 1936 prohibited wholesalers from giving large buyers a price break by different pricing of the same merchandise for different retailers, from foregoing brokerage fees or by giving other rebates (such as for advertising) that would discriminate between different classes of retailers. Other legislation was eventually passed to set minimum or "fair trade" prices that effectively prevented discount houses from selling national brand merchandise until the 1960s (Bluestone et al. 1981).

5. The specific technology designed for self-service stores existed before the Great Depression. Shopping baskets and basket carts, the turnstile, check-out stands, aisles for customers' circulation, and open display counters were all developed by the 1920s, or before World War II.

6. The demands of the customer for adequate labeling were not met entirely. For example, manufacturing specification labels were attached to some goods; the famous DO NOT REMOVE THIS LABEL UNDER PENALTY OF LAW listing content was attached to mattresses and seems to have terrorized generations of customers into a careful preservation of the tag! But it would be decades before manufacturers listed fabric contents of clothing and fabric-care instructions. Manufacturers' liability for product defects is a continual problem for buyers of new housing, clothing, automobiles, and electrical goods, especially as sellers have passed the responsibility for warrantees on to the manufacturer. In cosmetics and food labeling, technical terms are used that hide more than they reveal about products' contents.

7. By 1982, the concentration of capital in manufacturing and retailing was evident in the international Associated Merchandising Corporation (AMC). Through AMC, 28 major American department stores with a total of 353 branches and 17 affiliated overseas stores cooperated, rather than competed. Jointly owning AMC, the stores developed tactics for all aspects of retailing, provided monopoly-like conditions for sales, and created a homogenous market (Salmans 1982: 1).

8. The Keedoozle system removed the customer from the merchandise even more than packaging did, preventing customer examination as well as pilfering of fresh produce. As in the Horn and Hardart "Automat," the customer was presented with goods only after paying for them. The goods were assembled by drop-feeds, belts, and other electrical devices.

9. Harrington (1962) provides one of the rare analyses of the RCIPA, although his book concentrates, unfortunately, on the union after World War II.

10. Self-service was also adopted for the only product bought initially by men rather than women: gasoline. The marketing of gasoline is the history of competition between independents and monopolies, smaller independent refineries and their retailers, and the big oil corporations and brand dealers. Self-service was not adopted until the late 1960s. In the early 1970s, many independent dealers were driven out of business when major oil companies withheld

supplies from the independent refineries, allegedly because of shortages. The brand dealers, franchised by the oil monopolies, were forced to adopt self-service. By 1982 all but two states (Oregon and New Jersey) had self-service gas stations (Bluestone et al. 1981).

Chapter 5

1. Retail workers also include stock persons, delivery persons, cleaners, and other miscellaneous occupations, but the majority of workers are managers, cashiers, and salesclerks, to whom the analysis is limited.

2. The other two major unions for retail workers were the Retail, Wholesale and Department Store Employees of the CIO (split by the refusal of important locals to comply with the Taft-Hartley requirement that officers sign noncommunist affidavits) and the International Brotherhood of Teamsters of the AFL. The RCIPA merged with the United Food and Commercial Workers in the 1970s.

3. According to Harrington (1962: 6–8), RCIPA membership reached its first peak in 1903 (for which I did not have access to issues of *The Advocate*). In 1908, membership reached a major low point; in 1919, a postwar surge; in 1933, a low point followed by a postwar surge in 1954 and growth to 1962. I searched *The Advocate* during periods of its highest membership for discussions by, about, and for the woman clerk. The texts I found reflect, of course, the opinions and political views of the editors, who wrote the editorials and decided what letters, articles, news, and columns would be printed and reprinted. I thank Julie McKeehan and Nitza Hidalgo, graduate students at the Divinity School, Harvard, in 1983, for their help in researching *The Advocate*. All articles—editorials, feature articles, stories, poems, etc.—were searched for discussions about women. Financial and death reports, filler jokes, and ads were excluded.

4. The report on Kentucky noted that from 43.7 percent to 61.2 percent of white women working in tobacco (except cigars), cordage and thread, manufacturing, and laundries were or had been married, and that 20 to 30 percent were forty years of age or older. African American women worked in large numbers in tobacco processing, though not cigarmaking, and in laundries. Most were or had been married (71.7 percent in tobacco; 66.7 percent in laundries) (RCIPA 1924: 22).

5. A 1916–1917 study of Boston's retail industry also used nonsexist language, referring to women workers as "salespeople." Nonetheless, it reported discrimination against young women in all jobs in retailing and noted that this was identical to conditions in confectionary, metal trades, and clerical work (Ayars ca. 1917: 157). "Talk" is not social structure; the RCIPA may have been nonsexist for its time and supportive of women's equality in *The Advocate*, but

this may or may not have reflected union practices in shops, and the relations between women and men in union locals.

6. Data comparing women's and men's earnings by occupation within the retail industry are difficult to obtain. Bluestone et al. (1981) used the New England LEED sample for estimates.

7. Historically, women's lower wages also reflected their lower rates of unionization (Canfield 1948: 102). Many union organizers believed that women were difficult to organize because they were often temporary workers (Jay 1953).

8. In his history of the RCIPA, Harrington (1962) notes that clerks were difficult to organize because so many were women. Yet the 1946 Oakland general strike, which he also discusses briefly, was provoked by the militant strike action of women store clerks. This is not to fault Harrington, but to show how uncritically many analysts have accepted the view that women workers are difficult to organize.

9. Informants employed in one large West Coast chain store described their training to me as a course in encouraging customers to buy the most expensive items and in pushing these as the highest in quality (Interview 1982). An executive in a major eastern department store gave an interview on clerk training and supplied a copy of their sales manual, which includes weekly brochures on new goods with appropriate phrases to use in selling, for example, "This is really fashionable and very popular" (Interview 1983).

Chapter 6

1. Discussions by retailers and market analysts use *men* when referring to workers and *women* when referring to grocery shoppers.

2. Meeting the ideal of domesticated womenhood was not equally possible for all women. White working-class and even lower-middle-class women could only aspire to the ideal. Married women worked in their homes, too, taking in boarders and lodgers to supplement the earnings of the male breadwinner and employed children. Most unmarried women worked for pay, usually as domestics. The wages of married (or widowed or divorced) African American and immigrant women—the Irish, Polish, French Canadians, Jews, Asian Americans, Hispanics—and their offspring were needed for family survival. But racial and ethnic groups varied in their acceptance of married women doing paid work outside the home and in their access to alternative sources of income. Sometimes, bourgeois women and reformers used social Darwinism and the work ethic to argue that working-class women, unlike middle-class women, ought to do paid work outside the home.

3. From the 1830s onward, magazines advised young wives to learn housewifery so as to be able to supervise their servants adequately. William Alcott (1839) urged women to demand the help of their husbands and children in housekeeping, though his advice did not seem to have been accepted widely.

The dominant content of nineteenth-century advice centered on the supervision of servants by well-to-do women.

4. After price competition was virtually eliminated, retailers began to portray themselves as giving all variety of services to self-service customers. Retailers were seeking a substitute for low prices to attract customers. Other services retailers noted included adequate parking, nice wall colors, in-store music, shopping carts, a wide choice of shopping hours, clearly marked department and produce signs, convenient sizes and quantities of goods, check cashing, a rapid check-out system, and carrying purchases to cars (Cassady 1962). Air-conditioning, parcel pickup, and premium plans (Zimmerman 1955), as well as self-opening doors and hot-air curtains, have also been presented as services to self-service shoppers (Nell 1958).

5. Because prepackaging is used widely by most supermarkets, customers not only substitute for clerk-service by taking over "the unorderly marketing burden," but they also absorb the expensive *inventory* or *storage burden*. Insofar as customers buy in large quantities, the retailers have that much less inventory or waste losses. While home storage may be a convenience, it also means costly equipment, such as a large refrigerator, many cupboards and a freezer, and a large outlay for goods well in advance of their use. The European small refrigerators, so devalued by Americans, ensure frequent shopping trips, but also ensure fresh produce and less space reserved for turnips and potatoes, cereal and milk.

Chapter 7

1. See U.S. General Accounting Office (1982) and Hammond (1979) for assessments of the uncertain cost-effectiveness of home health services during the 1965–1981 period.

2. Thanks to Ellen Morrison for compiling these data on corporate reports.

3. Thanks to Hugh Lovell for the information on computation changes.

4. I examined *The Outlook* from 1959 through 1986.

5. Unpaid patient labor in clinics and hospitals includes the use of patients in place of runners to carry their own laboratory specimens from one office to another, and in place of clerical workers to fill out insurance claims that physicians and hospitals file. Sometimes family members and friends are expected to substitute for nurses and aides by doing minor tasks in hospital wards.

Chapter 8

1. The posts that nursing personnel occupy include top administrative positions (e.g., the director of home health, ambulatory care, and patient services, who reports directly to the chief executive officer, hospital administrator, or president), middle-level (e.g., the coordinator of home health) and lower-

level management (e.g., the charge nurse and the supervisor of health aides), and staff. The staff in turn are ordered hierarchically, with RNs at the top, LPNs in the middle, and HHAs at the bottom. RNs themselves are further differentiated by degree and advanced training: BSNs and graduate-prepared clinical specialists are labeled "professionals," while ADNs and diploma RNs are labeled "technical," though all RNs are still formally allowed to take the same entry-level jobs.

2. The preoccupation of RN leaders with professionalization is consistent through the history of nursing in the United States, with complex implications for both class and race relations among all women in nursing (see Glazer 1991).

3. I am not suggesting that more schooling is undesirable, but rather that some RNs believe that more training should be accessible to lower-grade workers and that a core curriculum for nursing would be beneficial for patient care and upward mobility.

4. Public health nursing, institutionalized in visiting nurses associations, originally treated the entire family as well as the sick person in order to improve health among the poor. Visiting nurses today are the basic labor force in the treatment of the acutely ill in their homes, but the work of the contemporary visiting nurse fits the individualized, genetic medical model rather than the older public health model.

Chapter 9

1. The National Committee of Nurses and the American Hospital Association agreed to use RIMs in all accredited hospitals. RIMs were calculated from RN reports and from observations of RNs and other hospital workers as they cared for patients. They include the work of technical evaluation ("assessment and planning"), housekeeping (e.g., exercise, hydration, and socio-emotional activities to meet "affective, psychological, and social needs"), technical implementation (giving drugs and treatments, appraising effects) and education (teaching self-care, providing information about patient condition). The RIM forms rely on precoded categories, eliminating all narrative except comments on flow charts (Interview, Betsy Potter, graduate-prepared RN and LPN educator).

Chapter 10

1. In old French, *amateur* means "lover of an activity." I use it to underscore that women tend others for love as well as duty. In English usage, *amateur* refers to activities done without professional training, and sometimes the term carries a derogatory connotation.

2. Gendered practices run through the organization of medical care. Women are treated as if they have less social value than men and so are more readily expected to sacrifice their jobs and personal life in order to tend. There are also gender differences in medical treatment; for example, women are less likely than men to get rehabilitation services after a stroke, and women are referred for bypass surgery at a much later stage of heart disease than men.

3. While the "technological fix" fascinates many in the United States, only a few sociologists have developed new theories and empirical research (Bijerk et al. 1987; Gaston 1984), even in health services, with its science-based technologies and use in home medical care (Aiken and Freeman 1984; Fox and Swazey 1974). Home-based technology may pose health hazards (Strasser 1982) and its high-tech features initially outstrip its possible use in home health care (Cowan 1983). Neither home health care nor the home use of high-technology medicine were considered in the extensive international debates among sociologists during the 1970s about unpaid domestic labor (Fox 1980; Glazer-Malbin 1976) or in studies of housewives (Lopata 1971; Oakley 1974) or the household division of labor (Berk and Berk 1979; Berk 1980; Vanek 1974). On the other hand, the effects of medical technology on ethics, bureaucratization and costs, marital relations, the poor, and women of color have been examined (Fox 1985; Kutner 1987; Lasker and Borg 1987; Mechanic 1977; Rothman 1986, 1987; Simmons and Marine 1984).

4. Hidden assumptions make this perspective on medical technology palatable. New medical technologies are viewed by corporate managers as benign phenomena, even if financial drains on advanced capitalist societies. Sociologists have too often adopted what social historians treat as ideology: technological change is welcomed as a sign of social progress, as something emerging from the inherent nature of research and technical accumulation and pushed on by disinterested researchers and engineers (Marx 1964; Segal 1985; Smith 1977; Winner 1977). Pauline Atwood, director of discharge planning at a major medical center, cites the use of intermittent positive pressure breathing machines (IPPB) for both pre- and post-operative pulmonary function as an example of the technological fix in medicine. According to her, ten years of research shows that the old methods of having patients walk, breath deeply, and cough are just as good as expensive IPPB machines.

5. A less benign concept of technology as implicated in the social relations of domination typifies a minority view among Americans, rooted more in Jeffersonian ideals of agrarian democracy or populist republicanism than in Marxism (see Hughes 1959; Marx 1964; Mumford 1934; Noble 1977).

6. Researchers, following the revival by Braverman (1974) of interest in Marx's analysis of the labor process, have examined technology as both an independent and dependent variable, studying how technologies have been introduced deliberately to circumvent affirmative action, discipline workers, and re-

duce wages and pension costs (Cockburn 1983; Glenn and Feldberg 1977; Hacker 1979; de Kadt 1979). Technology has also been used to cheapen labor costs and degrade labor in health services (Braverman 1974); for example, the computerization of clerical work has increased some work for RNs, shifting to them work once done by hospital ward clerks (Sacks 1988).

7. Total parenteral nutrition (TPN) administration allows recovery of functions or permits life to be sustained indefinitely when digestive organs are unlikely to heal. Enteral nutrition (EN) bypasses the throat, either temporarily to allow recovery or permanently. Intravenous (IV) antibiotics are used to treat infection in persons otherwise judged not to need hospitalization. IV chemotherapy is used to treat patients who want to be in their homes or do not need hospitalization after treatment. Oxygen therapy (permanent or temporary, continuous or intermittent) may be given to patients otherwise not judged to benefit from hospitalization. Apnea monitoring is used for breathing disturbances in babies, for awakening nonbreathers, and often for obese men, providing them with constant oxygen. Phototherapy uses light to enable newborn babies to manufacture a factor needed for liver metabolism.

8. Renal dialysis treatment was first given in hospitals, but by 1972 40 percent of patients were being treated by family caretakers. A drop in family caregiving to 20 percent by 1977 resulted from an interaction of social factors: government reimbursement for in-hospital rather than outpatient care, and broadened eligibility criteria (Russell 1979: 11–13).

9. A home health agency may try to get an adult day center to give respite to the caregiver and to support the family emotionally if they decide to place their sick member in a nursing home. Emotionally or physically disabled adults, usually over 65 years or at least 55 years of age, may be able to spend two or three days a week at these centers for meals, exercise, a bit of social life, lectures, and other activities. The goal of adult day care is to allow people to stay in their homes without deteriorating further.

Chapter 11

1. An analysis of national data on long-term informal care of the impaired elderly found that husbands were more likely than wives to report spending "extra time" doing household tasks because of the spouse's disability. This seems in accord with the finding that wives but not husbands consider household activities a usual responsibility (Stone et al. 1987).

References

Abbreviations

AESL   Archives of the Arthur and Elizabeth Schlesinger Library of the History of American Women, Radcliffe College, Harvard University

HCFA   Health Care Financing Administration

LHJ   *Ladies' Home Journal*

RCIA   *Retail Clerks International Advocate*

RCNA   *Retail Clerks National Advocate*

RCIPA   Retail Clerks International Protective Association

RCNPA   Retail Clerks National Protective Association

RW(DS)E   Retail and Wholesale (Department Store) Employee

Introduction

Brown, Michael K. 1988. "The Segmented Welfare System: Distributive Conflict and Retrenchment in the United States, 1968–1984." Pp. 182–200 in *Remaking the Welfare State*, ed. Michael K. Brown. Philadelphia: Temple University Press.

Hall, Stuart. 1988. "The Toad in the Garden: Thatcherism Among the Theorists." Pp. 58–74 in *Marxism and the Interpretation of Culture*, ed. Cary Nelson and Lawrence Grossberg. Urbana: University of Illinois Press.

Chapter 1

Abel, Emily, and Margaret Nelson (eds.). 1990. *Circles of Care*. Albany: SUNY Press.

Aldershoff, D. E., A. C. L. Zuidberg, and W. Baak. 1983. *Household Production in the Netherlands*. Institute for Scientific Research on Consumer Affairs, SWOKA, Interim Report No. 14 (summarized English version). Bezuidwenhoutseweg 231, Postcode 2594AM, Gravenhage, Netherlands.

Antill, John, and Sandra Cotton. 1988. "Factors Affecting the Division of Labor in the Household." *Sex Roles* 18: 531–553.

Atkinson, Jean, and Ted Huston. 1984. "Sex Roles in Marriage." *Journal of Personality and Social Psychology* 46:330–345.

Berk, Richard A., and Sarah F. Berk. 1979. *Labor and Leisure at Home*. Beverly Hills: Sage Publications.

Berk, Sarah F. 1985. *The Gender Factory*. New York: Plenum.

Braverman, Harry. 1974. *Labor and Monopoly Capital: The Degradation of Work in the Twentieth Century*. New York: Monthly Review Press.

Coverman, Shelley, and Joseph F. Sheley. 1986. "Change in Men's Housework and Child-Care Time, 1965–1975." *Journal of Marriage and the Family* 48: 413–422.

Finch, Janet. 1983. *Married to the Job*. London: Allen & Unwin.

Folkart, Burt. 1984. "Shopping Cart Inventor Dies." *Oregonian*, Nov. 27, D14.

Glazer, Nona Y. 1980. "Overworking the Working Woman: The Double Day in a Mass Magazine." *Women's Studies International Quarterly* 3:79–93.

Harvey, Andrew. 1989. "Time Use in Canada." Paper presented at the Henry A. Murray Center, Radcliffe College, Harvard University.

Hochschild, Arlie. 1983. *The Managed Heart: Commercialization of Human Feelings*. Berkeley: University of California Press.

————, and Anne Machung. 1989. *The Second Shift: Working Parents and the Revolution at Home*. New York: Viking Press.

Kilpio, Eila. 1981. *Housework Study*. Helsinki, Finland: Ministry of Social Affairs and Health Research Department.

Lapidus, Gail (ed.). 1982. *Women, Work and Family in the Soviet Union*. New York: M. E. Sharpe.

Meissner, Martin, E. W. Humphreys, S. M. Meis, and W. J. Sheu. 1975. "No Exit for Wives: Sexual Division of Labour and the Cumulation of Household Demands." *Canadian Review of Sociology and Anthropology* 12:424–439.

Nyquist, Linda, Karla Slivken, Janet T. Spence, and Robert L. Helmreich. 1985. "Household Responsibilities in Middle Class Couples: The Contribution of Demographic and Personality Variables." *Sex Roles* 12:15–33.

Oakley, Ann. 1974. *The Sociology of Housework*. New York: Pantheon.

Pleck, Joseph. 1982. "Husbands' and Wives' Family Work, Paid Work and Adjustment." Working Paper, Wellesley College Center for Research on Women.

————. 1985. *Working Wives, Working Husbands*. Beverly Hills: Sage Publications.

Robinson, John P., Janet Yerby, Margaret Fieweger, and Nancy Somerick. 1977. "Sex-Role Differences in Time Use." *Sex Roles* 3(5):443–458.

Santii, Riitta, Ritva-Anneli Otva, and Eila Kilpio. 1982. *Housework Study*. Part VIII, *Unpaid Housework: Time Use and Value*. Helsinki, Finland: Ministry of Social Affairs and Health Research Department.

Szalai, Alexander (ed.). 1972. *The Use of Time: Daily Activities of Urban and Suburban Populations in Twelve Countries*. The Hague, Netherlands: Mouton.

Waitzkin, Howard. 1983. *The Second Sickness*. New York: Free Press.

Zaretsky, Eli. 1973. "Capitalism, the Family and Personal Life." *Socialist Revolution* 3 (Jan.–April):69–125, (May–June):19–70.

Chapter 2

American Nurse. 1979. "New Care Unit to Cut Hospital Costs by 40 Percent." *American Nurse* 11:1–6.

Ames, Sarah C. 1989. "Report Lists Ways to Cut Police Load." *Oregonian*, Sept. 12, C1, C2.

Bell, Daniel. 1976. *The Coming of Post-Industrial Society*. New York: Basic Books.

Blitzer, Carol. 1981. "Cooperative Care Unit Cuts Costs 40% at NYU Hospital." *Business Insurance* 15:3, 27.

Clark, Colin. 1940. *The Conditions of Economic Progress*. New York: MacMillan.

Evans, Robert, and Geoffrey Robinson. 1983. "An Economic Study of Cost Savings on a Care-By-Parent Ward." *Medical Care* 21:768–782.

Galbraith, John Kenneth. 1973. *Economics and the Public Interest*. Boston: Houghton Mifflin.

Gershuny, Jonathan. 1978. *After Industrial Society? The Emerging Self-Service Economy*. Atlantic Highlands, N.J.: Humanities Press.

Gibson, Kathy R., and C. Beth Pulliam. 1987. "Cooperative Care: The Time Has Come." *Journal of Nursing Administration* 17:19–21.

Glazer, Nathan. 1983. "Towards a Self-Service Society?" *The Public Interest* 70:66–90.

Glenn, Evelyn N. 1986. *Issei, Nisei, War Bride: Three Generations of Japanese-American Women in Domestic Service*. Philadelphia: Temple University Press.

Henry, Stuart. 1987. "The Political Economy of Informal Economies." *Annals of the American Association of Political Science* 493:137–153.

Heskett, James. 1986. *Managing the Service Economy*. Boston: Harvard Business School Press.

Koren, Mary Jane. 1986. "Home Care—Who Cares?" *New England Journal of Medicine* 314:917–920.

Langeard, Eric, John Bateson, Christopher Lovelock, and Pierre I. Eiglier. 1981. *Services Marketing: New Insights from Consumers and Managers*. Report no. 81-104. Cambridge, Mass.: Marketing Services Institute.

Lovelock, Christopher, and Robert F. Young. 1979. "Look to Consumers to Increase Productivity." *Harvard Business Review*, May/June, 66–76.

Mandel, Ernest. 1975. *Late Capitalism*. London: New Left Review Press.

Meiksins, Peter. 1981. "Productive and Unproductive Labor and Marx's Theory of Class." *Review of Radical and Political Economics* 13(3):32–42.

Miles, Ian. 1985. "The New Post-Industrial State." *Futures* 17(6):588–617.

————, and Jonathan Gershuny. 1983. *The New Service Economy*. London: Frances Pinter.

National Retail Dry Goods Assocation. 1939. "Superfluous or Necessary? Retail Services Defined by Kirstein." *The Bulletin* 21(2):34–35.

Pollard, Sidney. 1979. "The Rise of the Service Industries and White Collar Employment." Pp. 17–42 in *Post-Industrial Society*, ed. Bo Gustafsson. London: Croom Helm.

Rollins, Judith. 1985. *Between Women*. Philadelphia: Temple University Press.

Schumacher, E. F. 1979. *Small Is Beautiful*. New York: Harper and Row.

Testa, William. 1989. "Telling Fortunes: Manufacturing and the Great Lakes Region." *Chicago Fed Letter* no. 25 (Sept.). Chicago: Federal Reserve Bank of Chicago.

Tunstall, Patricia. 1960. "Hospitals without Nurses." *Practical Nursing* 10:14–15.

Walker, Richard A. 1985. "Is There a Service Economy? The Changing Capitalist Division of Labor." *Science & Society* 1:42–83.

Williams, Raymond. 1980. *Culture and Materialism*. London: Verso.

Chapter 3

Acker, Joan. 1989. "The Problem with Patriarchy." *British Journal of Sociology* 23:235–240.

Armstrong, Pat, and Hugh Armstrong. 1986. "Beyond Sexless Class and Classless Sex." Pp. 208–271 in *The Politics of Diversity*, ed. Roberta Hamilton and Michele Barrett. London: Verso.

Barrett, Michele, and Mary McIntosh. 1984. *The Anti-Social Family*. London: Verso.

Beechey, Veronica. 1988. "Rethinking the Definition of Work." Pp. 45–62 in *Feminization of the Labour Force*, ed. Jane Jenson, Elisabeth Hagen, and Ceallaigh Reddy. Cambridge, Eng.: Polity Press.

Bennholdt-Thomsen, Veronika. 1984. "Subsistence Production and Extended Production." Pp. 41–54 in *Of Marriage and the Market*, ed. Kate Young, Carol Wolkowitz, and Roslyn McCullogh. London: Routledge and Kegan Paul.

Benston, Margaret. 1977. "The Political Economy of Women's Liberation." Pp. 216–226 in *Woman in a Man-Made World*, ed. Nona Glazer and Helen Waehrer. Chicago: Rand McNally.

Berk, Richard A., and Sarah F. Berk. 1979. *Labor and Leisure at Home*. Beverly Hills: Sage Publications.

Cowan, Ruth. 1983. *More Work for Mother*. New York: Basic Books.

Daniels, Arlene. 1987. "Invisible Work." *Social Problems* 34(5):403–415.

————. 1988. *Invisible Careers*. Chicago: University of Chicago Press.

Duane-Richard, Anne-Marie. 1988. "Gender Relations and Female Labor." Pp.

260–275 in *Feminization of the Labour Force*, ed. Jane Jenson, Elisabeth Hagen, and Ceallaigh Reddy. Cambridge, Eng.: Polity Press.

Fox-Genovese, Elizabeth, and Eugene Genovese. 1983. *The Fruits of Merchant Capital*. New York: Oxford University Press.

Fuchs, Victor. 1968. *The Service Economy*. New York: Columbia University Press.

Galbraith, John Kenneth. 1973. *Economics and the Public Interest*. Boston: Houghton Mifflin.

Gershuny, Jonathan. 1987. "The Future of Service Employment." Pp. 105–125 in *The Emerging Service Economy*, ed. Orio Giarini. New York: Pergamon.

Glazer-Malbin, Nona. 1976. "Housework: A Review Essay." *Signs* 1(4):360–369.

Hartmann, Heidi. 1974. "Capitalism and Women's Work in the Home, 1900–1930." Ph.D. diss., Yale University.

Hochschild, Arlie. 1983. *The Managed Heart: Commercialization of Human Feelings*. Berkeley: University of California Press.

———, and Anne Machung. 1989. *The Second Shift: Working Parents and the Revolution at Home*. New York: Viking Press.

Hohendahl, Peter. 1974. "Jurgen Habermas: The Public Sphere." *New German Critique* 3:46–55.

Humphries, Jane. 1977. "The Working Class Family, Women's Liberation, and Class Struggle: The Case of Nineteenth Century British History." *Review of Radical Political Economics* 9(3):25–41.

Illich, Ivan. 1981. *Shadow Work*. Boston: Marion Boyars.

Janiewski, Dolores. 1985. *Sisterhood Denied: Race, Gender and Class in a New South Community*. Philadelphia: Temple University Press.

Lasch, Christopher. 1979. *Haven in a Heartless World*. New York: Basic Books.

Leonard, Diane, and Mary Anne Speakman. 1986. "Women in the Family: Companions or Caretakers." Pp. 8–76 in *Women in Britain Today*, ed. Veronica Beechey and Elizabeth Whitelegg. Philadelphia: Open University Press.

Leuthold, Jane H. 1981. "Taxation and the Value of Nonmarket Time." *Social Science Research* 10:267–281.

Lopata, Helena Z. 1971. *Occupation: Housewife*. New York: Oxford University Press.

Mandel, Ernest. 1981. "Introduction." In Karl Marx, *Capital* vol. 2. New York: Vintage Books.

Marx, Karl. 1969. *The 18th Brumaire of Louis Bonaparte*. New York: International Publishers.

Mies, Maria. 1986. *Patriarchy and Accumulation on a World Scale*. London: Zed Books.

Milkman, Ruth. 1987. *Gender at Work*. Urbana: University of Illinois Press.

Oakley, Ann. 1976. *Women's Work*. New York: Vintage.

Offe, Claus. 1984. *Contradictions of the Welfare State*. London: Hutchinson.

Parker, Roy. 1981. "Tending and Social Policy." Pp. 17–34 in *A New Look at Social Services*, ed. Matilda Goldberg and Stephen Hatch. London: Policy Studies Institute.

Parsons, Talcott, and Robert F. Bales. 1955. *Family, Socialization and Interaction*. Glencoe, Ill.: Free Press.

Rapp, Rayna, Ellen Ross, and Renate Bridenthal. 1979. "Examining Family History." *Feminist Studies* 5:174–200.

Sacks, Karen. 1988. *Caring by the Hour: Women, Work and Organizing at Duke Medical Center*. Urbana: University of Illinois Press.

Seligman, Ben. 1968. *Economics of Dissent*. Chicago: Quadrangle Press.

Smith, Dorothy E. 1987. *The Everyday World as Problematic: A Feminist Sociology*. Boston: Northeastern University Press.

Stanback, Thomas M., Jr., Peter J. Bearee, Thierry Noyelle, and Robert Karasek. 1981. *Services: The New Economy*. Totowa, N.J.: Allanheld, Osmun and Co.

Strasser, Susan. 1982. *Never Done: A History of American Housework*. New York: Pantheon.

Strauss, Anselm L., Shizuko Fagerhaugh, Barbara Suczek, and Carolyn Weiner. 1981. "Patients' Work in the Technologized Hospital." *Nursing Outlook* 29(7):404–412.

Strong-Boag, Veronica. 1986. "Keeping House in God's Country: Canadian Women at Work in the Home." Pp. 124–151 in *On the Job*, ed. Craig Heron and Robert Storey. Montreal: McGill-Queen's University Press.

Szalai, Alexander (ed.), with Phillip E. Converse, P. Feldheim, E. K. Scheuch, and P. J. Stone. 1972. *The Use of Time: Daily Activities of Urban and Suburban Populations in Twelve Countries*. The Hague, Netherlands: Mouton.

Wadel, Cato. 1979. "The Hidden Work of Everyday Life." Pp. 365–384 in *Social Anthropology of Work*, ed. Sandra Wallman. London: Academic Press.

Weinbaum, Batya, and Amy Bridges. 1976. "The Other Side of the Paycheck." *Monthly Review* 28:88–103.

Williams, Raymond. 1983. *Keywords*. London: Verso.

Zaretsky, Eli. 1973. "Capitalism, the Family and Personal Life." *Socialist Revolution* 3 (Jan.–April):69–125, (May–June):19–70.

Chapter 4

Architectural Forum. 1948. "Automatic Merchandising Evolves as a Changing Force in the Nation's Stores." *Architectural Forum* 88(3):121–122.

Baker, James W. 1956. "What Price Services?" *Journal of Retailing* 32(2):86–89, 103.

Barmash, Isadore. 1989. "Bloomingdale's Commission Plan." *New York Times*, July 6, D5.

Bluestone, Barry, Patricia Hanna, Sarah Kuhn, and Laura Moore. 1981. *The Retail Revolution*. Boston: Auburn House.

Burros, Marian. 1989. "Supermarkets as Theatre, Service as Star." *New York Times*, Nov. 8, C1, 6.

Business Week. 1932. "Littman (Cash and Carry) Brightens 5th Ave. Week." *Business Week*, Oct. 12, 8–9.

———. 1934. "Piggly Wiggly Comeback." *Business Week*, Nov. 24, 14–15.

———. 1939. "Auto-Serv—A New Wrinkle in Self-Service Markets." *Business Week*, Oct. 11, 36.

———. 1946. "Shopping with a Key in a Saunders Keedoozle." *Business Week*, July 6, 41.

———. 1951. "Drug-O-Mat Saves Time for Shopper . . . Saves Work for Storekeeper." *Business Week*, July 28, 52.

Canfield, Bertrand. 1948. "Unionization of Salesmen—An Outline of the Present Situation." *Printers' Ink* 239(9):34–35, 97–98, 102, 104–105.

Carey, John L., and Phyllis Flohr Otto. 1977. "Output per Unit of Labor in the Retail Food Store Industry." *Monthly Labor Review* 100(1):42–47.

Castle, J. M. 1921. "The 'Eteria' Idea." *Printers' Ink* 117(13):113–114.

Collins, Kenneth. 1940. "The Trend toward Self-Service." *Journal of Retailing* 16(4):98–102.

Corina, John. 1947. *Spotlight on Self-Service*. Manchester, England: Co-operative Union Ltd.

Coulter, C. C. 1936. "Salespeople Resolutely Defend Right to Organize." *RCIA* 39(9):1–4.

Coutant, Frank R. 1942. "Women Now Read Advertising More Eagerly Than Ever." *Printers' Ink* 199(13):13–14.

Cowan, Ruth. 1983. *More Work for Mother*. New York: Basic Books.

Cumming, James C. 1943. "Retailers Turn to Self-Service: What Are You Doing About It?" *Sales Management* 52(8):64–66.

Curtiss, Donald. 1940. "Supermarkets and Self-Service Stores." *Advertising and Selling* 33(7):22–24.

Dameron, Kenneth. 1935. "The Retail Department Store and the NRA." *Harvard Business Review* 13(3):261–270.

Deutsch, Claudia. 1989. "The Powerful Push for Self-Service." *New York Times*, April 9, sec. 3, pp. 1, 15.

Dipman, Carl W., Robert W. Mueller, and Ralph E. Head. 1946. *Self-Service Food Stores*. New York: Butterick Co.

———, and John E. O'Brien. 1940. *Self-Service and Semi-Self-Service Food Stores*. New York: Butterick Co.

Edwards, Richard. 1979. *Contested Terrain*. New York: Basic Books.

Fredericks, Christine. 1917. "Brands Needed by Consumer as Economy of Time and Money, Says Mrs. Frederick." *Wear*, Oct. 29. MO 7, Reel 78-1, AESL.

Geschweschender, James, and Rhonda Levine. 1983. "Rationalization of Sugar Production in Hawaii, 1946–60." *Social Problems* 30(3):352–368.

Glave, H. E. 1943. "The Application of Self-Service to Department and Specialty Stores." *Journal of Retailing* 19(4):103–110.

Haas, Harold M. 1939. "Social and Economic Aspects of the Chain Store Movement." Ph.D. diss., University of Minnesota. Reprinted 1979.

Harrington, Michael. 1962. *The Retail Clerk*. New York: John Wiley.

Henksmeier, K. H. 1960. *The Economic Performance of Self-Service in Europe*. Paris: Organization for European Co-operation.

Jackson, John. 1925. "Increased Direct Selling Expense Unjustified." *Bulletin of the National Retail Dry Goods Association* 7(11):12–13.

Kingson, Jennifer. 1989. "At the Gas Station, Help Yourself to Less Service." *New York Times*, May 14, E7.

Langeard, Eric, John Bateson, Christopher Lovelock, and Pierre I. Eiglier. 1981. *Services Marketing: New Insights from Consumers and Managers*. Report no. 81–104. Cambridge, Mass.: Marketing Services Institute.

Lebow, Victor. 1955–1956. "Forced Consumption—The Prescription for 1956." *Journal of Retailing* 31(4):166–173, 200.

Lovelock, Christopher H., and Robert F. Young. 1979. "Look to Consumers to Increase Productivity." *Harvard Business Review*, May/June, 66–76.

Lutey, Kent. 1978. "Lutey's Marketeria—Self-Service Grocers." *Montana* 28(2):50–57.

Mapes, Jeffrey. 1989. "Groups to Battle Self-Service Gas." *Oregonian*, Feb. 24, D1, 3.

Markin, Rom J. 1963. *The Supermarket: An Analysis of Growth, Development and Change*. Pullman: Washington State University Press.

Murphy, John Allen. 1917. "In Piggly Wiggly Stores the Product Has to Sell Itself." *Printers' Ink* 101(12):17–20.

National Retail Dry Goods Association. 1939. "Superfluous or Necessary? Retail Services Defined by Kirstein." *Bulletin of the National Retail Dry Goods Association* 21(2):34–35.

———. 1942. "Wanamaker's Curtails Free Customer Service." *Bulletin of the National Retail Dry Goods Association* 24(2):58, 60.

Nordstrom. ca. 1991. *Nordstrom History/Philosophy*. Regional Customer Service Board. N.p.

Peak, Hugh S., and Glen Peak. 1977. *Supermarket Merchandising and Management*. Englewood Cliffs, N.J.: Prentice-Hall.

Personnel and Management Division. 1929. "Evaluation of Services to Customers." *Journal of Retailing* 5(3):24–26.

Phillips, Charles F. 1941. "Price Policies of Food Chains." *Harvard Business Review* 19(3):377–388.

Plant, George. 1942. "O.P.A. Readies for Action to Cut Customer Services." *Bulletin of the National Retail Dry Goods Association* 24(10):11–13, 60–62.

Printers' Ink. 1921a. "Piggly Wiggly in New Line of Merchandise." *Printers' Ink* 117(1).

———. 1921b. "Piggly Wiggly Develops a Chain Store Copy Angle." *Printers' Ink* 117(11):149–150.

———. 1945. "Stores Still Short of Help: Macy's Uses Complete Promotion." *Printers' Ink* 213 (Sept.):29.

Progressive Grocer. 1941. "Self-Service Layout Boosts Unit Sales From .72 to 1.60." *Progressive Grocer* (Oct.):65–66.

RCIPA. 1919. "Why Not Try Unionism?" *RCIA* 26(2):14.

———. 1936. "Seattle Chain Stores Decree Anti-Union War." *RCIA* 39(9):31.

RWDSE. 1941. "New Super-Markets Making Deep Inroads in Department Store Field." *Retail, Wholesale and Department Store Employee* 4(1):2.

———. 1942. "Drug Self-Service Aims to Cut Costs." *Retail, Wholesale and Department Store Employee* 5(5):11.

Sales Management. 1937. "Keedoozle, Electrical Self-Service Grocery, Makes Memphis Debut." *Sales Management* 49(6):520, 550.

———. 1938. "Why Advertisers Like Self-Service Stores." *Sales Management* 43(7):39.

Salmans, Sandra. 1982. "Seventh Avenue's Sharpest Eye." *New York Times*, May 23.

Schatz, Fred C. 1933. "Restriction of Free Delivery Service." *Bulletin of the National Retail Dry Goods Association* 15(6):49–50, 120–121.

Schwartzmann, David. 1971. *The Decline of Service in Retail Trades.* Washington: Washington State University.

Sibson, Robert E. 1971. *Managing Professional Services Enterprises.* New York: Pitman Publishing.

Sloane, Leonard. 1989. "Sales People Getting Incentives for Service." *New York Times*, Aug. 26, 41.

Smith, Bernard W., and Herman Radolf. 1960. "Self-Selection Challenges the Merchandising Division." *Journal of Retailing* 36(2):81–87.

Steagall, Jane, Viola Sylbert, and Shirley Victor. 1942. "Customer Services under War Conditions." *Journal of Retailing* 18(2):49–56.

Steinberg, Jack. 1989. "What's New in Vending Machines." *New York Times*, Oct. 8, F17.

Swan, Carroll J. 1947. "Cards Act as Salesmen in Self-Service Outlets." *Printers' Ink* 218(2):39–41.

Thompson, Morris. 1942. "What About Self-Service? Is It an Answer to the Problem of Personnel Shortage?" *Bulletin of the National Retail Dry Goods Association.* 24(11):14–15.

U.S. Department of Commerce. 1947. "Checking-Counter Bottleneck." *Domestic Commerce* 35(1):78–80.

Vestal, A. G. 1918. "The Cousin of the Cafeteria." *Scientific American* 119:193.

Wingate, John W. 1942. "Wartime Personnel Problems in Department Stores." *Journal of Retailing* 19(1):2–9, 17.

Zimmermann, M. M. 1955. *The Supermarket: A Revolution in Distribution*. New York: McGraw-Hill.

Chapter 5

Ayars, Christine. ca. 1917. *Young Persons Employed in Retail Selling*. Women's Educational and Industrial Union, unprocessed box, AESL.

Bane, Lita. 1929. "The Household Buyer." *LHJ*, Nov. 102, 129.

Barmarsh, Isadore. 1983. "Selling—Retailing's Lost Art." *New York Times*, March 15, D1.

Benson, Susan Porter. 1986. *Counter Cultures: Saleswomen, Managers and Customers in American Department Stores, 1890–1940*. Urbana: University of Illinois Press.

Bloodworth, Bess. 1930. "Utilization of Part-Time Workers." *Bulletin of the National Retail Dry Goods Association* 12(July):385.

Bluestone, Barry, Patricia Hanna, Sarah Kuhn, and Laura Moore. 1981. *The Retail Revolution*. Boston: Auburn House.

Brandt, Ellen. ca. 1978. Women in Shops: A Sociological Exploration of the Saleswoman Occupation. Paper, Norges Almenvitenskapelige Forkingsrad, Oslo, Norway.

Burke, Mary. 1893. "Proceedings of the Third Annual Convention, Held at Nashville, Tennessee, July 11, 12, 13 and 14, 1893." *RCNA* 1(1):1.

Canfield, Bertrand. 1948. "Unionization of Salesmen—An Outline of the Present Situation." *Printers' Ink* 239(9):34–35, 97–98, 102, 104–105.

Conway, H. J. 1920a. "Facts Regarding Minimum Wage for Women in Industry." *RCIA* 27(2):79.

———. 1920b. "Increased Activity among Associated Retailers." *RCIA* 27(5):9–11.

———. 1921. "Minimum Wage Laws Afford No Security." *RCIA* 28(10):11–12.

———. 1924. "A Fearless Arraignment." *RCIA* 31(10):14–15.

Estey, Marten S. 1956. "Unionism in the Retail Trades." *Business Topics* 3(6):23–25.

Ewen, Stuart. 1976. *Captains of Consciousness*. New York: McGraw-Hill.

Fletcher, Joseph A. 1942. "Overcoming Personnel Shortages with Partial Self-Service." *Chain Store Age*, Dec., 24–26, 84, 86.

Harrington, Michael. 1962. *The Retail Clerk*. New York: John Wiley.

Hoffman, William C. 1949. "A Study of Occupational Adjustment Problems of Retail Workers in the Louisville, Kentucky Metropolitan Area with Implications for Secondary School Retail Training Programs." Diss., Northwestern University.

Jay, Richard. 1953. "A Case Study in Retail Unionism." Ph.D. diss., University of California, Berkeley.

Kathrens, R. D. 1899. "Women Wage-Earners and the RCIPA." *RCNA* 7(1):14.

Kessler-Harris, Alice. 1986. "EEOC vs. Sears, Roebuck and Company: Testimony." *Signs* 11(4):767–779.

Klein, Julius. 1929. "Two Women at the Counter." *LHJ*, March, 35–36.

Lanphere [Lamphere], Emma. 1899. "Bright Woman's Views" (letter to the editor). *RCNA* 7(1):11.

Lawrence, William M. 1895. "For Women Who Work." *RCNA* 2(8):11.

Lens, Sidney. 1959. *The Crisis of American Labor*. New York: Barnes.

Lind, G. Edward. 1906. "Women's Sphere." *RCIA* 13(1):15.

Morris, Max. 1907a. "How the Conditions of the Clerk Contrast with Those of Other Workers." *RCIA* 14(1):24.

———. 1907b. "Women's and Men's Wages." *RCIA* 14(2):25.

———. 1907c. "The Girl in Business." *RCIA* 14(6):15.

———. 1908a. "International Plain Talk." *RCIA* 15(1):15.

———. 1908b. "Extracts from a Recent Address Made by International Secretary Treasurer Max Morris in Mobile, Alabama, as Appearing in the *Mobile Register*." *RCIA* 15(2):18.

———. 1908c. "International Plain Talk." *RCIA* 15(5):14.

———. 1908d. "Reform and Economics" (editorial). *RCIA* 15(6):23.

———. 1908e. "No Wage Reduction to Be Tolerated" (editorial). *RCIA* 15(2): 25.

———. 1908f. "International Plain Talk." *RCIA* 15(2):15.

Morrow, James. 1893. "Presidential Address, Third Annual Convention, Nashville, Tennessee, July 11, 12, 13 and 14, 1893." *RCNA* 1(1):3.

Ohrbach, Nathan M. 1943. "Meeting the Labor Shortage in Retailing." *Journal of Retailing* 19(2):33–34.

O'Leary, Iris P. 1916. *Department Stores Occupations: The Jarvey Committee of the Cleveland Foundation*. Philadelphia: William F. Fell Company.

Pickernell, A. 1931. "What About Customer Service." *Bulletin of the National Retail Dry Goods Association* 13(Aug.):481–482.

RCIPA. 1902. "Morality of Women Clerks" (editorial). *RCIA* 9(10):12.

———. 1903. "Women Wage Workers." *RCIA* 10(2):14.

———. 1905a. "To Our Lady Members." *RCIA* 12(10):17.

———. 1905b. "Minimum Scale of Wages." *RCIA* 12(8):52.

———. 1906. "The Salesladies Should Join the Local." *RCIA* 13(4):16–17.

———. 1908. "Are You Doing Your Own Thinking?" (editorial). *RCIA* 15(1):27

———. 1910. "Mary Boyle O'Reilly Condemns 'Bread Line' Wages for Girl Toiler." *RCIA* 17(4):13–14.

———. 1919. "Noblesse Oblige." *RCIA* 26(3):13–14.

———. 1920a. "First Saleswoman Caused Boycott of Saco Store." *RCIA* 27(9): 34.

———. 1920b. Editorial. *RCIA* 27(7):22.

———. 1924. "Women in Kentucky Industries." *RCIA* 31(2):22–23.

RCNPA. 1895. "How to Form a Local Union." *RCNA* 2(8):11.

———. 1899a. "Woman as a Competitor." *RCNA* 6(12):6.

———. 1899b. "Pertinent Suggestions." *RCNA* 7(1):1.

Rosenberg, Rosalind. 1986. "EEOC vs. Sears, Roebuck and Company: Testimony." *Signs* 11(4):757–766.

Rytina, Nancy F. 1982. "Earnings of Men and Women: A Look at Specific Occupations." *Monthly Labor Review* 105(4):25–31.

Schwartzmann, David. 1971. *The Decline of Service in Retail Trades*. Washington: Washington State University Press.

Simeral, Margaret. 1978. "Women and the Reserve Army of Labor." *Insurgent Sociologist* 7(2):164–179.

Smith, Charles. 1928. "Educating the Public to Changing Conditions in Retailing." *Journal of Retailing* 4(3):3–8.

Strasser, Susan. 1989. *Satisfaction Guaranteed: The Making of the American Mass Market*. New York: Pantheon.

Thompson, Morris. 1942. "What About Self-Service? Is It an Answer to the Problem of Personnel Shortage?" *Bulletin of the National Retail Dry Goods Association* 24(11):14–15.

U.S. Bureau of the Census. 1973. *Occupation by Industry*. 1970 Census of Population. PC(2)-7C. Washington, D.C.: U.S. Government Printing Office.

———. 1956. *Special Reports: Occupational Characteristics*. 1950 Census of Population. Report P-E no. 1B, preprint of vol. IV, pt. 1, chap. B. Washington, D.C.: U.S. Government Printing Office.

———. 1914. *Population 1910*. Occupation Statistics. Washington, D.C.: U.S. Government Printing Office.

Valesh, Eva McDonald. 1902. "Woman's Work." *RCIA* 9 (2):11–13, (3):11–15, (4):11–15, (5):9–11, (6):11–12, (9):11–19, (10):5–13, (11):5–7, (12):7–8.

———. 1903. "Woman's Work." *RCIA* 10(1):6–7.

Vestal, A. G. 1918. "The Cousin of the Cafeteria." *Scientific American* 119:193.

Weinbaum, Batya, and Amy Bridges. 1976. "The Other Side of the Paycheck." *Monthly Review* 28:88–103.

Whitehead, Frances M. 1942. "Hours and Wages of Retail Clerks in Illinois Outside Chicago, 1939." Ph.D. diss., University of Illinois.

Williams, Raymond. 1980. *Problems in Materialism and Culture*. London: Verso.

Williamson, Frances A. 1906. "Labor Movement Concerning Women." *RCIA* 13(4):16–17.

Wingate, Isabel. 1944. "Personnel Notes." *Journal of Retailing* 19(4):115–116, 120.

Chapter 6

A & P (Atlantic and Pacific) ad. 1929a. *LHJ*, Jan., 129.

———. 1929b. *LHJ*, July, 63.

———. 1929c. *LHJ*, Nov., 66.

Agnota ad. 1903. "The Improved Seamless Glove." *LHJ*, Sept., 33.

Alcott, William A. 1839. *The Young Housekeeper*. Boston: George W. Light.

Bane, Lita. 1929. "The Household Buyer." *LHJ*, Nov., 102, 129.

Barrington Coffee ad. 1916. *LHJ*, April, 66.

Benson, Susan Porter. 1986. *Counter Cultures: Saleswomen, Managers and Customers in American Department Stores, 1890–1940*. Urbana: University of Illinois Press.

Bluestone, Barry, Patricia Hanna, Sarah Kuhn, and Laura Moore. 1981. *The Retail Revolution*. Boston: Auburn House.

Business Week. 1934. "Piggly Wiggly Comeback." *Business Week*, Nov. 24, 14–15.

Carson, Eleanor. 1916. "The Hired Girl 'Co-ed.'" *LHJ*, Feb., 36.

Cassady, Ralph, Jr. 1962. *Competition and Price Making in Food Retailing*. New York: Ronald Press.

Cooke, Rose Terry. 1889. "Be Plucky." *LHJ*, July, 19.

Corina, John. ca. 1947. *Spotlight on Self-Service*. Manchester, England: Co-operative Union Ltd.

Coutant, Frank R. 1942. "Retailers Turn to Self-Services: What Are You Doing About It?" *Sales Management* 52(8):64–66.

Cowan, Ruth. 1983. *More Work for Mother*. New York: Basic Books.

Dudden, Faye E. 1983. *Serving Women*. Middletown, Conn.: Wesleyan University Press.

Edwards, Alice L. 1929. "Things That We All Want Alike." *LHJ*, March, 86, 96, 98.

Ewen, Stuart. 1976. *Captains of Consciousness*. New York: McGraw-Hill.

Fredericks, Christine. 1915. "The New Housekeeping." *LHJ*, Oct., 45.

———. 1917. "If I Could Begin Housework All Over Again." *LHJ*, Nov. M-107, Reel 78, AESL.

———. 1920a. "The Most Important Kitchen Tool." *LHJ*, March, 186.

———. 1920b. "How a 'Repair Day' Saves Money in My House." *LHJ*, March, 188.

———. 1926. "If I Could Begin Housework All Over Again." *Hardware Dealers Magazine*, Sept., 62.

George Batten Co. 1921. *Printers' Ink* 115(5): opposite p. 53.

Glazer, Nona. 1980. "Overworking the Working Woman: Portrayals of the Double Day in a Mass Magazine." *Women's Studies International Quarterly* 3:79–93.

Haas, Harold M. 1939. "Social and Economic Aspects of the Chain Store Movement." Ph.D. diss., University of Minnesota. Reprinted 1979.

Hartmann, Heidi. 1974. "Capitalism and Women's Work in the Home, 1900–1930." Ph.D. diss., Yale University.

Holt, Felicia. 1889. "Consideration of Maid for Mistress." *LHJ*, Nov., 7.

Hotpoint Automatic Electric Range ad. 1929. *LHJ*, Sept., 133.

Ideal Vacuum Cleaner ad. 1913. *LHJ*, Sept., 63.

Ivory Flakes ad. 1908a. *LHJ*, July, 2.

———. 1908b. *LHJ*, Sept., 4.

———. 1929. *LHJ*, Feb., 64.

Jewett, Sarah Orne. 1889. "The Sensible Housekeepers of the Future." *LHJ*, June, 10.

Katzman, David M. 1978. *Seven Days a Week: Women and Domestic Service in Industrializing America*. New York: Oxford University Press.

Klein, Julius. 1929. "Two Women at the Counter." *LHJ*, March, 35–36.

Knapp, Louisa. 1885. "Editorial Notes." *LHJ*, May, 3.

Ladies' Home Journal. 1886a. "Mistress vs. Maid." *LHJ*, Dec., 3.

———. 1886b. "Which Is Mistress?" *LHJ*, April, 7.

———. 1886c. "Household Help." *LHJ*, Dec., 3.

———. 1916a. "Dishwashing Made Easy." *LHJ*, June, 40.

———. 1916b. "The Wedding Present That Embarrasses." *LHJ*, Oct., 7.

———. 1929. "Announcing—The LHJ Clearing House of Consumer Information." *LHJ*, Dec., 84.

Lambert, Jan H. 1887. "New Dress Goods." *LHJ*, March, 10.

Lebow, Victor. 1955–1956. "Forced Consumption—The Prescription for 1956." *Journal of Retailing* 31(4):166–173, 200.

Liquid Veneer ad. 1908. *LHJ*, Nov., 78.

Lutey, Kent. 1978. "Lutey's Marketeria." *Montana* 28(2):50–57.

Markin, Rom J. 1963. *The Supermarket: An Analysis of Growth, Development and Change*. Pullman: Washington State University Press.

McConaught, Mrs. 1885. "The Housekeepers' Hard Problem." *LHJ*, May, 4.

Minute Tapioca ad. 1908. *LHJ*, May, 56.

Mennen Talcum Powder ad. 1916. *LHJ*, May, 87.

Nell, W. A. 1958. "Automation in Food Marketing—The Extension of Mechanized Shopping." *Agenda* 6 (Dec.):27–31.

North Bennet Street Industrial School. 1912. Readings for second year of girls' prevocational work. Box 79, series II, folder 77, AESL.

Old Dutch Cleanser ad. 1916. *LHJ*, May, 82.

———. 1908. *LHJ*, Jan., 47.

Parloa, Maria. 1908. *Miss Parloa's New Cookbook and Marketing Guide*. Boston: Colonial Press.

———. 1903a. "The Woman with No Servant." *LHJ*, March, 43.

———. 1903b. "The Woman with No Servant." *LHJ*, Sept., 32.

———. 1903c. "The Woman with No Servant." *LHJ*, Nov., 46.

Parrish, Ruth L. 1929. "Scoring Your Own Marketing Information." *LHJ*, May, 118, 145–146, 148, 151.

Phillips, Charles. 1941. "Price Policies of Food Chains." *Harvard Business Review* 19(3):377–388.

Piggly Wiggly ad. 1929a. "No Delays, No Hurry, When You Shop This Way." *LHJ*, April, 170.

———. 1929b. "Choose for Yourself . . . Help Yourself." *LHJ*, June, 114.

———. 1929c. "Select What You Please . . . By Yourself." *LHJ*, Dec., 137.

———. 1929d. "Here She Is Free—to Reach Her Own Decisions." *LHJ*, Oct., 185.

Pillsbury's Breakfast Food ad. 1908. *LHJ*, Nov., inside cover.

Practical Housekeeper. 1885. "Domestic Journalisms." *LHJ*, Jan., 5.

Printers' Ink. 1921. "Piggly Wiggly Develops a Chain Store Copy Angle." *Printers' Ink* 117(11):149–150.

Procter and Gamble, White Naptha Soap ad. 1913. *LHJ*, Aug., 29.

Quelch, John A., and Hirotaka Takeuchi. 1981. "Nonstore Marketing: Fast Track or Slow?" *Harvard Business Review* 59(4):75–84.

Savage Clothes Washer ad. 1929. *LHJ*, May, 216.

Simplex Ironer ad. 1913. *LHJ*, April, 81.

Sprague, Polly. 1916. "The Hired Girl in the Home." *LHJ*, Sept., 54.

Standard Porcelain Enameled Baths and Sanitary Ware ad. 1903. *LHJ*, Sept., 42.

Strasser, Susan. 1982. *Never Done: A History of American Housework*. New York: Pantheon.

———. 1989. *Satisfaction Guaranteed*. New York: Pantheon.

Sylbert, Viola P. 1942. "Self-Service Experiments in Department Stores." *Journal of Retailing* 18(3):74–81.

Vestal, A. G. 1918. "The Cousin of the Cafeteria." *Scientific American* 119:193.

Washburn-Crosby Gold Medal Flour ad. 1908. *LHJ*, Nov., 61.

Williams, Raymond. 1980. *Problems in Materialism and Culture*. London: New Left Review.

Women's Educational Industrial Union. 1897. Program Description. B-8, box 1, folder 9, AESL.

Wright, Gwendolyn. 1980. *Moralism and the Model Home: Domestic Architecture and Cultural Conflict in Chicago, 1873–1915*. Chicago: University of Chicago Press.

Zimmerman, M. M. 1955. *The Supermarket: A Revolution in Distribution*. New York: McGraw-Hill.

Chapter 7

Anderson, Joan, and Helen Elfert. 1989. "Managing Chronic Illness in the Family: Women as Caretakers." *Journal of Advanced Nursing* 14:735–73.

Archbold, Patricia G. 1982. "An Analysis of Parentcaring by Women." *Home Health Care Services Quarterly* 3:5–26.

Bergthold, Linda A. 1987. "Business and the Pushcart Vendors in an Age of Supermarkets." *International Journal of Health Services* 17(1):7–27.

Boffey, Phillip. 1988. "Three in House Ask Medicare Financing Chief to Resign." *New York Times*, Aug. 12, 24.

Brewster, Agnes W. 1958. "Voluntary Health Insurance and Medical Care Expenditures: A Ten-Year Review." *Social Security Bulletin* 21(12):8–15.

Brody, Elaine. 1985. "Parent Care as a Normative Family Stress." *The Gerontologist* 25:19–29.

———, and Claire Schoonover. 1986. "Patterns of Parent-Care When Adult Daughters Work and When They Do Not." *The Gerontologist* 26:372–381.

Buhler-Wilkerson, Karen. 1983. "False Dawn: The Rise and Decline of Public Health Nursing in America, 1900–1930." Pp. 89–106 in *Nursing History*, ed. Ellen Conliffe Lagemann. New York: Teachers' College and Columbia University Press.

Burck, Gilbert, and Todd May. 1959. "The Good Uses of $750 Billion." *Fortune* 59(4):104.

Caplan, R. 1981. "Pasteurized Patients and Profits: The Changing Nature of Self-Care in American Medicine." Ph.D., diss. University of Massachusetts.

Coe, Merilyn, Anne W. Wilkinson, Patricia Patterson, and Michael R. Goldwyn. 1986. "Dependency at Discharge: Impact of DRGs." In *Examination of Quality of Care under Medicare's Prospective Payment System*. Hearings Before Committee on Finance, 99th Congress, June 3, 143–197. Washington, D.C.: U.S. Government Printing Office.

Committee on Aging. 1984. *Building a Long-Term Care Policy: Home Care Data and Implications*. Subcommittee on Health and Long-Term Care, December. Pub. no. 98-484. Washington, D.C.: U.S. Government Printing Office.

Committee on the Costs of Medical Care. 1932. *Medical Care for the American People*. Chicago: University of Chicago Press. Reprinted 1970 by the U.S. Department of Health, Education, and Welfare.

Congressional Hearing. 1977. *Medicare-Medicaid Reimbursement Reform Act*. Appendix B, Health Care Expenditures and Their Control. Hearings Before Subcommittee on Health, June 7, 8, 9. Washington, D.C.: U.S. Government Printing Office.

Dewhurst, J. F., and Associates. 1955. *America's Needs and Resources*. New York: Twentieth Century Fund.

Economic Report of the President. 1991. 102d Congress, 1st sess., February 10. House doc. no. 102–2.

Ehrenreich, Barbara, and John Ehrenreich. 1971. *The American Health Empire: Power, Profits and Politics*. New York: Random House.

Embree, Edwin R. 1933. *Julius Rosenwald Fund: Review for the Two-Year Period 1931–33*. Chicago: University of Chicago Press.

Employee Benefit Plan. 1988. "Home Health Costs." *Employee Benefit Plan* 43(3): 13.

Falk, I. S., C. Rufus Rorem, and Martha D. King. 1933. *The Costs of Medical Care*. Chicago: University of Chicago Press.

Faltermayer, Edmund K. 1970. "Better Care at Less Cost without Miracles." *Fortune* 81(1):80–83, 126–128, 130.

Finch, Janet, and Dulcie Groves. 1983. *A Labour of Love*. London: Routledge and Kegan Paul.

Fortune. 1958. "AMA versus Miners." *Fortune* 58(3):199–200.

Freudenheim, Milt. 1988. "The Boom in Home Health Care." *New York Times*, May 2, 23–24.

Haber, David. 1986. "In-Home and Community-Based Long-Term Care Services." *Journal of Applied Gerontology* 5:37–50.

Halloran, E. J., and M. Kiley. 1987. "Nursing Dependency, Diagnosis-Related Groups and Length of Hospital Stay." *Health Care Financing* 8(3):27–35.

Hammond, John. 1979. "Home Health Care Cost Effectiveness: An Overview of the Literature." *Public Health Reports* 94(4):305–311.

Health Care Financing Administration. 1988a. *1988 HCFA Statistics*. HCFA pub. no. 03271, Dec., 28. Washington, D.C.: U.S. Government Printing Office.

———. 1988b. "Use and Cost of Home Health Agency Services Under Medicare: Selected Calendar Years 1974–86." *Research Brief No.* 88-4. Washington, D.C.: U.S. Government Printing Office.

Herzlinger, Regina E. 1986. "How Companies Tackle Health Costs." *Harvard Business Review* 64(1):70–80.

———, and J. Schwartz. 1985. "How Companies Tackle Health Costs, Part II." *Harvard Business Review* 63(4):69–81.

Hickey, Mary. 1987. "Prospective Payment and Patient Acuity Levels." *Rehabilitation Nursing* 12:132–134.

Home Care News. 1985. "HHS Reveals 80 Percent of All Medicare DRG Initial Discharges Go Home for Self-Care." *Home Care News* 3(24):1.

Horowitz, A. 1985. "Sons and Daughters as Caregivers to Older Parents." *The Gerontologist* 25:612–617.

Iglehart, John K. 1986. "Health Policy Report: Canada's Health Care System." *New England Journal of Medicine* 315(3):202–208.

Johnston, J. Bruce, and Uwe E. Reinhardt. 1989. "The Health of a Nation: Two Views." *Health Affairs* 8(2):5–23.

Jones, Dee A., and Norman J. Vetter. 1984. "A Survey of Those Who Care for the Elderly at Home: Their Problems and Their Needs." *Social Science in Medicine* 19:511–514.

Kilbane, Kathleen, and Beth Blacksin. 1988. "The Demise of Free Care: The Visiting Nurse Association of Chicago." *Nursing Clinics of North America* 23(2):435–442.

Kleinfield, N. R. 1983. "The Home Health Care Boom." *New York Times*, June 30, D1, 4.

Kramer, Andrew M., Peter W. Shaughnessy, Marjorie Bauman, and Kathryn Crister. 1990. "Assessing and Assuring the Quality of Home Health Care: A Conceptual Framework." *Milbank Quarterly* 68(3):413–444.

Krieger, Nancy, and M. Bassett. 1986. "The Health of Black Folk: Gender, Class and Ideology in Science." *Monthly Review* 38(3):74–85.

Littman, Theodor J. 1974. "The Family as a Basic Unit in Health and Medical Care: A Social Behavioral Overview." *Social Science Medicine* 8:495–519.

Maher, Walter. 1989. "Reform Medicare: The Rest Will Follow." *New York Times*, July 9, 3.

———. 1990. "Perspectives." *Health Affairs* 9:169–170.

Management Review. 1958. "Keeping the Lid on Health Insurance Costs." *Management Review* 47:58–59.

———. 1960. "Facts and Figures on Corporate Health Insurance." *Management Review* 49:57–58.

Matthews, Sarah H. 1987. "Provision of Care to Old Parents." *Research on Aging* 9:45–60.

Meier, Barry. 1989. "High-Tech Home Care Under Scrutiny." *New York Times*, December 8, 32.

Miller, Baila. 1990. "Gender Differences in the Spouse Management of the Caregiver Role." Pp. 92–104 in *Circles of Care*, ed. Emily K. Abel and Margaret K. Nelson. Albany: SUNY Press.

Morrissey, Michael, Frank A. Sloan, and Joseph Valvona. 1988. "Shifting Medicare Patients Out of the Hospital." *Health Affairs* 7(Winter):52–63.

Moss, Abigail J., and Mary A. Moien. 1987. "Recent Declines in Hospitalization: United States, 1982–86." *Advanced Data No. 140*, Sept. 24, 1–15. Washington, D.C.: National Center for Health Statistics, U.S. Department of Health and Human Services.

National Association for Home Care. 1986. *The Attempted Dismantling of the Medicare Home Care Benefit*. Select Committee on Aging, U.S. House of

Representatives, 99th Congress, 2d sess. Washington, D.C.: U.S. Government Printing Office.

Navarro, Vicente. 1987. "Federal Health Policies in the United States: An Alternative Explanation." *Milbank Quarterly* 65(1):81–111.

Office of Technology Assessment. 1984. *Medical Technology and Costs of the Medicare Program.* OTA-H-227, July. Washington, D.C.: U.S. Government Printing Office.

Paringer, L. 1985. "Forgotten Costs of Informal Long-Term Care." *Generations* 9:55–58.

Pesznecker, Betty, Barbara Horn, Joanne Werner, and Virginia Kenyon. 1987. "Home Health Services in a Climate of Cost Containment." *Home Health Care Services Quarterly* 8(1):5–21.

Roe, Wayne I., and Gary S. Schneider. 1985. "High-Tech Moves into Home Market with Cardiac, Nutritional Therapies." *Business and Health* 2(5):52–53. Washington Business Group on Health publication.

Rosenberg, Charles. 1987. *The Care of Strangers.* New York: Basic Books.

Salmon, J. W. 1975. "The Health Maintenance Organization Strategy: A Corporate Takeover of Health Services Delivery." *International Journal of Health Services* 5(4):609–624.

Sapolsky, Harvey M., Drew Altman, Richard Greene, and Judith D. Moore. 1981. "Corporate Attitudes toward Health Care Costs." *Health and Society* 59(4):561–585.

Schlesinger, Mark, Judy Bentkover, David Blumenthal, Robert Musacchio, and Janet Willer. 1987. "The Privatization of Health Care and Physicians' Perception of Access to Hospital Services." *Milbank Quarterly* 65(1):25–58.

SEIU. 1988. Strike pamphlet. Author's collection, Portland, Oregon.

Silberman, Charles E. 1959. "The Markets of the Sixties: The Money Left Over for the Good Life." *Fortune* 25(5):134–137.

Skolnick, A. 1962. "Employee-Benefit Plans, 1954–60." *Social Security Bulletin* 25(4):5–16.

Souhrada, L. 1988. "Suppliers Target Alternate Care Provider Networks." *Hospitals* 62(9):50–54.

Starr, Paul. 1982. *The Social Transformation of American Medicine.* New York: Basic Books.

Stoller, E., and E. L. Stoller. 1983. "Help with Activities of Everyday Life: Sources of Support for the Non-Institutionalized Elderly." *The Gerontologist* 23:64–70.

Stone, Robyn, Gail Lee Cafferata, and Judith Sangl. 1987. *Caregivers of the Frail Elderly: A National Profile.* Washington, D.C.: National Center for Health Services Research.

U.S. Department of Commerce. 1959–1986. *U.S. Industrial Outlook.* Washington, D.C.: Government Printing Office.

U.S. General Accounting Office. 1982. *The Elderly Should Benefit from Expanded*

Home Health Care But Increasing These Services Will Not Insure Cost Reductions. GAO/IPE-83-1. Gaithersburg, Md.: U.S. Government Printing Office.

U.S. Public Health Service. 1985. *Health—United States, 1985.* Washington, D.C.: U.S. Government Printing Office.

Waitzkin, Howard. 1979. "A Marxian Interpretation of the Growth and Development of Coronary Care Technology." *American Journal of Public Health* 69(12):1260–1268.

———. 1983. *The Second Sickness.* New York: Free Press.

Waldo, Daniel R., Katherine R. Levit, and Helen Lazenby. 1986. "National Health Expenditures, 1985." *Health Care Financing* 8(1):1–21.

Zink, Victor. 1976. "Greater Effort Needed to Control Costs." *Hospitals* 50(6): 65–67.

Chapter 8

American Nurse. 1979. "New Care Unit to Cut Hospital Costs by 40 Percent." *American Nurse* 11:1–6.

Blitzer, Carol. 1981. "Cooperative Care Unit Cuts Costs 40% at NYU Hospital." *Business Insurance* 15(52):3, 27.

Brown, Esther L. 1948. *Nursing for the Future.* New York: Russell Sage Foundation.

Butter, Irene, Eugenia Carpenter, Bonnie Kay, and Ruth Simmons. 1985. *Sex and Status: Hierarchies in the Health Workforce.* Ann Arbor: School of Public Health, University of Michigan.

Congressional Hearings. 1977. *Medicare-Medicaid Reimbursement Reform Act.* Appendix B, Health Care Expenditures and Their Control. Hearings Before Subcommittee on Health, June 7, 8, 9. Washington, D.C.: U.S. Government Printing Office.

Evans, Robert, and Geoffrey Robinson. 1983. "An Economic Study of Cost Savings on a Care-by-Parent Ward." *Medical Care* 21(8):768–782.

Farley, Dean. 1988. "Trends in Hospital Average Length of Stay, Casemix, and Discharge Rates, 1980–85." *Hospital Studies Program Research Note II.* DHHS pub. no. (PHS) 88–3420. Washington, D.C.: National Center for Health Services Research and Health Care Technology Assessment.

Glass, Alice L., and Leon W. Warshaw. 1978. "Minimal Care Units: Mechanisms for Hospital Cost Containment." *Healthcare Management Review* 3(2):33–41.

Glass, Leah, and Laurel Eisner. 1981. "CETA as a Vehicle to Recruit Welfare Recipients and the Unemployed into the Home Care Field." *Home Health Services Quarterly* 2(3):5–21.

Glazer, Nona. 1991. "'Between a Rock and a Hard Place': Women's Professional

Organizations in Nursing, and Class, Race, and Ethnic Inequalities." *Gender and Society* 5(3):351–372.

———. 1987. "Intragender Occupational Segmentation: Nurse Work, Race and Class." Paper presented at the Eastern Sociological Society meetings, May, Boston.

Haddad, Amy Marie. 1987. *High Tech Home Care*. Rockville, Md.: Aspen Publishers.

Hines, Darlene C. 1989. *Black Women in White*. Bloomington: Indiana University Press.

Melosh, Barbara. 1982. *"The Physician's Hand": Work Culture and Conflict in American Nursing*. Philadelphia: Temple University Press.

Rushmer, Robert F. 1976. "Home Care: A Biomedical Engineering Challenge." *Biomedical Engineering* 11(4):121–123.

Russell, Louise B. 1989. *Medicare's New Hospital Payment System: Is It Working?* Washington, D.C.: Brookings Institution.

Tunstall, Patricia. 1960. "Hospitals without Walls." *Practical Nursing* 10(5):14–15.

U.S. Department of Commerce. 1960–1987. *U.S. Industrial Outlook*. Washington, D.C.: U.S. Government Printing Office.

Chapter 9

Bly, Janet. 1981. "Measuring Productivity for Home Health Nurses." *Home Health Care Services Quarterly* 2(3):23–39.

Bontempo, Theresa, and Ellen Thomas Eggland. 1987. "Nursing Implications for Home Parenteral Therapy." *Home Healthcare Nurse* 6(4):14–17.

Cooper, Kenneth. 1987. "U.S. Accused of Withholding Medicare Payments." *Oregonian*, Feb. 17, A8.

Donavan, Rebecca. 1987. "Home Care Work: A Legacy of Slavery in U.S. Health Care." *Affilia*, Fall, 31–44.

———. 1989. "'We Care for the Most Important People in Your Life': Home Care Workers in New York City." *Women's Studies Quarterly* 1, 2:56–65.

Franz, Julie. 1984. "Challenge for Nursing: Hiking Productivity without Lowering Quality of Care." *Modern Healthcare* 61 (Sept.):60–68.

Glazer, Nona Y. 1991. "'Between a Rock and a Hard Place': Women's Professional Organizations in Nursing and Class, Race, and Ethnic Inequalities." *Gender and Society* 5(3):351–372.

Joel, Lucille A. 1984. "DRGs and RIMs: Implications." *Nursing Outlook* 32(1): 42–49.

Kilbane, Kathleen, and Beth Blacksin. 1988. "The Demise of Free Care." *Nursing Clinics of North America* 23(2):435–442.

Kosecoff, Jacqueline, Katherine Kahn, William Rogers, Ellen Reinisch, Marjorie Sherwood, Lisa Rubenstein, David Draper, Carol Roth, Carole Chew, and Robert Brook. 1991. "Prospective Payment System and Impairment at Discharge—The 'Quicker and Sicker' Story Revisted." *Journal of the American Medical Association* 264(15):1980–1983.

Koska, Mary T. 1988. "Aide Shortage Limits Home Health Delivery." *Hospitals* 62(9):63.

Madsen, Nancy, and Rosalind W. Harper. 1985. "Improving the Nursing Climate for Cost Containment." *Journal of Nursing Administration* (15):11–17.

Marek, Karen, and Beth McVan. 1987. "Home Transfusion Therapy: A New Dimension in Home Care." *Quality Review Bulletin* 13(1):17–20.

Morrisey, Michael, Frank A. Sloane, and Joseph Valvona. 1988. "Shifting Medicare Patients Out of the Hospital." *Health Affairs* 7(Winter):52–63.

Neu, C. R., Scott C. Harrison, and Joanna Z. Heilbrun. 1989. *Medical Patients and Postacute Care: Who Goes Where?* R-3780-MN. Santa Monica, Calif.: Rand.

Paget, Marianne. 1987. "Becoming Silent." Paper presented at the Eastern Sociology Society meetings, May, Boston.

Progress. 1990. "Who Is Going to Take Care of Your Mom?" *Progress: The Newsletter of Women for Economic Justice* 9(1):1, 3.

Roe, Wayne, and Gary S. Schneider. 1985. "High-Tech Moves into Home Market with Cardiac, Nutritional Therapies." *Business and Health* 2(5):52–53.

Rubinstein, Lisa, Katherine Kahn, Ellen Reinisch, Marjorie Sherwood, William Rogers, Caren Kamberg, David Draper, and Robert Brook. 1991. "Changes in Quality of Care for Five Diseases Measured by Implicit Review, 1981 to 1986." *Journal of the American Medical Association* 264(15): 1974–1979.

Ruther, Martin, and Charles Helbing. 1988. "Use and Cost of Home Health Agency Services Under Medicare." *Health Care Financing Review* 10(1): 105–108.

Weeks, L. C., and P. Darrah. 1985. "The Documentation Dilemma." *Journal of Nursing Administration* 15(11):22–27.

Chapter 10

Abel, Emily. 1990. "Family Care of the Frail Elderly." Pp. 63–91 in *Circles of Care*, ed. Emily Abel and Margaret Nelson. Albany: SUNY Press.

Aiken, Linda H., and Howard E. Freeman. 1984. "Medical Sociology and Science and Technology in Medicine." Pp. 527–580 in *A Guide to the Culture of Science, Technology, and Medicine*, ed. Paul Durbin. New York: Free Press.

American Nurses Association. 1978. *Health Care at Home*. Kansas City: American Nurses Association.

Barfoot, K. R., and K. L. Ross. 1988. "Intravenous Therapy at Home: An Overview." *Home Healthcare Nurse* 6(4):11–14.

Barrett, Michele, and Mary McIntosh. 1984. *The Anti-Social Family*. London: Verso.

Berk, Richard, and Sarah F. Berk. 1979. *Labor and Leisure at Home*. New York: Sage Publications.

Berk, Sarah F. (ed.). 1980. *Women and Household Labor*. New York: Sage Publications.

Bijerk, Weibe E., Thomas P. Hughes, and Trevor J. Pinch. 1987. *The Social Construction of Technological Systems*. Cambridge, Mass.: MIT Press.

Bontempo, Theresa, and Ellen Thomas Eggland. 1987. "Nursing Implications for Home Parenteral Therapy." *Home Healthcare Nurse* 6(4):14–17.

Braverman, Harry. 1974. *Labor and Monopoly Capital: The Degradation of Work in the Twentieth Century*. New York: Monthly Review Press.

Budrys, Grace. 1986. "Medical Technology Policy: Some Underlying Assumptions." Pp. 147–183 in *Research in the Sociology of Health Care*, vol. 4, ed. Julius Roth and Sheryl B. Ruzek. Greenwich, Conn.: Jai Press.

Bystydzienski, Jill M. 1989. "Women and Socialism: A Comparative Study of Women in Poland and the USSR." *Signs* 14:668–684.

Carpenter, Eugenia S. 1980. "Children's Health Care and the Changing Role of Women." *Medical Care* 18(12):1208–1218.

Cockburn, Cynthia. 1983. *Brothers*. London: Pluto Press.

———. 1985. *Machinery of Dominance: Women, Men and Technical Know-How*. London: Pluto Press.

Corbin, Julie, and Anselm Strauss. 1988. *Unending Work and Care*. San Francisco: Jossey-Bass.

Cowan, Ruth. 1983. *More Work for Mother*. New York: Basic Books.

Dolbee, S. F., and N. S. Creason. 1988. "Outcome Criteria for the Patient Using Intravenous Antibiotic Therapy at Home." *Home Healthcare Nurse* 6(4):22–29.

Edmonson, Brad. 1985. "The Home Health Care Worker." *American Demographics* 7(4):28–33.

Finch, Janet, and Dulcie Groves. 1983. *Labour of Love: Women, Work and Caring*. Boston: Routledge and Kegan Paul.

Folbre, Nancy. 1987. "The Pauperization of Motherhood: Patriarchy and Public Policy in the United States." Pp. 491–511 in *Families and Work*, ed. Naomi Gerstel and Harriet Gross. Philadelphia: Temple University Press.

Fox, Bonnie (ed.). 1980. *Hidden in the Household*. Toronto: Women's Press.

Fox, Renee. 1985. "Reflections and Opportunities in the Sociology of Medicine." *Journal of Health and Social Behavior* 26(1):6–14.

———, and Judith Swazey. 1974. *The Courage to Fail*. Chicago: University of Chicago Press.

Franz, Julie. 1984. "Challenge for Nursing: Hiking Productivity without Lowering Quality of Care." *Modern Healthcare* 61 (Sept.):60–68.

Gaston, J. 1984. "Sociology of Science and Technology." Pp. 465–526 in *A Guide to the Culture of Science, Technology, and Medicine*, ed. Paul T. Durbin. New York: Free Press.

Glazer-Malbin, Nona. 1976. "Housework." *Signs* 1(14):905–921.

Glenn, Evelyn Nakano, and Roslyn Feldberg. 1977. "Degraded and Deskilled: The Proletarianization of Clerical Work." *Social Problems* 25:52–64.

Goffman, Erving. 1961. *Asylums*. Garden City, N.Y.: Doubleday.

Greer, Ain L. 1986. "Medical Conservatism and Technological Acquisitiveness." Pp. 185–235 in *Research in the Sociology of Health Care*, vol. 4, ed. Julius Roth and Sheryl B. Ruzek. Greenwich, Conn.: Jai Press.

Hacker, Sally L. 1979. "Sex Stratification, Technology and Organization Change—A Longitudinal Case Study of AT&T." *Social Problems* 26(5):539–557.

———. 1981. "The Culture of Engineering: Woman, Workplace and Machine." *Women's Studies International Quarterly* 4(3):341–353.

Haddad, Amy Marie. 1987. *High Tech Home Care*. Rockville, Md.: Aspen Publishers.

Hughes, Everett. 1959. *Men and Their Work*. Glencoe, Ill.: Free Press.

de Kadt, Maarten. 1979. "Insurance: A Clerical Work Factory." Pp. 242–256 in *Case Studies in the Labor Process*, ed. Andrew Zimbalist. New York: Monthly Review Press.

Kind, Allan C., David N. Williams, Gary Persons, and Judith A. Gibson. 1979. "Intravenous Antibiotic Therapy at Home." *Archives of Internal Medicine* 139:413–415.

Krieger, Nancy, and M. Bassett. 1986. "The Health of Black Folks: Gender, Class and Ideology in Science." *Monthly Review* 38(3):74–85.

Kutner, N. J. 1987. "Issue in the Application of High Cost Medical Technology: The Case of Organ Transplantations." *Journal of Health and Social Behavior* 28(1):23–26.

Lasker, Judith N., and S. Borg. 1987. *In Search of Parenthood*. Boston: Beacon Press.

Litwak, Eugene. 1985. *Helping the Elderly*. New York: Guilford Press.

Lopata, Helena Z. 1971. *Occupation: Housewife*. New York: Oxford University Press.

Marx, Leonard. 1964. *The Machine in the Garden*. New York: Oxford University Press.

Mechanic, David. 1977. "The Growth of Medical Technology and Bureaucracy: Implications for Medical Care." *Milbank Fund Quarterly* 55(1):61–78.

Morrisey, Michael, Frank A. Sloan, and Joseph Valvona. 1988. "Shifting Medicare Patients Out of the Hospital." *Health Affairs* (Winter): 52–63.

Moss, Abigail J., and Mary A. Moien. 1987. "Recent Declines in Hospitalization: United States, 1982–86." *Advanced Data No. 140*, Sept. 24, 1–15. Washington, D.C.: National Center for Health Statistics.

Mumford, Lewis. 1934. *Technics and Civilization*. New York: Harcourt, Brace.

Neu, C. R., Scott C. Harrison, and Joanna Z. Heilbrun. 1989. *Medical Patients and Postacute Care. Who Goes Where?* R-3780-MN. Santa Monica, Calif.: Rand.

Noble, David. 1977. *America by Design*. New York: Alfred Knopf.

Oakley, Ann. 1974. *The Sociology of Housework*. New York: Pantheon.

Parker, Roy. 1981. "Tending and Social Policy." Pp. 17–34 in *A New Look at the Personal Social Services*, ed. E. Matilda Goldberg and Stephen Hatch. London: Policy Studies Institute.

Post, Stephen. 1989. "Technology and the Aging Society: Ethics and Public Policy." Pp. 202–222 in *Biomedical Technology and Public Policy*, ed. Robert H. Blank and Miriam K. Mills. Westport, Conn.: Greenwood Press.

Roe, Wayne I., and Gary S. Schneider. 1985. "High-Tech Moves into Home Market with Cardiac, Nutritional Therapies." *Business and Health* 2(5):52–53.

Rothman, Barbara K. 1986. *The Tentative Pregnancy*. New York: Viking Press.

———. 1987. "The Commodification of Motherhood." *Gender & Society* 1(3): 312–316.

Ruderman, Florence. 1986. "A Misdiagnosis of American Medicine." *Commentary* 81(1):43–49.

Russell, Louise B. 1979. *Technology in Hospitals: Medical Advances and Their Diffusion*. Washington, D.C.: Brookings Institution.

———. 1989. *Medicare's New Hospital Payment System: Is It Working?* Washington, D.C.: Brookings Institution.

Ruther, Martin, and Charles Helbing. 1988. "Use and Cost of Home Health Agency Services under Medicare." *Health Care Financing Review* 10(1):105–108.

Sacks, Karen B. 1988. *Caring by the Hour: Women, Work, and Organizing at Duke Medical Center*. Chicago: University of Illinois Press.

Salinger, J. D. 1960. *For Esme—With Love and Squalor*. London: Harborough Publishing.

Segal, Howard. 1985. *Technological Utopianism in American Culture*. Chicago: University of Chicago Press.

Simmons, Roberta, and Susan Klein Marine. 1984. "The Regulation of High-Cost Technology Medicine: The Case of Dialysis and Transplantation in the United Kingdom." *Journal of Health and Social Behavior* 25:320–334.

Smith, Merritt Roe. 1977. *Harpers Ferry Armory and the New Technology*. Ithaca, N.Y.: Cornell University Press.

Stone, Robyn, Gail L. Cafferata, and Judith Sangl. 1987. *Caregivers of the Frail*

Elderly: A National Profile. Washington, D.C.: National Center for Health Services Research.

Strasser, Susan. 1982. *Never Done.* New York: Pantheon.

Strong-Boag, Veronica. 1986. "Keeping House in God's Country: Canadian Women at Work in the Home." Pp. 124–151 in *On the Job*, ed. Craig Heron and Robert Storey. Montreal: McGill-Queen's University Press.

Vanek, Joanne. 1974. "Time Spent in Housework." *Scientific American* 231(5): 116–120.

Waitzkin, H. 1983. *The Second Sickness.* New York: Free Press.

Winner, Langdon. 1977. *Autonomous Technology.* Cambridge, Mass.: MIT Press.

Chapter 11

Dill, Bonnie Thornton. 1986. "Our Mothers' Grief: Racial Ethnic Women and the Maintenance of Families." Center for Research of Women, Memphis State University. Research Paper 4.

Ehrenreich, Barbara. 1985. "Defeating the ERA: A Right-Wing Mobilization of Women." *Journal of Sociology and Social Welfare* 9(3):389–398.

England, Paula. 1984. "Wage Appreciation and Depreciation: A Test of Neoclassical Economic Explanations of Occupational Sex Segregation." *Social Forces* 62(3):726–44.

Glenn, Evelyn Nakano, and Charles M. Tolbert III. 1987. "Technology and Emerging Patterns of Stratification for Women of Color: Race and Gender Segregation in Computer Operations." Pp. 318–331 in *Women, Work, and Technology*, ed. Barbara Drygulski Wright et al. Ann Arbor: University of Michigan Press.

Gwartney-Gibbs, Patricia, and P. A. Taylor. 1986. "Black Women Workers' Earnings Progress, 1960–1980 in Three Industrial Sectors." *Sage: A Scholarly Journal of Black Women* 3(1):20–25.

Hochschild, Arlie. 1989. *The Second Shift.* Berkeley: University of California.

Janiewski, Dolores E. 1985. *Sisterhood Denied: Race, Gender, and Class in a New South Community.* Philadelphia: Temple University Press.

Reskin, Barbara, and Heidi Hartmann. 1985. *Women's Work, Men's Work: Sex Segregation on the Job.* Washington, D.C.: National Academy of Sciences.

Sacks, Karen B. 1988. *Caring by the Hour: Women, Work and Organizing at Duke Medical Center.* Chicago: University of Illinois Press.

Stone, Robyn, Gail L. Cafferata, and Judith Sangl. 1987. *Caregivers of the Frail Elderly: A National Profile.* Washington, D.C.: National Center for Health Services Research.

Szasz, Andrew. 1990. "The Labor Impacts of Policy Change in Health Care: How Federal Policy Transformed Home Health Organizations and Their Labor Practices." *Journal of Health, Politics, Policy and Law* 15(1):191–210.

Zavella, Patricia. 1987. *Women's Work and Chicano Families*. Ithaca, N.Y.: Cornell University Press.

Appendix

Glaser, Barney, and Anselm Strauss. 1971. *The Discovery of Grounded Theory*. Chicago: Aldine.

Index

Acker, Joan, 42

Advertising: in *Ladies Home Journal*, 90–92; information on product standardization, 92–94; freedom of self-service shown in, 99–101, 105; loss of domestic servants portrayed in, 94–98; preselling through, 56, 58, 75; rationales for self-service in, 100–102; self-service as "women's work" in, 101–102; work status of women in *Ladies Home Journal*, 95–99; support for self-service shopping, 89–91

Advocate: and women's wages, 78–82; nonsexist language of, 82

Amalgamated Meat Cutters and Butchers Workmen, 70–71, 83

American Hospital Association, 109–110

American Medical Association, 109, 217, 218

American Nurses Association, 141

Blue Cross, 122–123, 137

Braverman, Harry, 5

Bridges, Amy, 34–35, 72

Capitalism: and relation between paid and unpaid work, 42–43; domination of, 207–208; familial responsibility under, 12–13; hegemony and, 69, 208–209

Caregivers: and lack of resources, 197–198; learning medical technologies, 193–194, 195–196; other problems faced by, 198–199; refusal to learn nursing procedures, 197; women as, 112

Caregiving: before patients are hospitalized, 184; early discharge from hospital and increasing difficulty of, 184; individual versus familial ideologies and, 43–45, 182–183; gender differences in, 112

Centralization, in retailing and health care, 28

Class: and use of home health care, 112–114; definition of, 39; effects of self-service by, 103–105; in Marxist theory, 39–40; implications of RN "professionalization" by, 144–145; intersection with race/ethnicity and gender, 38–42

Client. *See* Customer

Commodification, explanation of, 5. *See* Decommodification

Congress of Industrial Organizations (CIO), 61

Consumer, use of term, 16, 104

Consumption, mainstream versus radical views of, 34–35

Corporations: adoption of work transfer, 207–208; competition and cooperation among retailing, 8–9; competition and cooperation among health care, 9–10, 115–116; profitability of health care for, 121–122; investing in home health care, 189, 191, 211

Cost containment: and changes in health care work of women, 134–135; and limits on work of home health care aides, 170–171; corporate concerns with, 118; corporate profitability and, 117–118, 119–120; home health care as means of, 114; minimal care units as means of, 136–137

Customer, use of term, 16

Customer labor, control over, 63–64

Customer service, reduction by retailers, 62; resistance to reduction, 65

Daniels, Arlene, 37

Decommodification, in capitalism, 6, 210–211, 215–218

Diagnosis-Related Groups (DRGs), 110–112; and increased discharge to home care, 157–158; hospital versus home care under, 126–131; increased outpatient